still
STANDING

still STANDING

Finding Light Inside a Guatemalan Prison

ANAITÉ ALVARADO

APOLLO
PUBLISHERS

Apollo Publishers books may be purchased for educational, business, or sales promotional use. Special editions may be made available upon request. For details, contact Apollo Publishers at info@apollopublishers.com.

Visit our website at www.apollopublishers.

Library of Congress Cataloging-in-Publication Data is available on file.

Cover design by Rain Saukas.

Print ISBN: 978-1-948062-05-3
Ebook ISBN: 978-1-948062-12-1

Printed in the United States of America ·

CONTENTS

My name is Anaité Alvarado and on January 5, 2016, I was arrested, taken away from my two five-year-old children, and sent to preventive detention for sixty-five days, accused of a crime I did not commit, with no evidence to justify my arrest and imprisonment. I hope my account of this harrowing experience will help shed light on the broken prison and justice system in Guatemala—one that, as this book goes to print, I am still dealing with—and that one day soon justice will prevail and absolve every innocent prisoner from the crimes they did not commit. This is my story . . . an ongoing battle with the hope that the truth will set me free.

CHAPTER 1

A Warrant for My Arrest

—

The intercom rang at 6:05 a.m., like every other weekday morning. It was the security guard at the first gate of our neighborhood complex, letting us know that my children's school bus was on its way to my home. And like every other weekday morning, I opened my front door to send them off, only this time I was surprised by three police cars waiting outside. After the bus drove up to my house, I managed to say goodbye to my children and wish them a wonderful day. Then I stood there, watching the bus speed away, as I waited for the officers to approach me.

"Good morning," said one of the officers. "We have a warrant to search your home."

I wasn't scared or surprised. Given the circumstances, my first thought was, *Here we go. They are about to turn my home upside down!*

Six or seven officers walked into my home, but they did not seem to touch or move anything. I entered my study and compliantly opened the only place in my house where I kept documents under lock and key. And since I tend to suffer from a sort of compulsion to over-organize, all my

personal documents were in plain sight, in alphabetical order, and organized by size or color. From the binder clearly labeled "Banks," they took an
old folder that read "Green Millennium Precious Woods," which contained
a document that stated that I had been the first investor to believe in my
husband years before. What had once been a proud moment in our lives,
would now be used as evidence against me.

The officers were courteous, respectful, and well-mannered. Among
them was a young man dressed in plainclothes who asked me about my
husband, his whereabouts, and his phone number.

"I don't know where he is," I replied politely. "I don't know where he
lives, and I am not going to give you his phone number because, as civil as
we all seem to be right now, you are my enemy."

"We have a warrant for his arrest," explained the officer calmly,
and seemingly embarrassed, he added, "and we have a warrant for your
arrest too."

In that instant, still in my nightgown, surrounded by strangers with
guns and warrants, I realized that my husband's problems, which I had so
vehemently tried to separate from my children and myself, were now closer
and more destructive than ever before.

"I'm not sure I understand. Could you please explain what this means?"

He patiently explained that I would have to accompany them to the
Torre de Tribunales, Guatemala City's courthouse, where I would be brought
before a judge to make my statement. The arrest warrants he flashed before
my eyes included three names—my husband and his accountant were being
charged with money laundering, fraud, and criminal association. Under my
name, I only read "criminal association." Little did I know I was on the cusp
of a crash course in legal terminology.

As I continued to read the warrants, I also noticed that the officers
would be going to a house where my husband once lived with his first wife.
Fortunately, she and her children no longer resided there, but I couldn't
help thinking about the family who now lived there and whose home

would soon be invaded by officers while they were flooded with questions.

When I looked up from the documents, the officer suggested that I eat some breakfast because it was uncertain when I would eat again. How could I eat? My stomach was in knots, but I remained calm.

"Would it be OK if I took a shower and got dressed instead?" I asked.

"Well, that's certainly not normal procedure, but yes, go ahead," he replied, and stood back filling out forms while a female agent, Delmi, was assigned to escort me, becoming my shadow for the rest of the morning.

Delmi and I went up to my bedroom on the second floor. She waited patiently and respectfully while I showered, got dressed, and prepared for the unknown. I grabbed a handbag from my closet and began filling it with the basics. Just as I was about to place my cell phone inside, I decided to ask Delmi what she suggested I do about my purse.

"Don't bring anything other than your ID," she said immediately, and explained that everything else would be confiscated when I entered the building.

Still in shock, I followed her advice, leaving my bag behind and taking only my ID. Before leaving my bedroom, I asked Delmi if I could make a few phone calls. She kindly agreed, so I began the slew of calls to attempt to explain my fate that day, one that I did not yet understand completely.

I called my mother, who immediately began to scream, painfully, "No, mija, no, no, no!" Somehow, I sheltered myself from any despair and remained as practical as possible given the circumstances.

My next call was to my employer. I was scheduled to meet my colleague Carlos that morning because we had planned to take several cars filled with artwork to Antigua, Guatemala. We were working on the exhibition phase of a beautiful art project that would soon culminate in an auction to benefit a foundation for children with cancer. All I could say to him was that I would not be able to meet him at 8 a.m. as planned, that I could not explain any further, and that the situation was out of my control.

I then called my father to let him know what was going on and he sprang into action. The only commitment I was unable to cancel that day was with my friend Steve, whom I was to meet for lunch in Antigua after delivering the artwork to Casa Santo Domingo Hotel.

When all was said and done, I walked out of my bedroom with Delmi by my side, wearing a pair of black jeans, a white tank top, a light black-and-white scarf, black flats, and a black sweater over my shoulders. I placed my ID, lip balm, some mints, and a small compact in my pockets, and said goodbye to my housekeeper, Olga. As we left my home, I once again saw the three police cars, which I now realized were pickup trucks, as well as fourteen agents waiting outside. Delmi explained to me that the proper procedure was to handcuff me then, but that she would spare me for now and do so as soon as we arrived at the courthouse.

They decided I should travel inside the last truck. The other two trucks would continue their journey to search for my husband and his accountant. Two agents got in the front seat, while Delmi and I climbed into the back, careful not to step on the ten pineapples that were on the floor. The rest of the officers took their places in the flatbed. I will never forget the gardeners' and guard's astonished faces as they watched us speed by, knowing me well from my neighborhood walks and our daily greetings. Those were the last familiar faces I would see for the next few hours.

———

I had never been to the courthouse before and had never thought this was how my first visit would happen. I had also never imagined that it would become a familiar place to me.

The pickup truck entered a guarded side street and parked at the end of the road, near the underground parking lot entrance. Delmi handcuffed me and we walked to the main gate, where cars would normally enter the building. There were two guards at a tiny table who asked for my ID and I formally entered the courthouse as an arrestee. They confiscated my compact, but let me keep my lip balm and mints.

We walked down the ramp toward the building's basement level and passed the male inmate holding cells. I had imagined they'd get rowdy every time a woman went by, but the noise, the whistling, and the remarks were truly deafening. I noticed what felt like an endless blur of inmates and police officers, but I felt protected by Delmi, who never left my side. And, although police in Guatemala aren't usually regarded as gentlemen, all the agents I had contact with that day behaved professionally.

After waiting for some paperwork to be cleared, I was taken to the second floor, to the Fourth Court of First Instance, or trial court, where my hearing would be held. And lo and behold, among the strangers, I recognized a face from my world. It was David, my dear friend Kali's husband. As we approached him, I finally burst into tears . . . the first tears I had shed all morning. I am not sure if I cried out of fear or sheer gratefulness that he was there, all I know is that there are moments in one's life that one never forgets, and this was just the first of many that occurred that day.

David and I sat together in some broken-down chairs and chatted for a bit, as I let my situation sink in. Then, when he got up to say hello to an attorney friend of his, a TV reporter suddenly headed straight toward me. Without even saying good morning, he asked, "Anaité?"

I shook my head and simply responded, "No." When the reporter left to make a phone call, I quickly got up, told David what had just happened, and then walked over and stood right next to the reporter. I knew he was from Channel 7 because the microphone in his hand said so. When he realized that I was very close to him, he asked me if I had been apprehended that day.

"And who are you and why are you interested in knowing?" I asked in response.

"I'm from Channel 7 and we interview everyone here."

By now, the cameraman was busy trying to set up his tripod and camera to film me, but I remained with my back to him, continuously shifting to avoid the camera lens each time he moved his gear to get me on screen.

For the first time, I began to wonder if everything that was happening that day was more than just a terrible misunderstanding. Could someone be targeting me deliberately? I told Delmi that I was scared, that the reporter referred to me by name, and that I would appreciate it if she could take me to the restroom. She immediately asked her superior for permission and we left.

Once in the safety of the women's restroom four floors down, I took a deep breath and turned my attention to Delmi for a minute; I needed some small talk to calm my nerves and I was curious about the woman before me, assigned to guard my every step.

"Did you always want to be a police officer?" I asked.

She smiled and said, "No. I've been on the force for a year now, but I had never touched a weapon before this, not even a toy gun. I actually graduated from college with a degree in business administration, but after unsuccessfully looking for work for more than a year, I came across this opportunity and took it." Little did I know this would be the first of many more stories I would encounter in the following year . . . stories that would teach me that life is never simply black or white, right or wrong, as I had believed for most of my life.

By the time we returned to the second floor, the reporter and his cameraman were gone. I later learned that his inquiry had not been personal and he didn't have a specific interest in my case. Reporters simply make it their job to know who has been arrested and try to get an interview at the courthouse on a daily basis.

In the meantime, my father, my brother Rodrigo, and other loved ones had been frantically trying to figure out what was going on. They were contacting attorneys and gathering any information they could get their hands on, but for some very unusual reason, there was nothing on my case in the system yet.

David had gone down to meet my father and brother, who were already in the building trying to find my case number. I then remembered that I had a copy of the arrest warrants with me. I read through them and found the number. But how could I contact them when I had no cell phone? Luckily, a tall agent, who seemed to be of much higher rank than the others, offered me his cell phone to call my father. "But do it quickly, because this is not allowed and there are cameras everywhere," he said.

When I got my father on the phone, I quickly gave him my case number, and he was finally able to find out what was going on that day.

I honestly don't remember the exact order of events after this, it was an emotional and stressful whirlwind, but I do recall that at some point we were informed that my hearing would take place the next day, which basically meant, to my dismay, that I would be spending the rest of the day and that night locked up in the women's *carceleta*, a communal holding cell located inside the courthouse's underground parking lot. That's where the authorities keep the newly apprehended people who arrive daily, and where they hold inmates that come from prisons to attend their hearings at the courthouse each day. The only people who spend the night in the carceleta are those whose hearing is scheduled for the next day. The law states that everyone has the right to be heard within twenty-four hours of their arrest, but this is not always the case.

Delmi and I went down the stairs to the lobby, where I was able to speak to David, my father, and my brother. I handed them my belt and scarf. My father gave me his jacket. We said goodbye and I continued descending in what felt like a downward spiral into hell.

The women's carceleta is located beyond the view of the men's, around the corner, next to a ramp that descends to the subbasement. The communal holding cell is approximately 40 by 5 feet. There is a cement bench against one of the longer walls. Another wall is a solid half wall with metal bars extending from it into the ceiling. Since the lower levels of the building also serve as a parking lot, cars are constantly going down the adjacent ramp, driving by approximately 30 inches from the bars. As if that weren't enough, the bathroom inside the communal cell holds a toilet and a sink, with no toilet paper, soap, or door. Meanwhile, the media is allowed to enter and film inmates inside this cell at any time, day or night.

Apparently, there was still not enough interest in my case to send reporters my way, but the media was a constant presence in the carceleta that week because of the high-profile case of a high government official named Carmen. Authorities had arrested her three days earlier, on Monday, September 14, and she had already spent three nights in the carceleta by the time I arrived.

At the entrance to the cell, Delmi uncuffed me and told me to go inside. I walked in and occupied a tiny space on the bench. Survival instincts kicked into full gear and I quietly studied my surroundings. There were close to twelve women locked inside. Most of them were lying on the floor or sitting on the bench. Many were chatting, all were waiting. I noticed two women on the floor, their arms loosely around each other, sleeping on some blankets. Two things immediately caught my attention. One was a pile of things on the bench—two plastic bags filled with stuff, two neatly folded coverlets, and several bottles of water—that seemed to belong to nobody. Not only did they occupy precious sitting space, but no one touched them. The second was a tall, young, pretty woman who was obviously different from the rest of the inmates. She was sitting on the bench right next to me.

I soon learned that nothing can be brought into the carceleta. This is why Delmi suggested I leave my handbag at home. And this is why she also suggested that I take off my belt and scarf and leave them with my father before bringing me down there. The other thing I quickly learned was that the only people allowed to visit holding cells are attorneys. They do not need to be hired by prisoners, they simply must have their credentials available. They do not enter the carceleta per se, they simply visit through the bars.

Once I was inside, I also learned that such things as water, food, and toilet paper are only available to first-timers in the carceleta through attorneys or family members who manage to get attorneys to deliver these items. There is a schedule for food delivery: 6 a.m., 1 p.m., and 6 p.m. My lunch came courtesy of my brother Rodrigo. He sent a cheeseburger with French fries and a bottle of water. I was not very hungry, and it was not my preferred choice of food, but I decided to eat the cheeseburger anyway.

I offered the fries to my cellmates and someone took them. That was my first real encounter with them. I had been watching them, listening to their conversations and their laughter, but I had not yet spoken to anyone, except the pretty woman sitting next to me. She told me, among other things, that she had turned herself in the day before, had spent the night in the carceleta, had had her hearing that morning, and God willing, would be going home later that day. She was released a few hours later.

Meanwhile, my family figured out that my brother-in-law's wife, Vania, could come see me because she's an attorney. It was great to see a familiar face, but she came bearing bad news: I was now officially unemployed. My employer was suddenly claiming that they had not renewed my one-year contract, which coincidentally had ended on September 16, the day prior to my arrest.

It's true that the renewal had not been officially signed, but no one had been in a hurry to get my first contract signed either. I had started working for them the previous September, but we only got around to signing that contract in December, so it had really seemed like a formality more than a necessity. And I was obviously on board for another year because I was clearly in the middle of a project. Additionally, my approved fundraising project included a benefit auction planned for October 28, and it had been agreed that my fundraising efforts would come in on that date. Talks had always revolved around renewing, so much so that on several occasions the foundation's executive director had teased me, in public, about how she was worried that I may ask for a raise. It was clear that they were pleased with my performance and the success so far of the art project I had devised and implemented to benefit the children's cancer hospital. Furthermore, I was scheduled to deliver artwork the very morning of my apprehension.

In any event, they were suddenly singing another tune. It seemed they were now claiming that I had breached my contract when I had failed to raise a certain amount of money during my first year on the job. I understood their predicament regarding this new turn of events, and I had bigger problems to attend to at the time, but the way it was handled left much to be desired. Later, they refused to give my father a letter stating that I worked there, a letter my attorney had requested in the hope of convincing the judge that I had a job and was not a flight risk.

The news left me speechless. All I can say now is that working to benefit Guatemala's children with cancer was one of the biggest joys of my professional career; it gave me a wonderful purpose at a time when my personal life was crumbling around me, and I met and worked alongside fantastic people. The decision made by the board, which included people I have known most of my life, will always be a sad memory for me.

When Vania arrived with this news, I was reading for the first time the accusations that Juan Pablo Olyslager Muñoz, one of my husband's alleged victims, had made against me the year before. My attorney had brought them by earlier so I would know what I was up against and in the hope that I could give him some insight into the case. Since Vania had not yet read them, she pulled out her cell phone and snapped pictures of every page. As she did this, we were interrupted by the women in the holding cell suddenly screaming for help and calling out for a doctor. I turned and realized it was one of the girls I had observed sleeping with her arms around another on the floor earlier; her body was stiff and straight as a board. It was clear she was having a seizure. Her partner, distraught, sat by her side not knowing what to do. Finally, the guards opened the gate, carried the girl out, and set her on the floor, at Vania's feet, while her partner remained helplessly behind bars. Vania quickly took out a key chain with a stuffed monkey from her purse and put it in the girl's mouth, trying to prevent her from swallowing her tongue. The girl was left there, on the floor, until the seizure passed.

After the shock of the moment subsided, Vania gave me a bottle of water, a small packet of baby wipes, and a tiny pillow she had managed to put inside her purse, and then left to meet my family on the outside and continue working on getting me out of there.

As if the morning chaos hadn't been enough, later that afternoon, some of the ladies grew concerned about another young woman and began asking if she was feeling well. She responded that she was eighteen years old, had not eaten anything all day, was pregnant, and really wanted to vomit. Everyone cleared the way and the woman rushed to the bathroom. The ladies began yelling once again, slamming their hands against the bars, and demanding that the guards bring a doctor or an ambulance. It all sounds terrifying, but for what it's worth, at no point did I feel I was in danger. On the contrary, their concern felt reassuring. I quickly realized that we were all in this together and, should that have been me, these women would have done the same thing. For the first time that day, I began to feel the sisterhood that forms among women who find themselves in this predicament, who are deprived of their freedom and their basic human rights.

It was in that interim that Carmen was brought back down to the carceleta. She had been at her hearing, and since she had been in the carceleta for several days, she was welcomed back by inmates who had seen her during that time. It was Carmen who gave the young pregnant woman some yogurt and water when she came out of the bathroom.

A short time later, an ambulance arrived for the young pregnant woman. However, there were so many of us in that holding cell by then that none of us had realized that she had returned to the bathroom, fainted, and was bleeding. She was quickly taken away.

It must have been around 5 p.m. when the inmates were called to leave the carceleta for their ride back to prison. As they all scurried away, I realized only Carmen and I were left behind, and so did the reporters. They swiftly arrived and set up their cameras, while I lay on the now empty bench and covered my face with my father's jacket.

It must have been around 6 p.m. when my name was called. My brother

Rodrigo had sent a chicken Caesar wrap and chicken soup for dinner. I originally thought the container with the hot liquid was coffee and I almost left it in the bag, but I got curious and discovered the delicious soup. I had no appetite for the wrap Rodrigo had so thoughtfully sent me, but underneath it I found a small piece of folded paper. *Please let it be a note, please!* And it was! I immediately unfolded it and read:

> *We are all with you.*
> *We support you; you are not alone.*
> *Everything will be OK.*
> *We are all with you. Be strong.*
> *I love you,*
> *Rodri*

> *P.S. Chicken Caesar Wrap! :-)*

It is very difficult to explain what it feels like to be suddenly taken physically from your usual environment, and locked up in an underground cell, with no communication with the outside world. Reading that simple yet heartfelt note meant the world to me. For a long time, that handwritten note was displayed in a picture frame in my bedroom. In that moment, and forever, it will always be my treasure.

Later, I received a visit from another family acquaintance, also a lawyer. He had come to see how I was doing and to assure me that my children would be safe no matter what happened. I had had no reason to think otherwise until then, but as this person explained to me, with an absent father and a mother in custody, my children were apparently now legally orphaned. Because of this legality, my mother and brother had contacted my brother-in-law, Ed, and had asked him to pick up my children from school. They figured that, given the malicious way things had been unfolding, anything was possible, including the public prosecutor requesting that my children be sent to a state-run orphanage, due to our new circumstances.

Now, as if the idea of spending a night in jail wasn't tortuous enough, I'd had a bombshell dropped on me. I was being advised that, in order to protect my children, I had to move quickly and temporarily hand over custody of my children to my mother. I thanked my lucky stars that amid the drama unfolding before my eyes, I knew that my children and I were surrounded and protected by an amazing family. My mother, my brother Turi, and my brother-in-law Ed and his wife, Vania, were all ready to step forward and become my children's legal guardians. My mother was my first choice, but due to her age, we knew there was a possibility that a judge might not grant her that right. Luckily, because my mother is so youthful and my children love her, the judge agreed and chose her.

So, one morning you wake up expecting an ordinary day, with two beautiful children on their way to school, a full day of work ahead, activities, friends, freedom, and just when you begin to think that all your hard work in the past year to lift your family back from a terrible ordeal is beginning to pay off, it is all taken away from you, in the blink of an eye, with no sense or purpose to speak of other than to get back at your husband. I still can't believe someone would go to such lengths for revenge.

As I was pondering this new information and my reactions, I returned to the holding cell, flabbergasted by the latest news, and then remembered I was not alone.

I honestly had never heard of Carmen before that Thursday, although she was quite famous at the time. She seemed to be very anxious, sitting, standing, walking around, and constantly searching for stuff inside the two bags on the bench. Several times that evening, we sat and spoke for a while. She told me she had been in the carceleta since Monday, without access to a shower, and she had just been awarded a judge's order to go freshen up somewhere inside the courthouse. As she began to undo her beautiful fishtail braid, I asked her how she made it. "The other inmates did it for me," she said.

It turns out the other inmates had taunted her when she first arrived, with remarks such as, "Well, look who's in jail now! Baldetti's dear friend!" But Carmen immediately set them straight, explaining that it was actually because of Guatemala's former vice president Roxana Baldetti that she was in jail in the first place. If they'd really been friends, Carmen wouldn't have been used as a scapegoat for crimes she didn't commit. And her remarks and explanations paid off. When all the cards seemed to be stacked against her, the inmates believed she was telling the truth, so much so, that they went from taunting her to protecting her, even going as far as making sure she looked beautiful for her public hearings. I saw this with my own eyes the following morning when Carmen put her hair up in a simple ponytail and the inmates insisted on styling her hair with another beautiful braid before she left the holding cell to attend her hearing. The inmates later told me that they had even protected Carmen from some nasty reporters who had come by to aggravate her. They were very proud to recount how they had been showcased on the nightly news yelling at the reporters to leave Carmen alone.

At some time that evening, I remember seeing Carmen take out a toothbrush and some toothpaste.

"Would you mind sharing some toothpaste with me?" I asked as I extended one of my father's interdental brushes, so small that it went undetected by the guards when they had searched me earlier.

"On that?" she asked.

"It's all I have," I responded.

She immediately pulled out a new regular-sized toothbrush from her supply bag and gave it to me. Moved by her generosity, I thanked her and asked her how she was holding up. She went on to tell me a bit about her family and friends, and how helpless she felt with such a high-profile case, where she felt she was being tried by the media rather than a jury of her peers. It certainly looked like an uphill battle for her, given that the public prosecutor, the CICIG (Comisión Internacional Contra la Impunidad en

Guatemala—a relatively new commission in Guatemala backed by the UN and allegedly formed to combat corruption), the media, former president Otto Perez Molina, and former vice president Roxana Baldetti were all against her. She knew that Friday's hearing was crucial and she was preparing herself for it, but behind the hope that she might go home the following day was a latent fear that her fate had already been decided.

Before we went to sleep, if one can call that sleep, Carmen handed me one of her coverlets. She said her friends had brought her two, the pretty woman who'd been released earlier had used one the night before, and now it was mine to use for the night. I placed the tiny pillow Vania had brought me under my head, used the borrowed coverlet as a sleeping mat, wrapped myself in my father's jacket, and suddenly realized my sleeping arrangements weren't as terrible as I had imagined. Not even the hundreds of baby cockroaches wandering about bothered me. My biggest problem was caused by the many mosquitoes biting my feet throughout the night. Never did I imagine that I was only beginning a journey that would turn into an ongoing and arduous battle for my freedom, with the hope that justice would finally prevail.

CHAPTER 2

The Beginning of the End

—

As I tried to sleep on the carceleta's cold concrete bench, I could not
help thinking of the journey that had somehow brought me there.
My world collapsed on July 29, 2014. It had actually begun collapsing quite
a while before that fateful day, but I was none the wiser.

How could I have not seen the storm that was heading my way?

—

On the morning of July 29, 2014, I woke up on the forty-sixth floor in our
apartment overlooking Biscayne Bay, the Port of Miami, and South Beach,
as I'd done on so many other mornings. I loved sleeping with the blinds
open, falling asleep with a billion lights shining in the night, and opening
my eyes the next day as the sun rose over the ocean on the horizon.

Miami was a familiar place to me; it was where I was born, and after
being raised in Guatemala City, it is where I returned as a young woman to
attend the University of Miami in Coral Gables, and it is the city I called

home during the following seventeen years after graduation, where I became an adult. When I finally moved back to Guatemala in 2003, within weeks of my arrival, I found love. I was thirty-five years old, had been engaged twice before, but had never gotten married. Marriage had not been a goal in my life, but that suddenly changed.

My husband and I got married in 2008 and a year later, God blessed us with twins: a girl, Nina, and a boy, Fabián. I could not have been happier or felt more fortunate. My husband had been doing very well with his business endeavors, and every year seemed to bring more projects and more possibilities. He had managed to bring a forestry investment firm to Guatemala and began creating one of the largest teak plantations in the world. Every year, more trees were planted and his management revenues grew. He also had other plans; he seemed to never stand still.

That year, my husband had decided to run the IRONMAN race in Nice, France. As with his other interests in life, he prepared, training hard, and was ready to tackle what he'd set his mind to do. Since it was scheduled for the middle of the summer, we decided to bring the children along. We rented a small apartment in the center of Nice, packed our bags, and enjoyed a wonderful month-long vacation in the south of France. When we returned, my husband flew to Guatemala, while the kids and I made one last stop in Miami before continuing home. The children were to start school at the American School of Guatemala, the same school my husband and I had attended as children. Life seemed to be smiling in our direction, and there was no reason for me to think otherwise. Until that one day, when I woke up and realized that soon my life would never be the same again.

It must have been around 9 p.m. The children were already sleeping in their room, exhausted after another fun-filled summer day in Miami. As I sat on my bed watching TV, the phone rang. It was my husband calling me from Guatemala.

"I have something very important I need to tell you. Are you sitting down?" he asked. "I have gotten myself in deep financial troubles. I have been trying to get it all sorted out for a while now, and I was hoping to fix things before you ever found out, but it has become impossible. I needed you to hear it from me."

I remember hearing something about his taking something he should not have, and in my ingenuity, I simply said, "Well, give it back."

"It's not possible," he said, "I can't say anything else about this over the phone. I'll be back in Miami tomorrow."

My entire life changed with those words. They were simple, but I knew my world would never be the same again. I hung up, still sitting on my bed, overlooking the magnificent bay, and suddenly felt as if my life were not mine, as if I was now in a movie and my life was happening to someone else—these things didn't happen to people like me. And even though at that moment nothing had changed, everything was suddenly different. I was paralyzed, yet my brain was going a million miles an hour. My life was still intact, I was seemingly safe, but those words had changed everything. I did not understand what had just happened, or how I felt, and I did not have enough information to devise a plan or figure out a course of action. All I knew for sure was that I had to focus on the important things, what was left: Nina and Fabián. Yes, Nina and Fabián, and all that I could not see at that moment but would surely be there when the storm passed . . . because this too shall pass . . . or so I had been told.

For the next two days I was in a fog. I thought I would go crazy. I was exhausted, I could not sleep, I could not eat, I knew a devastating tornado was about to make landfall in our lives, and yet I was going through the day doing things that changed nothing. And my husband, whom I loved for so many wonderful reasons, was suddenly a stranger to me. He needed my support and I had no idea how to help him. We were both drowning in the ocean, unable to save each other. And despite my indescribable fear and my anger at realizing that my own husband had destroyed my young family, I still felt the need to protect him. If someone had asked me just a few days prior to receiving this news, what I would have done if I had found myself in this very predicament, I would most likely have said that I would not tolerate such deceit and would never be able to stand by someone capable of so many lies. And yet there I stood, crying and overwhelmed by fear, bombarded by news that grew worse by the hour.

Upon his return to Miami, I tried helplessly to understand everything my husband was attempting to explain to me. I needed to know what had happened, what was going on, and yet my brain could not make sense out of any of it. At some point during those first days after his return, I found myself taking his hands in mine and telling him, "Listen, we all make mistakes and we are all so much more than our worst missteps." It was at that moment that he finally broke down and cried.

Everything about my life had suddenly become uncertain. I assumed he would have to face the consequences of his actions, and I would have to build a new life. My husband insisted I did not deserve any of this. I could not say what it was I deserved, but the fact of the matter was that my life had changed forever. If these changes were for better or for worse, only time would tell.

While we navigated through the following week, my husband suddenly claimed he could not go on. He talked about how months had passed while he desperately tried to plan a way out of this mess. He said that the only reason he had not taken his life was to protect his children and me. Every day came with new pieces of information regarding his predicament and what he had been trying to do these past years, all while I had obliviously been enjoying my so-called perfect life. It was all very complicated, but I kept holding on to one truth: he had not killed anyone. Yes, he would have to pay the consequences for his actions, but I truly believed that eventually we'd be able to figure it all out.

As I tried to understand everything that was happening, as I tried to put all the pieces of the puzzle together, and figure out how to continue living my life, I was overwhelmed by deep sadness when I slowly realized that my husband and I had not been partners for a while, and that my family would never be whole again.

At first, I thought it would be best for my husband to move out of the house as soon as we returned to Guatemala, because the tension between us was making the children uneasy, and because if I was to remain separate from his actions to avoid becoming an accomplice, we could not live under the same roof.

But then my feelings shifted. I decided that precisely because our time as a family unit might come to an end sooner rather than later, it would be best if we tried to remain together as long as possible. The rupture might be inevitable, but I was still not ready to be the one to cause it. I wasn't ready to let go. Up until that moment, I truly believed that I had my life under control, that my husband and I were a team, and that we had our life as figured out as possible. As it turned out, NOTHING was in my control.

I called my father, seeking comfort and advice.

"Papá, I have nothing, I have no idea what's to come. I don't know what to do."

And, just as he'd done at other times in my life when my own thoughts had made me feel helpless, he cleared my mind with his wisdom.

"This too shall pass," he said calmly. "There is a solution to every problem, there are inevitable consequences, but there's no need to fret and worry so much beforehand. We do not know what is to come. Don't let your mind be your worst enemy. There is no point in letting negative and destructive thoughts control us."

My father continued to call me from Guatemala every twelve hours to ask how I was, to tell me that I was not alone, and that I had all his support; I felt blessed.

On August 5, 2014, my children, the nanny, and I returned to Guatemala as originally planned. Back home, I spent weeks suffering panic attacks, falling prey to my worst thoughts, going over every detail that was available to me to see if it could all finally make sense in my mind. But nothing made sense. I was inside a whirlwind of change, and I would've been sucked into its vacuum had it not been for the one thing that remained constant in my life: the continuous and determined support of my family and friends. They say you learn how few friends you can truly count on when you are in the hospital, in prison, or in financial trouble. I now know how many wonderful people surround my life's journey, a ray of light during dark and stormy times.

And when I asked myself how I could remain by my husband's side after the devastating news, the answers were simple: because I loved him for so many other reasons, because he was my partner, because he made a mistake, and because my family without him still made no sense to me.

——

Exactly a month after the devastating news, I decided to go on my first job interview in over twenty years. I had no idea whether I would get the job, but I knew I had to do something. Given the circumstances, it was likely I would have to sell everything, learn to live a simpler life, and work for a living. I really had no idea what was in store for me, but I knew I needed to keep moving forward. So, I interviewed at AYUVI, Fundación Ayúdame a Vivir, which raises funds to benefit children with cancer in Guatemala. Drowning in my personal and financial worries, I had been blind to truly unimaginable sadness until that day.

When I arrived, I was given a tour of the hospital, and met very sick children from extremely low-income families who were battling for their lives. And yet they were the lucky ones, benefitting from the amazing work AYUVI does on their behalf to get them the treatment they deserve. I was so inspired that I left the interview praying I would get the job, hoping to be part of that team dedicated to saving lives. I threw my wish out into the universe and thought, *God knows best.*

I have never considered myself a religious person, but I do believe in God and feel that the best way to honor Him is to trust that He knows best. So, even as my life was being turned upside down, as fear and anxiety invaded every cell of my body, I stood by that statement. I felt comfort in believing that even though I may not understand God's will at any given time, there is a divine purpose to everything.

A few days later, the phone rang: I got the job! On September 16, 2014, I began working as Fundraising and Public Relations Coordinator for the USA at AYUVI. Visiting that hospital changed my life forever. Witnessing firsthand how those children fought for their lives gave me the courage I needed to continue moving forward with mine. They will continue to be an inspiration to me for the rest of my life.

———

As 2014 came to a close, I found that once again I had purpose in my life. I had devised a wonderful art project and was looking forward to implementing it, sure that it would raise much-needed funds to benefit the children's cancer hospital. I was meeting new people, enjoying the Guatemalan art scene, and working comfortably from home, near my children. I felt useful and productive, and truly believed I was beginning to rebuild my life.

Meanwhile, my relationship with my husband was nonexistent. We lived in the same house but led separate lives. I was doing all I could to mitigate any other drastic changes in my children's lives, but my marriage had crumbled and could not be put back together again. My husband claimed that he had no money and no place to go, and I was at a loss. After all, he was the father of our two wonderful children. How could I possibly explain to them one day that I had thrown him out on the street when he was destitute? So, he remained at home.

Months passed, living in this surreal world where nothing made much sense, yet it existed and seemed to move along somehow. My art project was making amazing headway, my children were adapting to their new school, and life continued.

Then, in early 2015, my husband informed me that he would be moving out of the house, which meant newfound peace for me, but I knew it would be a blow for Nina and Fabián. As much as we both tried to make it all seem OK to our children, such feeling is usually not possible when families break up. I know this to be true since I was Nina and Fabi's age when my family fell apart.

So suddenly there I was, a forty-six-year-old woman, a single mother to five-year-old twins, starting a new life after a devastating heartbreak. But I was now free to choose my new path, I was free to reinvent myself, free to start over, free from so many lies. Or so I thought . . .

CHAPTER 3

My First Hearing

—

I woke up startled. As I opened my eyes and turned my head away from the concrete wall I was facing, I saw a guard on the other side of the metal bars staring at me. Carmen was awake and asked him for the time. It was impossible for us to know the time since we had no watch, no cell phone, there was no clock, and the sunlight did not reach our underground cell. "It's 4:10 a.m.," replied the guard. The basement was calmer at this time of night, but there was still constant yelling, metal doors clanking, and electric lights buzzing overhead. I turned my head back around, closed my eyes, and did my best to continue sleeping a little while longer.

It must have been around 6:30 a.m. when the doors clanked open and the first prisoners of the day—two women from a prison called Centro de Orientación Femenina (COF)—walked into our cell. I got up from my bench, used the restroom, and began to think about what I would say to the judge. Unlike Carmen, who had spent months preparing for this possibility, I had only learned about my predicament less than twenty-four hours earlier, when my attorney, whom I had met for the first time the day before, had brought a copy of Olyslager's accusations against me and had asked me to read it. "Prepare to give a statement in front of the judge," he had said, and added that I should claim my innocence, explain that I did not know this man, and even cry, if possible. Welcome to the world of justice, where he who tells the best story wins.

My hearing was scheduled for 9 a.m., and I still had no idea what I should or would say. While I waited for news or contact of any kind from the outside world, I folded Carmen's blanket and offered what food I had left to the newly arrived women. Meanwhile, Carmen changed into a blouse and a pair of pants, which were way too long for the flat shoes she was wearing. She sat on the bench next to me and began applying her makeup, wielding magic with the tiny makeup case she had been given. Once done, she glanced over at me and asked, "Do I look OK?" To which I quickly answered in amazement, "Yes!" She looked great.

After spending four days and four nights in that holding cell, about to face the hearing of her life, Carmen was an example to us all. She managed to prepare herself, remain calm and focused, and with very little sleep, if any, she walked out of the carceleta with her head high, her makeup on, and yet another beautiful braid, which would later become famous, dangling down her back. As she left the cell later that Friday morning, the inmates all cheered and wished her well. "God be with you, *Licenciada*," they said, using the title you give people with academic degrees.

Her hearing before a judge, and the media spotlight lasted eight hours, and after all was said and done, the judge sent her to preventive custody at El Centro de Detención Preventiva para Mujeres Santa Teresa. In the ensuing months, I could not stop thinking about her. When I met her, I had known nothing about her case, despite how public it had been. All I knew was that I met someone who was going through one of the worst moments of her life and still managed to be generous to me. Little did I know that that would not be the last time we crossed paths.

Soon after the women from COF arrived, another group of inmates from Santa Teresa came into our cell. I struck up a conversation with a young woman whom I recognized from the previous day. She had stood out that day, amusing us with her antics when she hung out by the open prison bars and asked people for cigarettes as they drove by in their cars. She was probably close to thirty years old, short, chubby, and spunky, and was wearing white jeans and a skimpy black and yellow tank top—one of those people who are hard to forget. As we talked, she told me she had already spent three years in Santa Teresa while she waited for the Attorney General's Office to finish its investigation. She was accused of being a gang member and an extortionist, along with five other women and several men, but she claimed that they were all from different parts of Guatemala and that none of them knew one another on the streets; however, she did confess that after being unemployed for months, when a friend offered her $13.50 to go to the bank and cash a check for her, knowing she needed the money, she accepted. She was well aware this was not kosher, but she agreed anyway and decided to not ask questions. However, she claimed to have never partaken in gang member activities.

Meanwhile, she'd been separated from her eleven-year-old daughter for the past three years, not only because she was behind bars, but because her sister had refused to bring the girl to prison to visit her. This was one of the many stories I would continue to encounter in the following years, stories that shed light on different realities I had been unaware of in the past, realities and people that would soon become a piece of the fabric that makes up who I am today.

———

After sending Carmen off to her fate before the judge, we all returned to our places and waited. There was not much else to do in the carceleta but wait. I glanced over the copy of Olyslager's accusations and read it once again, scribbling notes beside every statement that involved me. I had no idea what they were basing their accusations on, but I was quite sure it was very unlikely that they had any documents incriminating me because I am one of those rare people who actually read every word on a document before signing it. However, I was married to the main defendant, so I could have inadvertently signed something along the way. Everything else regarding this situation was out of my hands, so I reminded myself that all I had to do was tell the truth.

At around 8:30 a.m., my name was called. The women wished me good luck and repeated, "*¡Que Dios la acompañe, Seño!*" Yes, may God be with me. The guards opened the door and my newly appointed young male guard handcuffed me. I was searched by a female courthouse security officer before I was allowed to enter the tower and walk up the four flights of stairs. I was speechless when I reached the second floor and found my friends Karla and Tuffy; my two brothers; my sister, Gaby, and her husband, Carlos; and my dad waiting for me. A short while later, my stepmother, Anamaría, and my dear friends Kali and Christie joined us.

While my 9 a.m. hearing kept getting pushed back, we managed to use the extra time together that morning to chat, cry, and even laugh. How blessed I felt in spite of the situation. Karla had brought me a small makeup bag with a bit of everything, a small treasure in that barren place.

I cannot begin to imagine what my loved ones felt as they waited in the same hallway as Olyslager. It was surreal for me, too. I couldn't believe what he was putting us through, but somehow, we all managed to keep calm. If he had done this to someone I love, rather than to me, I am not sure I could have contained my fury.

My name was finally called and it was time to face the judge. My loved ones hugged me, Christie put a Saint Benito bracelet on my wrist, and Tuffy placed a religious commemorative stamp in my back pocket and said, "You are going in holding the Virgin Mary's hand." I am not a religious person, because I have never needed religion to feel God as ever-present in my life, but I must confess that Tuffy's statement did make me feel protected as I walked toward my unknown fate.

I entered the courtroom handcuffed, next to my attorney and followed by my guard, with a clear conscience, because I had nothing to hide. Olyslager came in with his attorney, the state's public prosecutor, and two other men. I had no idea why there were so many people there, carrying suitcases full of papers, while I had nothing but my scribbled notes on the copy of Olyslager's accusation against me, and an attorney who was a stranger I had just briefly met the day before, holding a couple of folders in his hands. The day I was apprehended, my family was forced to find a lawyer as quickly as possible to try to mend the unforeseen circumstances I was suddenly facing. Arturo Miranda was recommended by one of our acquaintances and was immediately hired. I could only pray that Miranda had prepared sufficiently and was good at his job.

The room was small, but it managed to hold the judge's bench, a young man seated next to the judge working on a computer, and two other desks facing the judge: one for my attorney and me, the other for the opposing team. As I sat there observing my surroundings, the judge finally walked in and we all stood up. While we waited for the judge's instructions, I asked my guard to loosen my cuffs because they were hurting me.

I now knew that this day had been in the works for over a year, because Olyslager's statements against me at the Attorney General's Office were dated October 15, 2014. This indicates how long it had taken for a judge to sign an arrest warrant against me, and the time it had taken the accusers to execute the master plan to include me as the third person necessary to make this a criminal case. They could have chosen my husband's assistant, or maybe a junior accountant, but they had chosen me. They had had over a year to reconsider, to realize that there was no evidence against me, that I was already a victim, that I had two small children. But they obviously did not care. I was not human to them. I was simply a dispensable object they were going to use to get to my husband.

The legal proceeding that followed is a bit murky in my mind because I frankly did not understand much of what was happening; I was completely overwhelmed by the circumstances. I do remember that one of the first things Olyslager's attorney did was ask the judge to recuse herself. Why? Because the attorney represented the law firm of Hector and Frank Trujillo, and they were the judge's first cousins. I couldn't believe my ears. If the judge recused herself due to this conflict, I would have to spend the entire weekend in the courthouse's holding cell until another judge could hear my case on Monday or Tuesday. To my dismay, the judge agreed; however, she clarified that she would recuse herself from this case only after she had heard my first declaration, as it was my right to be heard by a judge within twenty-four hours of my apprehension. And so, I survived the first blow of many still to come.

It was now my turn, time to give my statement, which was basically a response to Olyslager's accusatory testimony against me. I looked him straight in the eye and stated that I did not know him, that I had never spoken to him, that I had never asked him for money, that I had never accepted or received money from him, nor had I ever managed his money. I said I considered it an act of cowardice to attack me in response to the hatred he held for my husband, and that I considered his accusations violence against my integrity, my reputation, my emotional state, and my financial well-being. I continued with my statement, explaining that I had only become aware of my husband's financial troubles on July 29, 2014, and had been fortunate to have been hired as fundraising and public relations coordinator for AYUVI shortly thereafter. Furthermore, I made it clear that that job had allowed me to put food on the table, and today, because of these false accusations, I had lost that precious employment.

I spoke about the Entrepreneur Organization (EO), where Olyslager claimed he had met my husband, and where he claimed he had met me. I explained that I had never been a member of that organization, and that if I had assisted, it had been on very few occasions when the organization hosted family activities. I was sure they could contact the organization and learn exactly how many events I had ever attended.

Then I went one step further: I asked them to present any e-mails, mes-sages, times, places, dates, or any other form of communication between Olyslager and myself. I was sure not a single one existed and they would come up empty-handed. I then added that I had tried to save my marriage during the ten months after I had become aware of my husband's dire finan-cial situation, but that I had not succeeded. I told them that my husband and I had been separated for the past five months, and divorce was now inevitable.

I also made sure to remind the court that I am a dual US-Guatemalan citizen. I was born in Miami and I pay US taxes. I told them that my finances are an open book and that my bank accounts speak for themselves, yet no one had asked me to disclose them. Finally, I told the judge that I needed to go home to my children.

I am sure there was more, but this is all I remember. Maybe one day I will be able to read the court transcripts or hear the audio.

Then came the questions. I was interrogated by Olyslager's attorney, the attorneys representing Global Forest Partners, and the public prosecu-tor, and I responded as best I could. My accusers were ruthless and made horrifying statements, accusing me of awful things as they presented piles of documents for the judge to review. They claimed it was evidence, but there was no way any human could go through all that paperwork in the short time we had before us. According to them, all the evidence was against my husband, but I had been instrumental in getting investors to invest. They claimed that when my husband received the money, he transferred it to my accounts, where I managed it further. Where was the evidence of these transactions? I was flabbergasted. I had to sit there, handcuffed and silent, while they went on and on about me with accusations that they had to know were false, with no regard for the damage they were causing an innocent person, and all before a judge who did not know me, but held my future in her hands. After my accusers finished destroying my name with unsubstantiated lies, the judge had to come to a decision, without having time to even flip through the piles of documents, simply going on what was stated thus far in court that day.

To my surprise, she concluded that since there was no report from IVE (Intendencia de Verificación Especial, also known internationally as Unidad de Análisis Financiero or UAF, a special department created in 2001 aimed to prevent money laundering and the financing of terrorism in Guatemala), the money laundering accusation should be thrown out. She then said she didn't understand why there were attorneys representing Global Forest Partners (GFP) present during a hearing where Olyslager was the claimant, to which GFP's attorneys from the law firm of Mayora & Mayora revealed that they were joint plaintiffs.

Finally, the judge asked all parties what they were requesting from the court. The public prosecutor, who was there on behalf of the state, alleging that a law had been broken, and the two attorneys from Mayora & Mayora representing GFP requested preventive detention, claiming that since I am a US citizen, as well as a Guatemalan citizen, and had means, I was a flight risk and could flee the country as the other two accused already had. Up until the day before, my husband and his accountant weren't officially fleeing; however, when a warrant for their arrest was issued and they were nowhere to be found, they officially became fugitives of the law.

When the judge asked Olyslager's attorney what they were asking for, Olyslager leaned over to his attorney and whispered something in his ear. Startled, the attorney stared back at him speechless and Olyslager simply said, "Will you say it, or should I?" The attorney reluctantly proceeded, "My client, Mr. Olyslager, wants the court to know that he will soon be a father and he does not request the court to send the accused to prison."

The last one to speak was my attorney, Arturo Miranda. Up until that moment, I had no idea if my attorney was any good, but as soon as he began, nobody in that courtroom could take their eyes off him. It was as if the lion had woken up and everyone present was wishing to one day be like him.

Unlike the insignificant attorney representing Olyslager, attorney Juan Ignacio Gómez-Cuevas from Mayora & Mayora representing GFP, and the attorney general's public prosecutor, Miranda was not only well prepared and efficient, but he had the necessary ammunition to counter the attacks. His passion left me in awe. Among other things, he claimed that the only option was to let me go home, since there was not a single piece of evidence hinting at my involvement.

The judge linked me to due process and declared that I could go home during the following three months of investigation. She stated that I should not leave the country without prior authorization, and that I should sign the book at the Attorney General's Office every fifteen days to prove that I had not fled the country. She did not set bail, deciding that it wasn't needed. I'd be going home that same afternoon.

We left the courtroom and my loved ones were waiting outside with open arms. We were all relieved, but I knew the nightmare was just beginning; it would continue its course and I had no choice but to let it. I still could not believe it. I had returned to Guatemala and stayed there, knowing that I had done no wrong and naively thinking there was no reason to fear or to hide. How wrong I had been. No wonder most people in this country decide to flee at the first sight of legal trouble, instead of trusting the justice system. In Guatemala's defense, and notwithstanding my husband's alleged actions, this legal strategy orchestrated by Olyslager and his attorney, the law firm of Mayora & Mayora representing Global Forest Partners, and an apparently partial public prosecutor, is one of the vilest I have witnessed and experienced in my life. But then again, I am not an attorney and I had never been in legal trouble before.

——

I was sent back to the carceleta to wait as the officers prepared the paperwork for my release. The moment I stepped inside the holding cell, the women asked me how it had gone and if I was to go home that day. I was still in shock and couldn't allow myself to be happy about the news, because I didn't feel I could trust the court to efficiently process and guarantee my release that day. That was immediately followed by another thought: how could I show happiness about going home when I was surrounded by so many women who may not have the same privilege that day? So, I quietly answered, "God willing, I should go home today." And to my utmost surprise, these women, each one dealing with her own personal story, many facing years behind bars far away from their loved ones, and most lacking the support and resources I had, approached me one by one to hug me and wish me well. That pure and humane gesture moved me to the core.

I'm not sure how much time went by, but eventually my name was called and I was asked to step out of the carceleta. I said my goodbyes and wished the women luck, never imagining I would see this place again so soon. I was then taken to sign the exit book, where we waited for some paperwork to come through. Finally, I was led back up the same ramp I had walked down less than thirty-six hours before. Once again, as we passed the men's holding cell, the male inmates got rowdy while the police officers were gentlemen. Miranda was by my side every step of the way, until he delivered me safely to my family, waiting outside on the street. I gave him a long heartfelt hug and thanked him.

Once I'd got into the car, I spoke to my friends on my cell phone and they asked me if they could come over to my house to see me. I was exhausted, but how could I say no? I warned them I had nothing to offer them at home but that I needed to see them, hug them, share my story with them in the flesh, and simply have the same wonderful and blessed time we always have when we are together.

As I walked through my front door, I was lovingly greeted by my dogs, Sidney and Chelsea, and warmly welcomed with a hug by my housekeeper, Olga. My children were supposed to come home that night, but they were so happy spending time with their cousins at my brother Turi's home, that my mother decided to let them stay the night. This worked out fine. It would give me time to celebrate with my family and friends, and allow me a desperately needed good night's sleep in my own bed that night.

I managed to take a warm shower and change into sweatpants. My freshly washed hair was wet and gathered in a messy bun, and I was makeup-free. Several weeks would pass before I was able to wear makeup again. It seemed useless because any eye makeup I put on was inevitably washed away by tears. Vanity had become irrelevant.

Soon, my angels, my chosen brothers and sisters, began to pour into my home, each bearing a bottle of wine, cheese, or some other goody to share, along with those quiet, long hugs that say it all. We have spent a lifetime growing and learning together, sharing success, defeat, sadness, and joy, and here they were once again, by my side, replenishing my soul, allowing me to share my experience, letting me cry and laugh at the absurdity of it all.

I had just been through thirty-six of the most intense hours of personal growth I had ever experienced, and I had verified that I have an amazing family and unconditional friends, and that the love I am showered with is much more powerful than the hate Juan Pablo Olyslager Muñoz and a team of well-known attorneys could throw my way. I knew the battle would be long and hard, but now I also knew it would not be impossible.

CHAPTER 4

Months of Turmoil

—

The three months that followed were a blur of emotions. I was trying to get my life back on track, but I was now unemployed, I did not know where my husband was, and I had to deal with my ongoing legal issues. Nothing brought me more joy and a sense of purpose than my children.

I woke up on Saturday, the first morning back after a night in jail, rested and eagerly awaiting my children's arrival. My mother and I had decided to treat their two nights away at Tío Turi's house as if it had been their idea. I'd worry later about any questions they might have about where I'd been. They came home delighted, as five-year-old children tend to do, and I couldn't hug them enough.

Later that Saturday morning, I remembered Christie's words from the night before, "The first thing you should do tomorrow is read our classmates' chat. It will be food for your soul." I grabbed my cell phone, turned it on, and went straight to the chat. Tears started rolling down my cheeks. I was so moved by all the messages of love and support. That's how I learned that my longtime friends had not only been vigilant about my situation, but had even opened a bank account to raise funds in the event the judge required me to pay bail. They had also managed to have two bail bond companies ready so that I would not have to spend another night in jail.

———

A month went by and my home received visitors on a daily basis. My friends, family, and loved ones continued to make sure I was never alone. My therapist had once again diagnosed me with post-traumatic stress syndrome, which I had already suffered a year earlier when my husband told me of his financial troubles. I left my house only for the essentials or to meet in safe places with the people I loved. While at home, I was anxious and worried, thinking that "they" would come back to take me once again. My attorney insisted that this would not happen, but I didn't feel reassured. If I had been taken once from the safety of my home to the carceleta, courtesy of a false statement against me and with no tangible proof to back it up, why would it not happen again? What was to stop them? I had seen with my own eyes at my hearing how the Mayora & Mayora attorneys representing Global Forest Partners had requested preventive detention, and my attorney had told me that after that judge recused herself from my case, they had gone to the new judge with the same request, which thankfully had been denied . . . for the time being. Only an idiot would not worry in my case.

Meanwhile, as the law firms of Mayora & Mayora and Frank Trujillo, who represented Olyslager, continued working together to make their false accusations stick in their evidence-less case against me, my original judge, the one who'd conducted my hearing on Friday, September 18, 2015, had been apprehended the following Monday, September 21, 2015, and taken into custody, charged with several crimes. I later saw an online video recorded during her preliminary hearing, when she said that judges are no longer able to judge justly in Guatemala, that they can no longer do their jobs and do what is best, since they are now coerced into doing what the public prosecutor's office and the CICIG say must be done. She said that as long as CICIG is in Guatemala, all judges must say yes to the public prosecutor's office and yes to CICIG in order to avoid finding themselves in the same predicament she was currently in: in custody.

I do not know if her statement was true, but I witnessed firsthand what unfounded accusations on paper can do in this country. All I know is that this judge allowed me due process, but she must have doubted the intentions of Mayora & Mayora, the public prosecutor, and her cousin Frank Trujillo's law firm, because even though they were requesting my imprisonment, she refused, and instead sent me home to my children without having to pay bail.

As this court drama unfolded before my eyes, I had yet another battle to fight back at home: my children's custody. Some ten days after having been advised while in the carceleta to transfer my children's guardianship to my mother, in order to protect them from being taken by the state, my mother, my brother, my children, and I were summoned to a children's court to explain to a judge that I, the mother of the children in question, had been released and was in full capacity to regain custody of my children. Under the guidance of our family attorney, we planned to request that the judge remove my mother as guardian and legally return my children to me. However, the process was not as simple as logic may imply, and so began my new nightmare. After hearing our statement, the judge decided that, aside from the fact that her own people did not make the required visits nor present the required reports to her, my children were now in the system and there was nothing she could do but follow protocol.

To determine if I, the mother, was the ideal person to care for Nina and Fabián, my mother and I were ordered to attend a twelve-meeting course called "Parenting School." In addition, my mother, my children, and I would have to undergo psychological evaluations (state, not private), and receive psychological therapy until the state doctor determined that we were fine. This was ludicrous! I had freely taken an attorney's advice thinking that this was the best course of action to protect my children, and once again I was verifying that the government and its intensions were the last thing anyone should allow into their private matters. Even though my children would live with me, my mother would continue being their legal guardian until we sorted all of this out. I was devastated. My family attorney urged me to focus on the positive and insisted that at least my children had not been physically taken away from me.

We left the courthouse flabbergasted by what had just happened. Our next hearing was scheduled for November 17, 2015. In the meantime, my mother and I were ordered to find a government-approved center for our therapy and to attend parenting classes, go to INACIF (the National Institute of Forensic Sciences) with the children for our psychological evaluations, and to the PNG (Procuraduría General de la Nación) for another evaluation. As if I didn't already have enough on my plate! How do people who work manage to navigate these processes?

I called several state-approved centers and finally found a place quite far away from my home called CAIFGUA (Centro de Atención Integral Para el Fortalecimiento de las Familias Guatemaltecas). It was located just one block away from a designated red zone, areas known for having especially high crime rates, but it was the only place where my mother and I could attend parenting classes on Saturdays, and all of us together to therapy during the week.

Our first parenting class took place on Saturday, October 31, 2015. The subject was domestic violence and child abuse, irrelevant in our home, but interesting nonetheless. We had no option but to go through the motions, follow the judge's orders, and hope that the issue would be resolved at our next hearing.

The following Tuesday, my mother, my children, and I were scheduled for another court-ordered psychological evaluation at INACIF. This doctor was the first one to ask me who was the person claiming I was an unfit parent. He insisted that someone must have declared that I wasn't taking proper care of my children. I clarified my circumstances and explained the predicament I was in. He insisted there was no reason for me to be there, and after interviewing my children, he promised that we would have no trouble from him or his report to the judge.

The following Thursday, my mother, children, and I returned to CAIFGUA to begin our individual therapy sessions—forty minutes each. After the therapist concluded the private sessions with my children, he asked me to join in. He wanted the three of us to play a board game so he could see how we interacted. My children and I are so used to playing games together that we had a blast, and the doctor had to stop us. He said to me, "I am delighted by your relationship with your children. You cannot imagine how many five-year-olds get frustrated because they can't play well."

Before we left, he asked me how many sessions the judge had ordered, to which I responded that I was under the impression that as the therapist, he should decide that. I told him my next hearing was on November 17, so he graciously set our next appointment for November 19, reasoning that if our case was resolved during the hearing, there would be no need for us to attend this next appointment.

Meanwhile, on Tuesday, November 10, we drove to the Attorney General's Office at 8 a.m. for the other psychological evaluations required by the judge. After more than an hour's wait, the therapist came down to the waiting room to get us. I went up first. This was the second doctor to inform me that this entire situation with the custody of my children had been unnecessary from the start. The PGN does not remove children who have other family members willing and able to care for them, as in my case. However, since we had been ill-advised and my mother and brother had requested from the state that my children be protected legally, we were now in this insufferable system created to protect children from their parents . . . in this case, from me.

While my children had their sessions that day at the PGN, I decided to make an appointment with the social worker, as had been ordered by the court. This social worker, who was assigned by name, had failed to visit my home as the judge had ordered and I was not happy with her. As it turned out, she had tried to do her job, but had attempted to visit my brother's home since that was the address originally entered in my case file. She showed me the paperwork and I realized that my address and my cell number were also incorrect.

"My hearing is scheduled for next week," I said, "so I would appreciate it if you could visit us and report before then."

"Let's begin working on the socioeconomic study right now then," she responded. "I will do my best to visit your home on Wednesday or Thursday, but please be patient with me because I do not have a car."

Here was yet another good person filled with good intentions and ready to do her job, but drowning in a bureaucratic, inefficient, state system that lacks the resources and the tools to help people carry out their duties.

It was close to noon when my mother, my son, Fabián, and the therapist came down the stairs after their sessions had concluded. To my dismay, just as Fabián was placing his foot on the second-to-last step, he tripped on his rubber boots, hit his face against my mother's knee, and fell to the floor. I ran to him, picked him up, made sure he was fine, and then immediately noticed his left eye was red. Our next hearing before the judge was in a week's time, and by then it would surely be purple! Thank God it all happened in front of the therapist, the receptionist, and a waiting area full of patients. I told the receptionist I was worried about Fabian's eye turning purple and the judge thinking it had been abuse. She suggested I take him next door to see the PGN doctor. He would give me a letter explaining what had happened. By now I knew that anything could and would be used against me. Before I left, I turned around and saw the people in the waiting area, all nodding their heads in unison. It was a comical reaction. We were all there because of a judge's order; we understood one another.

That day, after dropping my mom off at her house, I kept going over what the therapist had told me, how I had been ill-advised and how this whole situation with my children was completely unnecessary and could've been avoided. I had tried my best to remain positive and calm throughout all this upheaval, but that day my rage got the best of me. What I had been led to believe was the sound decision had turned out to be one of the worst decisions of my life, filling my days with pain and anguish and causing me to lose precious time with court-mandated therapy sessions that none of us needed. I was so frustrated and angry with myself for having allowed this into our lives that tears welled up in my eyes, and for the first time since this entire ordeal exploded with my husband more than a year earlier, I cried in front of my children.

As we drove home, they chatted away in the back seat, asking me questions that I could not answer because I was choked up inside. It was not until we got home and they got out of the car that they saw my red, swollen eyes. Immediately they sprang into action, hugging me and kissing me all over, just as I do with them when they are sad. Moved by their reaction, I took a deep breath and said, "Mami also gets sad sometimes and that's OK. Soon I will be fine, because your kisses and hugs cure everything."

The following day, Wednesday, November 11, at 2:30 p.m., we received a visit from the social worker at the PGN, who came to assess my children's current living conditions at my home. "It is obvious that your children are very well taken care of in every sense," she said before she left.

———

During those three months after my time in the holding cell, I found myself crying constantly, sometimes it seemed as if for days on end. My body, my mind, and my heart were spent. Not only was I dealing with an accusation of criminal association in a criminal case for embezzlement (fraud), and a family case at PGN in the hope of regaining custody of my children, I had also decided to file a lawsuit against the magazine *Contrapoder*, which had written articles about my husband and me, but most importantly, had published unblurred photos of my children's faces, which they had taken from my Facebook page. This was unforgivable and as much as I did not want another legal battle, I could not let this go unpunished. My children had already been harmed, and I was now determined to try and make sure that this did not happen to anyone else.

So, there I was, suddenly facing the abrupt end of my marriage, an impending divorce, my unforeseen unemployment, unexpected legal proceedings, and the damage caused by tarnishing my good name and reputation in the public eye. I'm sure any single one of these situations would cause most people to temporarily crumble, yet somehow, I was still standing.

As much as my loved ones insisted that I should remain strong, that I could do it, that I had everything it takes to survive this enormous blow in my life, there were times when I couldn't see it clearly and I just needed to vent and rest. Despite every word of wisdom and gesture of love and support, I felt no one truly understood me; I sometimes felt very alone.

———

November 17, 2015, finally arrived and I anxiously set out for my hearing before a family judge, hoping that we'd be able to resolve this issue once and for all. I was much calmer this time. I had wonderful people attesting to my ability as a mother and I had concluded that the worst thing that could happen had already happened. The situation could only remain the same or change for the better. We went through two hours of legal proceedings, testimonies, reports, and finally the judge decided to suspend my mother's temporary guardianship and return it to me. The social worker would still visit us every two months for the next six months, my mother and I would continue with our designated parenting classes, and my children and I would continue our state therapy until the therapist deemed it no longer necessary.

I was hopeful that the state therapist who had told us on our first visit that we were fine would give us the all clear, and my children and I would be allowed to put this latest episode behind us. So, after our hearing, I eagerly called this therapist to tell him the news and to cancel our appointment, but I was informed that therapists cannot speak to their patients unless it is during scheduled appointments. Bureaucracy = ineptitude = inefficiency = no logic = lack of common sense . . . welcome to my new world.

———

November 27 rolled in and I turned forty-seven years old. I wasn't planning on celebrating my birthday that year, so my mother invited her best friend, her friend's daughter, my children, and me out for breakfast. Later, my friend Anabelle invited us to her yearly Friday Thanksgiving celebration and she had a surprise cake for me. Then, several friends insisted on coming over to my home to celebrate. So I went from not wanting to celebrate to rejoicing in the presence of my loved ones, regardless of the current circumstances.

On December 1, I went back to the courthouse for my pretrial hearing. I arrived with my mother—my father arrived later. I was quickly learning that my best plan was to have no expectations, so I entered the building at peace with whatever might transpire. When my attorney Miranda arrived, he was surprised to see that our counterparts were not there. Our name was called and we entered the courtroom. Miranda argued that since my accuser had already made a civil claim against my husband and his accountant before he included me in his second claim, this one criminal, this second process should be stopped until a decision had been made regarding the first. Because my first judge had recused herself, we were now beginning what would be a very long list of temporary judges serving on my case. This new judge required that my attorney's petition be made in writing instead of verbally, which meant the actual hearing was postponed until December 14.

I went home that day and continued my life as I had done thus far. A couple of days later, I was on my way to meet several of my girlfriends for lunch to celebrate our birthdays, but was running late because my children had ballet practice that morning, so I told them to start without me. When I finally arrived, I bumped into one of my friends at the entrance. She was talking on her cell phone but quickly stopped and asked, "Have you seen our group chat?"

"No," I replied. "Is our lunch canceled?"

"No," she said, "but Olyslager is sitting at the table next to ours! We were wondering if you would rather change venues."

Incredibly, I felt nothing but the arrival of an unexpected opportunity. If anyone should be uncomfortable and leave under these circumstances, it should be him, not me. I was not about to cower away from him. So, I entered the restaurant, walked right by him, and received a warm welcome by my dear friends. I sat in the chair they had saved for me, with my back to Olyslager and his two friends. My friends later told me that he seemed fidgety and uncomfortable, putting on his sunglasses and taking them off constantly. Several other people I knew left their tables to come say hello and give me a hug. Eventually, he left. A small yet priceless victory for me.

One of the most common questions I am asked regarding Olyslager's accusations against me is, "What do the Mayora & Mayora law firm and the US timber investment company Global Forest Partners have to do with any of it?" My first judge, Jisela Reinoso Trujillo, the one who recused herself for being first cousin to Olyslager's attorney, Frank Trujillo, expressed the exact same sentiment during my first hearing. It was explained to her that my husband had allegedly awarded Olyslager a farm belonging to GFP as a guarantee for the personal investment that Olyslager had extended him. Mayora & Mayora are GFP's legal counsel, hired to protect their interests in Guatemala (GFP owns Forestal Ceibal and Forestal Chaklum, the entities said farms belong to). I can only imagine that somewhere along the line, Trujillo and Mayora & Mayora realized that if one party had the farm that the other party wanted returned, their best bet was to join forces instead of fight against each other. All Mayora & Mayora needed to get Olyslager on their side was for him to believe that a judge would never award him the farm, and that he would lose everything if he did not join them by giving his statement against me. But, after another judge declared that my husband did have the legal faculty to award those farms as a guarantee to Olyslager, he no longer needed GFP or this entire situation he had agreed to. Unfortunately, by then, he had already given a false statement to the authorities and could not get out of it so easily. This is what I believe happened behind the scenes before this case was brought before a judge.

In addition, Mayora & Mayora, as GFP's legal counsel hired to protect their interests in Guatemala, were also most likely the party responsible for allowing my husband's actions, leaving them in a very awkward and humiliating position. As much as I understood their predicament, in my eyes, they will never be able to justify how their actions against me and my family were appropriate. If Mayora & Mayora considered themselves victims once, I have been a victim twice; once from my husband's alleged actions, and a second time from theirs. How a group of attorneys came up with such a legal strategy, I can almost understand, but how Olyslager, a businessman, husband, and father-to-be, ever agreed to give a false statement against a housewife and cause so much pain and suffering, I will never understand. There is no amount of anger, frustration, or revenge possible to ever justify that. His declaration against me says so much more about him than it ever said about me.

—

Time never stands still, and in the blink of an eye, Christmastime was upon us. My usual Christmas tradition had always involved waiting for the imported Canadian Christmas trees to arrive at the end of November, which meant my decorated tree would be up and ready before my birthday. However, this year was different. I did not have the money to spend on such an extravagance, and had no desire to bother with the purchase, transport, and care of a live tree. Suddenly, I realized that this gave me the freedom to set up our tree whenever I wished, and so, by early November, I dusted off our fake tree, and it was up and shining a light on our difficult circumstances in no time. Not only did we celebrate the longest Christmas season in my life to this day, but I also relished the tranquility of not having the money to buy Christmas gifts. It was fabulous and liberating. The season was solely focused on spending time with the ones we love, a life lesson for me and an invaluable way to teach my children that gifts are only one of many ways in which we can express love.

In the meantime, I realized that time goes on with or without me, that I cannot control everything, and that that's OK. And so, when I heard that Miranda had requested our December 14 hearing be postponed because he had another hearing on that same date, I just took another breath, and wrote the new date in my calendar, a day that would seal my fate and change my life forever: January 5, 2016.

CHAPTER 5

Pray for Me

A new year began, and with it came so much uncertainty that I had a very difficult time welcoming it properly. As much as we all tried to keep things as normal as possible, nothing was normal. My brother-in-law's invitation to spend New Year's Eve at my mother-in-law's beach house was a welcome one. I can imagine they were trying to let me know that they loved my children and me, and that, in spite of everything, and especially since my husband was nowhere to be found, they were still there for us. Furthermore, regardless of the difficult circumstances, we managed to have a wonderful time.

The teakwood beach house sits on concrete stilts, less than one hundred feet from the Pacific Ocean. It is small and simple compared to the many mansions that have been built lately on the beaches of Monterrico, Guatemala, but it has always been a place where we are in touch with nature, can spend quality time with one another, and have made so many fantastic family memories. From the front of the house, one enjoys a constant fresh breeze and an amazing ocean view. From the back, early in the morning or on extremely clear days, several majestic volcanoes and mountain ranges are visible in the horizon. In addition, the house is nestled close to a turtle sanctuary, and at this time of the year the baby turtles, who have been saved from constant poaching, are born and set free. We all loved visiting the Tortugario and being a part of the turtle release effort. This time of year is also the season for whale and dolphin migrations, and we've been lucky enough to have witnessed them swimming along the coast on several occasions—a truly life-changing experience.

Following our usual tradition, we welcomed the New Year on the beach, roasting marshmallows by the campfire and waiting for the midnight fireworks to light up the entire coastline. When the clock struck twelve, we toasted, hugged, and wished one another a wonderful New Year. This is what we have often done during the past twelve years, since the house was built with so much effort, so much promise, and so much love. As we embraced and welcomed 2016, I felt grateful that my husband's family had opened their home and invited my children and me to celebrate together one more time.

After our warm family holiday, we returned home and reality was upon us once again. I did my best to keep calm and stay positive regarding my fast-approaching hearing date—easier said than done.

———

January 5 proved to be a chilly day, around 65 degrees Fahrenheit, not terribly cold, but cold enough for Guatemala. What do you wear to a courthouse in a third world country when you have been accused of embezzlement, fraud, and criminal association; when the judge you are about to face is new on the case and will hear the most awful charges against you; when the Attorney General's Office and a powerful well-known law firm insists you are guilty? I decided to stay true to myself and chose a pair of black pants, a pink cashmere sweater set, and black boots. I figured I would be elegant enough to be respectful of the court, warm enough if needed, comfortable, and true to my usual attire. The last thing I wanted was to feel like I was a fake.

My father, my mother, and I arrived at the courthouse on time. Eventually my case number and name were called and Miranda and I went into the now familiar courtroom. We all sat in our usual spots, except for Juan Pablo Olyslager Muñoz, who was courageous enough to give the Attorney General's Office a false statement against me, but would never again show up at court. That's right, from that moment forward, he was a no-show; however, that didn't stop the proceedings from moving on as usual. The attorneys all greeted one another, following professional protocol, but their familiarity and niceties felt insulting to me. They were all there, being paid to do their jobs, while my life was hanging in the balance. As we settled into our seats, Julia Marisol Rivera Aguilar, the new judge assigned to my case, walked in. And so began the hearing.

The attorneys did their thing, maligning my name and character, while the judge listened, and once again, the opposing parties requested that the judge send me to preventive detention. Two separate judges had denied their request so far. The judge then proceeded to speak, analyzing the case for what to me felt like an eternity, until I suddenly heard her say, "I therefore have decided that the accused should be sent to preventive custody." What? Her words took Miranda and me by surprise. He glanced over at me, speechless. However, as shocked as I was by her decision, it seemed in line with everything I had witnessed and experienced in the courthouse so far, a courthouse where I had yet to see any reason, any truth, or any justice.

Nevertheless, at that moment I couldn't help thinking, *How can this be?* How could this new judge, a woman and an officer sworn to uphold the laws of the land and protect citizens from injustice, so blatantly violate my rights? Does the law not clearly state that preventive custody is a last resort, that all people are innocent until proven guilty? What could have possibly led her to believe, with such certainly, that I was guilty of anything? Where was the proof? Had she not noticed that, three months earlier, a judge had sent me home, that I had complied with everything the court had asked of me, that I had remained in the country, facing the system head-on, trying to still believe in it? Wasn't that evidence enough that I wasn't a flight risk?

As my mind raced through all these thoughts, the remaining time in the courtroom was a blur. All I remember was that I was led out of the courtroom and into a small office right next door, followed by my parents, who had been waiting outside and had just heard the news from Miranda. There was a woman working at her desk in this office, who let my mother and me sit on the sofa and told me to stay there until they came to get me.

I don't remember crying; I simply dove into full survival mode, trying to understand and envision what the judge's statement meant for my life. I removed my jewelry, put it in my purse, and gave it to my mother. I grabbed my cell phone and somehow had the clarity of mind to write a Facebook post. I knew it was the only tool I had to let the world know what these people were doing to me. The post read: "I am on my way to Santa Teresita courtesy of Mayora & Mayora's legal strategy against Roberto Montano [my husband]. Pray for me. Take care of my children."

My friend Melly immediately called and asked, "What is going on?" I told her I was being taken to El Centro de Detención Preventiva para Mujeres Santa Teresa. She was as flabbergasted as we all were and quickly replied, "Make your post *public* so that we can all share it." I did and less than thirty minutes later, I added one last post: "Friends—I need you to tell my story to those who will listen. Many of you are friends, clients, and you can exercise some form of pressure at Mayora. Thank you for believing in me." And that is how the people who knew me, loved me, and believed in me began an incredible sixty-five-day quest and movement to free me from prison.

Prison. I was going to prison. I couldn't completely wrap my head around this predicament, but had no choice but to be strong. My parents and I stayed in that little adjacent office with the friendly court worker for a couple of hours. We tried to get me some more appropriate prison clothes (there are no uniforms for inmates in Guatemalan prisons), but there was not enough time. Eventually, I was handcuffed and taken down to the carceleta one more time. However, this time I was to go straight to jail. No going home, no saying goodbye to my children or having the chance to explain my sudden absence to them, nothing. A single sentence from a judge who had examined no evidence against me and I went from being a free woman to a prison inmate.

I spent the rest of the day and well into the night in that holding cell waiting for the last of the inmates to finish their legal proceedings, so we could all be herded into the prison truck and hauled off to jail. By then, my world had reached unfathomable depths, and my life as I knew it was being deleted from my mind, seemingly making room for whatever I was to confront next. I focused on this new reality, on this new circumstance. Little Miss Planner was now being forced to improvise. Only time would tell how successful I would be.

CHAPTER 6

El Centro de Detención Preventiva para Mujeres Santa Teresa

WEEK ONE

I arrived at Santa Teresa Women's Correctional Facility in Guatemala City on Wednesday, January 6, 2016, slightly past midnight. After less than twenty-four hours in jail, I had already accumulated a wealth of new experiences that I was anxious to share with the outside world, but my brain was a wreck and my heart so broken that I sometimes felt like I couldn't even breathe. Every time I thought of my two lovely, innocent children, I broke down and cried.

The road from the courthouse's carceleta in Guatemala City to Santa Teresa was dark and unknown to me, and the prison was darker still. A dim light bulb here and there made my eyes struggle to see. Handcuffed and guarded, we stepped out of the gray pickup truck and descended many steps toward the prison. My first memory will probably always be the terrible stench from cat urine overpowering my senses as soon as we entered the warden's office area. I felt like I was being buried alive.

The check-in process is still a blur to me. I was asked about my academic background, about the reason for my imprisonment, and was assigned to Cellblock One. The word was that I was lucky to have been placed in that cellblock, but I couldn't fathom it. I was registered as inmate number 104, in a block originally designed for an estimated sixty-four women, with thirty-two bunk beds. Needless to say, this situation forced us to sleep in unconventional ways. At 1:30 a.m., I walked into a dark cellblock, lit only by a colorful Christmas tree and the traditional Guatemalan crèche.

After the guards locked the gates behind me, I was welcomed by Mimi, whom I would soon learn was the cellblock's voice. It is common for new inmates to arrive at the prison late at night, so Mimi was used to this situation. When I say Mimi welcomed me, I literally mean she welcomed me to share her twin bed. I was overcome by such exhaustion after spending twelve hours in the carceleta, that I didn't think twice about my newfound situation and simply crawled into bed next to this big woman, who generously let me have one-third of the space on her sleeping bunk and even lent me a blanket. Before long, I fell asleep.

I did wake up several times during the night, a bit disoriented, but fully aware of my circumstances; having no watch, and therefore no way of knowing what time it was, I closed my eyes and went back to sleep. At 4 a.m., I was startled awake by a bell, like the ones you may hear in schools or firehouses. However, this was no school recess or fire emergency. This is what they call an *inmate count* or *head count*. I quickly learned this was to be part of my new daily prison routine. When that bell rang at 4 a.m., every last one of us had to get out of our beds, line up in a predetermined manner in the main cellblock hall, and wait for the prison warden and her lieutenants to complete the 104-inmate head count. After the officers locked the gates behind them and were on their way to count inmates in the other cellblocks, we were finally allowed to go back to bed. I also learned that on Saturdays and Sundays our head count was mercifully moved to 6 a.m., giving us two extra hours before we were rattled awake to have our presence confirmed.

Inmates must be up by 9 a.m. and taking a shower is mandatory. The queue is long and the water cold. One shower curtain covers two showers with no showerheads, but most inmates shower one at a time. Some inmates shower in pairs to save time, but that is optional. Since showering there was not a pleasant ordeal, few inmates took their time. There is also a pila (a basin) where you can wash yourself in the open, but as I found out throughout the day, the pila is also used to wash hands, brush teeth, and scrub dishes and clothes.

Since I had nothing but the clothes I had chosen for my court hearing the day before and my father's jacket, I thought I'd have to skip my shower that morning, but several women came to my rescue. One lent me a small towel and a packet of shampoo and conditioner, but I did not have to use them because Mimi lent me a larger towel and her dandruff shampoo. I was not ready to wash my hair in that cold water, so I used the shampoo to wash my body. I was a champion at my two first traumatic events: sleeping and bathing.

I spent the rest of the day learning the ropes. There were six toilet stalls in my cellblock and, per Mimi's orders, I was to use toilet stall number three. The toilet handles did not work, so one had to pour water from a huge bucket into the toilet bowl to flush it. To my surprise, the system worked well. No doors were allowed, so curtains were used for privacy. Curtains were also used to mark each separate bunk area. They were all uniform curtains, paid for by the inmates, and were changed every three to four months. The ones hanging during my stay were satiny and pink, which made the cellblock look like a cheap brothel. Regardless of looks, the privacy they brought was greatly appreciated.

Even though my first day in prison was not officially a visitor's day, my father managed to stop by to check on me and see how I was holding up. In addition to giving me his love and words of wisdom, he also told me to find an apparently well-known inmate named Lili. Later, while searching for her to introduce myself, I learned that the stories about her power were legendary, and many inmates even feared her. Our meeting was brief, but I accomplished the mission my dad had given me.

Before he left, my father also made sure to give me some money. The prison system provides inmates with nothing, and you can't survive your prison sentence without money, no matter how long or short it may be. I had to pay Mimi seven dollars for some sort of cellblock entrance fee, seventy cents per week for a so-called communal account, and fourteen cents for weekly bathroom cleanup. There was a well-established prison economy and rules for just about everything; if you broke them, you got a punishment referred to as *plancha* (same word used for our concrete beds) where you had to clean the entire cellblock for a full day. This included sweeping and mopping before dawn, at noon, and at 5 p.m., and buying all the needed cleaning supplies with your own money. You were allowed to pay someone else to do it, but it would cost an estimated ten dollars, which was considered a small fortune in Santa Teresa. Water bottles cost seventy cents each and there were several food stands to purchase lunch, although I wasn't prepared to trust my luck with any of them. The prison system provided inmates three inedible meals per day, a food service commonly referred to as "Rancho," so access to any other type of food was priceless.

Rancho food came into the prison several times per day, in huge plastic barrels or buckets. According to prison rumors, Rancho suppliers were paid per meal per inmate per day, yet only a small fraction of it was spent on the food. Some inmates also believed that this is part of the reason why inmates are kept in prison beyond their sentences, to continue getting paid per inmate. I do not know if this is true, but it makes some sense. Inmates also claimed that Rancho food was much better not long ago, but that the contract had since been awarded to someone else. I wonder who the players are. Prisons must be a big business for somebody.

There was no cafeteria, so Rancho food was distributed at each cellblock three times per day. Inmates had to have their own plastic plates and cutlery since the prison did not offer any. Bread or machine-made tortillas were a staple, along with black beans, which many inmates wash, drain, and recook, adding their own spices to make them edible. Vegetables were a rare commodity, and when they were available, usually included plantains, potatoes, chayote, and zucchini. Sometimes a ham and spinach concoction was served that I mistook for pasta when I first saw it. Sundays were usually cereal and banana days. Sometimes coffee was available, delivered in a huge transparent plastic bag, and was so weak that it could easily be mistaken for iced tea. A prized lunch came on Wednesdays when plain boiled chicken was served. The women would rinse it and finish cooking it properly by adding their own spices, onions, and other vegetables, which were available for purchase inside the prison. Some inmates had permits for their own individual electric burners, and there were two communal burners available for the rest of us. As with everything else, you had to wait in line.

Cellblock gates were opened between 9 and 10 a.m. and inmates were allowed to wander around until noon. There were many women and not much to do. Inmates were locked in again from 12 p.m. to 2 p.m. Final daily lockdown happened at 4:30 p.m. This meant that enjoying the night sky was forbidden.

There was one public telephone in my cellblock and official Guatemalan Penitentiary System Calling Cards had to be used. Calling cards could be purchased from Mimi, but they cost twenty percent more than stated on the card, which was the fee she charged and most likely went straight to her pocket. I was warned to be very careful about one's calling card number because if another inmate should see it, she would use your minutes before you did. There was a system to call and a woman named Enma was in charge of the calling queue at that time. I put my name in at 8:40 a.m.; however, the day rolled on and by 4:50 p.m. I still hadn't been able to make my call. This new prison reality had me completely disconnected from the outside world.

To keep busy that afternoon, I set out in search of a book, another rare commodity in this prison. I had been told there was a library of sorts at the prison school, but books could only be used by official students and they couldn't be checked out. I was then directed to the Social Services office, and to my surprise, the prison's social worker, Marta, had begun a small project she liked to call "The Reading Corner." She had managed to get hold of close to thirty books. The options were limited, but there were about ten novels and Marta happily let me borrow one. I chose *Amor*, by Isabel Allende. My quest was over. I had a book—but a book I was unable to dig into like I usually did due to a newly acquired lack of concentration on my part—so I set out to visit Carmen, the woman I had met months earlier during my overnight stint in the carceleta. On the day she'd been sent to this prison back in September, I never imagined that I would be looking for her a few months later, in search of the only familiar face in this new world I was thrown into.

I found her in a section of the prison called *encamamiento*, a former prison hospital that was now the designated cellblock for inmates whom a judge had deemed unfit to live within the general prison population. The reasons for being placed in encamamiento varied, but usually they had to do with inmate health or safety. Carmen remembered me. We spoke for a little while and I thanked her for her generosity during our first encounter in the carceleta, but she did not seem very happy to see me. That shouldn't have come as a surprise. We barely knew each other, and I had already been advised by Mimi of one clear prison rule: one did not make or have friends in prison. We were all in that dark hole together, doing the best we could while trying to survive. That became the most important thing: survival.

In my efforts to make myself useful, busy my mind, and survive, I visited the labor department to offer my services as an English teacher at the prison school. María, the woman in charge, was very pleased with my offer and asked me to come to a special meeting the next day at 10 a.m.

As I observed how my new prison society worked, I realized there were several unofficial jobs available for inmates. One such position was an *inmate caller*. Callers received no pay, but many visitors tipped them or gave them a little thank-you gift for locating the inmate in question. That afternoon one of these callers came looking for me to tell me I had a visitor. I went to the prison's inmate gates and found Emilio, an attorney and member of my extended family, waiting for me. He had stopped by to visit a client, but also wanted to check up on me, thinking I might appreciate a familiar face and a break.

I was let out through the inmate gates, the normal practice when an attorney visits an inmate, and sat waiting for Emilio to finish his professional visit. To my surprise, in that moment, my brother-in-law Ed, his wife, Vania, and their friend Yvethe walked into the visiting room. Since Vania and Yvethe are both attorneys, they were allowed to visit me outside of regular visiting hours, while Ed posed as their assistant. They were all carrying supplies: a pillow, two blankets, pants, T-shirts, sweatshirts, Crocs, bathroom items, a towel, toilet paper, money, bread, and some extra goodies. I also received two boxes of cereal courtesy of another dear friend, and six new undies courtesy of an angel I had never met from Vania's office. Once Emilio finished with his client, he joined us, and we took advantage of his expertise as a former Vice Minister of the Interior, a position that put him in charge of prisons, to make a list of other things I might need. Their visit and the plentiful supplies were all a godsend on such a bleak day.

When I finally returned to my cellblock, I found that Mimi had assigned me new living quarters. I was to move into a bunk bed area (also referred to as plancha, the same word inmates use for punishments) with Clara, Mimi's maid and assistant. Mimi considered it a safe place for me, but there were already three women sleeping there: fifty-three-year-old Clara had the top bed; twenty-seven-year-old Verónica had the lower bed; and thirty-seven-year-old Mariana, a foreigner who had arrived a couple of days earlier than me, slept on the floor. Since the weather had recently turned cold, Mariana had begun sleeping with Verónica on her bed. However, with my addition to the group, it was decided that I was to sleep with Verónica, and Mariana would return to the floor. I felt bad for Mariana, but maybe having the floor to oneself was better than a small cement bunk bed for two. So far, they all seemed like nice women, each going through tough times and experiencing indescribable pain. As my first day in prison came to a close, I realized that some of these women, whom we may normally fear in the outside world due to their crimes, had been nothing but helpful and supportive to me so far.

At 5 p.m., right after we were required to return to our cellblocks for lockdown, I climbed onto Clara's upper bunk hoping to read for a while. It was *Día de los Reyes* (Three Kings' Day) and a celebration was underway, but all I wanted to do was dive into a fictional world and disappear. As I opened my book, I was suddenly overcome by sadness and tears started rolling down my cheeks. I thought I would cry for a while, let it all out, and then try to read again, but the tears didn't quit. It was all too much. This new reality, the thought of Nina and Fabián without a father and now missing their mother, how I was aching to kiss and hug them, not knowing how long this nightmare would last . . . it devastated me. While the party, loud music, games, and jokes grew louder, I felt worse and worse, incessant tears turning into a full-fledged anxiety attack. So, I climbed down from the bed, headed toward the cellblock entrance gates, and sat down, concentrating on regulating my breath. Before I knew it, I was surrounded by several women who came over, sat next to me, and coached me through deep breaths to calm me down, while inside I just wanted to die . . . anything to get out of that place.

I finally managed to calm down and swiftly became aware of the chill in the air coming in through the entrance's open bars. As I stood up and walked to my room, the music was at full blast, burning incense filled the cellblock, and baby Jesus was brought in by "The Three Wise Men." I climbed into my part of the lower bunk bed and, exhausted, at long last fell asleep. It was 7:30 p.m. The party lasted until midnight and I slept right through it. I think I asked God to let me sleep forever that night.

—

As the days of my first week in prison proceeded, I slowly fell into the prison routine. Four a.m. head count, sleep a few more hours, get up, wait in line for a freezing shower, add my name to the phone call list, and busy myself as best I could to endure another day without freedom. On weekdays, Mimi let us watch local television channels from 3 p.m. to 10 p.m., the general preference being the news and soap operas. Our cellblock's go-to series on one of the TVs was *El Señor de los Cielos*, a Mexican series about an infamous drug trafficker that had many on the edge of their seats. Later, from 10 p.m. to midnight, a nightly religious vigil was held inside the cellblock near the main entrance. The women would pray and sing, filling the night's silence with a bit of joy. It was quite beautiful.

On my second morning, I was called to the warden's office, where I was officially registered as a prisoner. From now on, if anyone inquired about my criminal record, it would show that I was an inmate in Santa Teresa. With wet hair, no makeup, and enlarged eyes from crying the night before, I was fingerprinted and then told to stand against a height chart with my inmate number in hand while my picture was taken. I was now an official inmate.

My new roommate Mariana was also being registered that morning. As we got to talking, I learned that she had come here like the rest of us, with nothing but the clothes on her back, while her fifteen-year-old son had also been taken into custody. Mariana was a foreigner, had no family in Guatemala, no money, and no way to contact her child. She told me she had been living in Guatemala with her partner and her fifteen-year-old son from another marriage. She claimed that her partner had gone out to buy sodas on December 31, and had never returned; his burned body turned up on the property where they lived on January 1. The next day, the police came to take her and her son away, charging them with the man's murder, based on a neighbor's statement claiming that the couple fought a lot. After having experienced firsthand how the Attorney General's Office had come after me, I was now readily inclined to believe an inmate rather than our own attorney general. Little did I know how many more similar heart-wrenching stories I would hear during my stay in prison. It changed my life forever.

Later that day, as I roamed around the prison compound, I bumped into a young, tall American woman whom I had noticed the day before. "Are you Anaité?" she asked, and I nodded. "I have a message from a fellow Rotary member who asked me to find you and let you know that everyone is in disbelief and outraged by what they are doing to you!" She introduced herself as Ashley Williams and even though she was not an inmate in Santa Teresa, she spent most of her time here because she ran a screen-printing company (Serigrafía) inside the prison. Ashley didn't remember the person's name, but her message brought me joy. I spent the rest of the afternoon at Serigrafía chatting away with Ashley, who told me I was welcome there anytime I wanted to sit down, read, write, or relax.

Serigrafía is located in the same section of the prison that houses Social Services, encamamiento, the infirmary, and the inmate maternity ward. The general prison population, which includes me, does not have access to that area, but I had received authorization from Lili from encamamiento and now Ashley from Serigrafía, so I was the exception to the rule.

The following day, after the gates to my cellblock were unlocked, I headed to Serigrafía, my newly found safe haven. Ashley wasn't there, but six inmates carefully chosen by Ashley to work for her were present and they gave me a warm welcome. I was quickly approached by one of them, Daniela, who wanted to ask me a question.

"We have been talking amongst ourselves and we would like to know if you would be willing to be our English teacher here at Serigrafía," she said. I could not believe my ears.

"It would be my joy and pleasure, but Ashley has to approve first," I said, to which they happily replied that she had already signed off on this.

Without skipping a beat, they handed me a dry-erase marker to write on their board and the lessons began. Because I was not expecting to teach my first English lesson so soon, I began with the alphabet, fully aware that professional English teachers would be horrified by this, but my students were thrilled . . . it was a hit, and I had found a purpose to impel me through the unknown number of days ahead, however many it would take until justice would prevail.

Meanwhile, I didn't have any other visitors, but I had managed to get access to the phone and speak to my beloved children. Their sweet voices telling me they were well was music to my ears. All I could think after that was, *God, give me the strength to survive.*

As I found my way in prison, I noticed that most activities took place in our community hall, everything from religious worship to inmate visiting hours, sports, and exercise classes, the latter of which I decided to try during my first week in jail. I left my flip-flops on throughout the class, knowing the floor had yet to be cleaned after the many events that had taken place earlier in the day. I was hoping all the exercises would be done standing up, but that was absurd wishful thinking on my part. Next thing I knew, I was rolling around on the floor, bare hands and all, and I survived! At the end of the class, I followed the others over to one of the inmate instructors to sign the attendance sheet. When she heard my name, she introduced herself and said her mother sent me her regards and was praying for me. I did not recognize her name, but I thanked her anyway. I was grateful for all the prayers I could get.

———

Saturday came along—four days in prison and counting. This was a special day for inmates in Cellblocks One and Two because we were allowed to receive visitors, watch movies on our three communal TVs and two DVD players, and end the night with either a dance party or a religious vigil. Our 6 a.m. head count also allowed us the luxury of two extra hours of uninterrupted sleep. Small details that mean the world when you're locked up.

I managed to fit in a call to my children early in the morning and was relieved to hear their happy voices. I then received a visit from my attorney, Miranda, who walked into the prison carrying a huge laundry basket from my mother full of bags for me. Setting the basket aside, we spoke briefly through the bars and he gave me a quick update on my case. He thought there were three possible legal fronts: 1) that my primary accuser, Juan Pablo Olyslager Muñoz, would desist and not show up to my next hearing, which was scheduled for the following Tuesday, and if he desisted the case would be void; 2) the judge would change her mind (Miranda had spoken to the judge, and it seemed that she now had a better understanding of the case and thought she had made a mistake, but her decision was made and she could not change it); 3) after discussing my case with some magistrates, particularly how the judge had sent me to preventive incarceration, Miranda filed an appeal to a higher court, but it would take a miracle for me to go home on Tuesday.

He assured me that he was doing everything possible to fix this atrocity. He also said that GFP and Mayora & Mayora were alleging I was now trying to ruin or damage their reputation with the statement I had posted on Facebook just before I was handcuffed and brought to Santa Teresa on January 5. I couldn't believe my ears! If their reputation had been damaged in any way, it had been completely of their own doing.

Miranda left, and as I walked back to Serigrafía, tears welled up in my eyes while I tried to deal with the possibility of not going home on January 12. Hope was suddenly a double-edged sword in my life, pushing me forward with the belief that the truth would eventually set me free, but also digging a dagger deep into my heart each time I faced the failing justice system.

Wiping away my tears, I settled into my routine at Serigrafía, and was chatting away with the other women, when in came Ashley accompanied by my mother. My heart skipped a beat and I ran to my mother like a little girl, hugging her tight, telling her I loved her, and thanking her for taking care of my children. Ashley kindly suggested we take a couple of chairs into another room and spend our visit there rather than in the communal hall with everyone else, with the loud music blasting, the smells of food, and the people. In the privacy of the new space, my mother told me not to worry about the children because everyone had been calling and making sure that they were OK. At first, we simply told them I had gone away on a trip, but as my absence grew longer, I eventually told them I had gotten a job that would keep me away a little longer than expected. Knowing that they were under her care was an immense relief during those terrible uncertain days. The moment I was sentenced to preventive detention, my mother immediately moved into my home to make sure that my children suffered as little as possible, doing all she could to mitigate the damage to our family.

A couple of minutes later, my brother Turi walked in. I don't think I had ever hugged him for so long or so tight. We sat down and I filled them both in regarding my living conditions, but all I really wanted to talk about was how they were doing, how my children were holding up, and any news about my case. During our conversation, I turned to my mother and reminded her that I urgently needed antibacterial gel to disinfect my hands. She told me that, together with such things as cookies, granola bars, and beans, which I had received inside the huge basket, she had also sent a large bottle of gel, along with apples, grapes, and fruit juice. Then it dawned on me: the guards had certainly confiscated those items at the prison entrance since the only fruit allowed into the prison were papaya, watermelon, cantaloupe, and avocado because these don't ferment and alcohol cannot be produced from them.

When the bell rang signaling the end of visiting hours, I accompanied them to the visitor exit area where there seemed to be an unusually long line to exit the premises. I later learned that the long line was due to extra security implemented because a minor had been caught trying to bring a cell phone into the prison. Since that incident, no more minors were allowed to enter the prison unless accompanied by an adult immediate family member. Many inmates were furious because some of them only got to see their children when a friend managed to bring them to visit. Women who had no immediate family members who could bring their children to Santa Teresa would now not be able to see them.

I said my goodbyes and watched my mother and brother go up the stairs and disappear into the exiting mob. My mother looked older and frailer than ever. My heart ached at having caused her so much pain. Thank God for her—I truly don't know what I would have done without her.

———

While I don't consider myself a religious person, I am spiritual and I do believe in a higher power. Although my hope was failing, my faith inspired me to come up with a prayer during that first week in prison, which I would continue to repeat to myself as the days dragged on, to serve as a reminder of my priorities during that frightening time:

DEAR GOD,
please give me the strength to
allow joy and gratitude into my heart today,
to make myself useful,
to let my light shine,
and to give Nina and Fabián all the love I can
from wherever I may be.
Amen.

—

At 9:30 a.m. on my first Sunday in prison, I was told I had an *encomienda* (a delivery). I assumed it was Miranda coming to have a more formal meeting with me, but I was wrong. A man I did not recognize introduced himself as Henry. He said he worked in operations with Miranda, was in charge of my case and wanted to know if I was being treated well, if I was being taken care of, or if I felt assaulted in any way. I wasn't even sure if he really worked with Miranda, but I answered his questions nevertheless:

"The women treat me well, but daily living conditions are deplorable; sharing a small concrete bed with another woman, sharing one shower and a public telephone with 103 women, and don't get me started on the fact that the food provided is most likely not even fit for animal consumption."

After carefully listening to me, he handed me two bags full of books, magazines, and cookies from my friend Tuffy; this was when I finally believed he was who he said he was. "Mimi and other inmates are looking out for you and reporting daily on your well-being," he said.

I may have been in the cellblock with the least dangerous inmates, but I was still a part of the general prison population. I wasn't expecting preferential treatment, but if there was anything that could help make my stay in prison any better, I wanted to know about it, so I also made sure to ask if being transferred to encamamiento was an option and inquired about the status of the sleeping pad donation we were expecting.

"We're working on your transfer and on the permit for the mattress. You may have a mattress to sleep on by Tuesday," he replied.

I walked back to my cellblock and had some cereal with milk and a banana—yes, a banana!—for breakfast. Bananas were not permitted in prison, but almost every Sunday morning we were served cornflakes, milk, and a banana. I had my own cereal from *the outside* and was advised by my cellmates NOT to drink the Rancho milk because it made everyone sick. Instead, I was advised to buy a bag of milk from the tiny convenience store in Cellblock Five—another expense that could've been avoided if the prison simply made sure to provide drinkable milk.

After breakfast, I headed to Serigrafía to teach my group of students another English lesson, which they were thrilled to receive—a challenging task, since, even though I was fluent, I had never stopped to analyze the language; yet somehow, we were making it work.

Later that afternoon, I headed downstairs to the preschool. I had offered my time to read to the children, but other than reading to my own two kids, I had no experience in a classroom filled with children. The teacher welcomed me, and the kids pretty much attacked me when they saw the books in my hands. They seemed excited to learn, but as much as I tried to keep them seated and away from me, they insisted on climbing all over me. It was quite an experience. Most of them were two years old, several were three and, although children were only allowed by law to live with their mothers until they reached the age of four, one of them was already five. They had some toys, a small indoor play area, and a small covered playground outdoors, which was also used for other activities. As the hour progressed, the eldest boy gathered the courage to speak to me.

"I have a butterfly in the trunk of my car," he said, as he showed me his toy car and opened up the trunk to reveal an actual living butterfly.

"This little creature, like all other animals, is a part of God's creation and each one of us has a purpose," I said as I observed the trapped butterfly. "This butterfly was meant to fly, so we should set it free."

He stared at me for a couple of seconds and then, agreeing that this was a good idea, he let the butterfly go. Such a simple action took on a whole new meaning under those circumstances.

———

Shortly after 5:30 p.m. that Sunday, I was back at my cellblock when six to eight lieutenants, men of higher rank than regular guards, probably intending trouble for us inmates, marched into our cellblock, asking for Mimi and conducting a quick check of the premises. Apparently, the electric fuse for our cellblock had been popping, which led the guards to believe there were too many electronic articles plugged into the wall outlets. They walked by each inmate and asked if we had any contraband items in our possession, such as drugs, alcohol, mirrors, grapes, apples, knives, hair dryers, curling irons, electric burners, or cell phones. I had none, so I was calm; however, the stress in the room from the guards invading our privacy and our routine was palpable.

I was later told that it had been over a year since the last *requisa*—a deep search or inspection performed by prison officials to confiscate illegal objects such as cell phones, knives, drugs, liquor, and electrical equipment. These inspections are always unannounced for obvious reasons and tend to be violent. Prisoners are removed from their living quarters while guards go through every possession. Things are cut, opened, thrown, discarded, confiscated, and stolen. Once the lieutenants leave, the place is in complete disarray and inmates do their best to recover and reorganize their belongings. Everyone agreed it was quite a traumatic event. The list of prohibited articles is so extensive and includes so many normal everyday things, that it is easy to find yourself owning something illegal. By this, I mean a nail clipper, a mirror, a glass container of any kind, or any fruit other than watermelon, papaya, cantaloupe, and avocado. The thought of a requisa is stressful enough for well-behaved inmates. I cannot imagine what it must be like for inmates who do have weapons, drugs, or a cell phone. There has apparently been a law in place for some time now that carries a minimum six-year penalty for anyone (inmate, prison personnel, or visitor) caught with a cell phone on prison grounds. Because of this, I assumed most inmates wouldn't even consider trying to get a cell phone, but not everyone thinks the same way. As I would soon learn, there were cell phones in prison, plenty of them.

The lieutenants asked Mimi about the two freezers in the hallway. She told them that one was used for her ice cream business and the other for meats and items that she allowed inmates to store there. She added that her permits were in order. They also asked about the three TV sets and Mimi explained that they were communal property and also had proper permits. Eventually, the lieutenants proceeded to the next cellblock and everyone breathed a sigh of relief, especially Daniela, one of my English students at Serigrafía. I learned the next day that their unexpected check had almost caused her to have a heart attack because she did have a cell phone.

As if the atmosphere wasn't jumpy enough, at around 2 a.m., my neighbor, who was sleeping on the floor less than ten centimeters away from me, with just a piece of cloth separating our bodies, was startled awake by one of the many Santa Teresa cats, and in a knee-jerk reaction, screamed at it, which made it screech at the top of its lungs, waking me with a jolt of terror and causing a huge commotion in our bunk area. When we realized that it was just a cat, everyone settled back into their assigned places and fell asleep once again. Better cats than a rat-infested hellhole.

When I woke up the next day, I managed to get a phone call in with my mother. I was unable to speak with my children because they were still asleep. How I missed their tiny voices, their warm kisses, and their tight hugs! I then got dressed and quickly headed out. I decided to go to the Social Services offices to return the Isabel Allende book I had borrowed but was not going to read. I took Mariana, one of my bunkmates, with me to introduce her to Marta, in the hope that she could help locate Mariana's son. There was little else I could do to help her.

Later that morning, I received a cherished visit from my father. Again, we were lucky enough to have Serigrafía as our meeting place, which was wonderful for all the obvious reasons, but mainly because my father's hearing is not perfect in one ear, and it would have been impossible for us to hold any sort of conversation in the terribly crowded and noisy communal hall. He brought me bottled water and *alfajores* (butter cookies coated in powdered sugar with caramel filling) from San Martín Bakery and we spoke about my case and upcoming hearing the following day.

Since I knew my father had taken a special interest in Carmen's case back in September after I had spent the night in the carceleta, I wanted to introduce them. She joined us when she returned from the religious service of the day, and they had a chance to speak for a while. I also introduced him to Ashley and the women working at Serigrafía. Having my loved ones know where and with whom I *lived* somehow made me feel less lonely.

My father left the prison with Ashley at 11:15 a.m. because he wanted to talk to the warden about the possibility of donating medications. It is common for people to become inspired to help in some way when they visit a place like Santa Teresa, especially when one of the inmates is a loved one. It is unbelievable to me that the former vice president of Guatemala, Roxana Baldetti, could visit Santa Teresa while in office and not do something to better this place—ironically enough, she later became an inmate at this very prison.

In the afternoon, a caller came looking for me at Serigrafía to let me know that I had visitors waiting for me in the communal hall. When I walked into the room, I was elated to see my friends Tina, Christie, Karlita, and Anabelle. They are the wind beneath my wings. Because having guests visit me at Serigrafía is a privilege, and I didn't want to push it by trying to bring in so many people at once, we remained in the communal hall—plus, when I got there, the chairs and tables used at the communal hall had already been paid for. Yes, that was yet another side business in prison. A few inmates had bought plastic tables and chairs and managed to rent them out to other inmates and their family and friends, so they could sit comfortably during visiting hours.

I have always been proud of my lifetime friends from school because they are everything I admire and everything I strive to be, and within this dark place, they seemed much more precious and brighter to me. I could only imagine what a sight I must have been to them, but they could not have been kinder, more loving, or more supportive. We can pretty much say now that we have been through almost everything together, as family. During that visit, we cried, laughed, and prayed. My stepmother, Anamaría, also arrived and was able to join us. She touched me and caressed my back the entire time. She may not even remember this, but I will never forget that loving gesture.

Once our visit was over, I said my goodbyes and took the goodies they brought me to my bunk. My bunkmates had been very generous in making room for my things; however, my plastic baskets, even though they were quite small, did not fit anywhere because there was no more room available under the bed. That's when I experienced yet another act of kindness in prison: my bunkmate Verónica went above and beyond by allowing me to place my baskets by her feet, next to where I put my pillow, on top of our tiny shared bed.

———

Tuesday, January 12, 2016, finally arrived. A week had passed since my last hearing had landed me in jail, and now I had another chance to plead my case before a judge. I woke up with the morning's head count, put on the clothes I had neatly laid out the previous night, so I could dress efficiently and quickly, brushed my teeth in a flash, and tied my hair in a bun. I had approximately ten minutes to get ready while the guards counted inmates in the other cellblocks, before they came back to get me.

At 4:15 a.m. all inmates going to the courthouse were taken to the warden's office for prison checkout. Our pictures were taken and we were then put in a holding area surrounded by an iron fence and topped with a tin roof. It was very cold out, but it was a beautiful crisp night and the stars were amazing in the sky. We must have waited in there for over an hour. Once the inmates were processed, our names were called one by one, we were lined up in pairs, and taken up the dark stairs to where *la perrera* (the kennel truck) was waiting for us.

Getting on this truck is no easy feat; it's very high and has no handlebars or steps. Usually the truck driver will give inmates a hand up, but that is not always the case. Once we were loaded and locked inside, most of us took seats on a cold metal bench located around the inside perimeter, while others, mostly the younger women, rode standing on the bench while grasping the bars on the small upper windows of the truck, hoping to catch a glimpse of the outside world as we drove by. I had no interest in seeing the view, so I stayed on the corner of the bench closest to the exit door in the back.

After a loud and chaotic drive, with our driver honking and swerving through the regular traffic, we arrived at the courthouse. The truck backed up to unload us, and we were handcuffed in pairs. Before entering the building, we were thoroughly searched once again. We were allowed to bring almost nothing with us—no books to read, pencil or paper to write with, or lip balm or combs. Anything found was thrown into a huge garbage can, never to be seen again. We were, however, allowed to bring toilet paper and money.

Once we had been searched, we were escorted down the now familiar ramp, accompanied by our guard, the one who held the keys to our handcuffs, and finally, around the corner. Out of sight of the men's holding cells, we were uncuffed and locked into the female carceleta, where we spent the entire day and part of the night, only allowed to leave it to attend our hearings.

At 7:30 a.m. my name was called and I was handcuffed, searched, and taken up to the Fourth Criminal Court. My jailer, Julia, and I were the first ones there, along with an annoying photographer who would not leave me alone. Noticing this situation, Julia and another court worker took me straight into the courtroom so that I could avoid the photographer. Soon after, Miranda came into the courtroom followed by one of the opposing attorneys. We waited for the prosecutor from the Attorney General's Office, but he did not show up. Juan Pablo Olyslager Muñoz was also a no-show, so the hearing was postponed until Monday. I cried. Another week in prison, and the rest of the day waiting in the carceleta until the last inmate finished her hearing and we could all go "home."

We exited the courtroom and found the waiting room filled with my family and friends' loving eyes and embracing arms, blessing my day with a cherished moment with my loved ones, as my guard allowed me to remain with them for a couple of hours. I thought about calling my babies, but I was too distraught.

Meanwhile, the public prosecutor arrived at 8:45 a.m., claiming that he thought the hearing was at 8:30 a.m. when it was actually scheduled for 8:15 a.m. How was that possible? Was this a cruel legal tactic to leave me in prison until the next available hearing date? Were they waiting for another judge to be assigned? Were they waiting for my husband to show up? Did they really believe that I knew where my husband was, or that I had access to any of his money? What did they hope to gain from incarcerating me? I knew they had no evidence to make them believe I was involved in any way.

At around 11:30 a.m., Julia said I had to go back down to the carceleta. I finished eating a black bean sandwich and drinking some coffee that my brother Rodrigo had bought for me, then I thanked, kissed, and received a hug from each of my loved ones, and was taken down to spend the next ten hours in that awful holding cell. There must have been eighteen of us locked up in there, six of whom were to be released that night. It gave me hope to see that inmates did get out of this place, but it terrified me that five of them were already bragging about what they had done and what they would do as soon as they got out. It scared me for the rest of the people out there. The system was not working.

Later that day, as we waited for the time to pass until we could leave, my guard Julia and a lieutenant ran to our cell, opened the lock, and started shouting at an inmate carrying a baby to follow them immediately. As other guards rushed her down the ramp to the second underground garage, Julia told the rest of us to prepare as well as we could because a gas bomb had just been detonated. I covered my head and nose with the pashmina scarf my mother had just given me and waited for the unknown, my heart racing, trapped in a locked cell with nowhere to take cover. However, less than a minute later, the other guards came back to inform us that it had been a false alarm. The maintenance crew had been burning paper on the other side of the parking lot and they'd confused the smoke with a gas bomb. I noticed the other guards making fun of Julia, so I went to her and said, "I congratulate you, Julia, because as soon as you thought it could be a gas bomb, your first instinct was to save the baby."

While I was in the carceleta my mind began to wander and I couldn't help but think about how there were over a thousand women incarcerated in Santa Teresa with me, each with a story to tell. I was now one of these women, and we all seemed to need our stories to be heard. Among the many stories I had heard thus far was a young woman's account of how she had become an extortionist. Her first husband had died in a motorcycle accident, leaving her a widow with two small children. She had worked at a fried chicken food chain for some time, but she had left that job to help her sister sell fruit at a market. Every day at 4 a.m., she bought fruit that Walmart deemed no longer fresh enough from their outlet in Guatemala City's Zone 1, and then retailed it at the local market. She not only made more money this way, but also managed to be done with work and be back with her children by noon on most days.

Her second husband, whom she called El Canche, which refers to a person who has fair-colored hair, was a tuk-tuk (auto-rickshaw) taxi driver. He was expected to pay a weekly extortion fee of twenty-six dollars. A man came every week to collect from him and his fellow drivers. Eventually, this man was murdered and the dark powers decided that from that day on, the tuk-tuk drivers would be responsible for collecting the weekly extortions around the neighborhood. The drivers took turns on the job and this was how her second husband found himself participating in the extortion business. He was intending to return to his prior job as a mechanic at a formal business when he, too, was murdered.

At the funeral, the young woman overheard one of the tuk-tuk drivers saying, "Javier will do the pick-ups this week replacing El Canche because, if he doesn't, he will end up dead just like him." They even mentioned his killer's name. The widow blurted out, "What did you say? You know who killed him?" After this, threats started pouring in against her and her family. On one occasion, while selling fruit, she noticed a stranger coming toward her; when her instincts prompted her to run, the man immediately chased after her. She managed to escape, but it was now clear: they wanted her dead.

After considering her options, and in the hope of resolving her situation, she decided to get in touch with a person she knew who had ties to that gang. This acquaintance put her in contact with Sparky, who suggested that the widow become his woman in exchange for protection. This implied having sexual relations, along with doing all types of favors and deliveries for the gang. She negotiated and agreed to do deliveries for her survival. Sparky then sent her money and told her to deliver products to him in prison, personally; however, she never saw him in person because she conveniently forgot her ID on that particular delivery day and wasn't allowed to enter the prison.

That same afternoon, she was also supposed to deliver a cell phone to a business so that the gang members could extort money from the owners. The widow was scared, so she asked her twenty-year-old niece to accompany her. The next day, they were instructed to pick up the extortion money. They refused, but agreed to be the lookouts from a block away. Once there, the widow, the niece, and the acquaintance were captured by the police because the business owner had reported the situation the day before. They were tried in a court of law and sentenced to ten years in prison each. While in Santa Teresa, waiting to hear about their appeal, the widow now barely left her cellblock, for fear that the acquaintance, who resided in another cellblock in Santa Teresa, might harm her.

This kind of story is so common in this prison that it is almost a cliché.

This widow didn't excuse her actions. She was totally aware of her involvement and she cried because of the damage and hurt she had caused. This reality is part of daily life for many women from Guatemala City's Zone 6 neighborhood, for most gang member girlfriends, and for many hardworking women who simply want to make enough money to feed their children. It is common for them to be threatened by gang members and used for their purposes. The police and the state are not capable of protecting them beforehand, yet they are capable of capturing and convicting them once the crime has been committed. They are victims of the oppressors, and then victims of the state.

———

Since we were under the impression that attorneys could visit the carceleta at any time and bring their clients food, Vania came by that day to bring the chicken soup that I had asked for, only to be told that this was no longer possible. Attorneys are allowed to bring their clients food and other approved items only when their clients have just been arrested. Once the client is a prison system inmate, attorneys are no longer allowed to bring anything in. So that meant no lunch for me; however, we did manage to talk for a while. Vania told me about an article that came out in the newspaper, which included my now apparently famous Facebook post. She claimed it was an amazingly smart post and that the public's perception was that I was a victim. I didn't want to be a victim, all I wanted was for the complicated yet simple truth to come out.

The truth will set me free . . . but when?

CHAPTER 7

Prison Drama

WEEK TWO

I was exhausted from the day before, so I made a conscious decision to sleep in (4 a.m. head count excluded). Miranda had said he would come see me that morning so I was expecting to get called at some point, and I was, but to the warden's office.

"Are you being treated well?" asked Warden Leah, once I entered her office. "Are you feeling safe, is all going well?"

"It's *going*, but *well* is a stretch, considering the circumstances," I said.

"Are you being given food?" she continued.

"I usually do not eat the food the prison gives us because I'm frequently not at my cellblock during lunchtime, but nobody has denied me food," I replied. When I asked her what this was about, she informed me that the Department of Human Rights was requesting that she investigate these allegations, which someone had called them and made. Since I did not want to get anybody in trouble, especially not Mimi, who had been good to me so far, I explained that I was OK in Cellblock One, but that a newspaper had published an article regarding my case and I feared that the information now publicly available could put me at risk.

"I've been trying to be very low-key and not answer any questions inmates pose regarding my case, but now all that has changed because it is public knowledge," I explained.

"Very well, go visit the doctor at the infirmary so that he may certify whether you are well or not," she said. I did, and fortunately, or unfortunately, I was given a clean bill of health.

I had initially been determined to survive that first week of imprisonment in Cellblock One, since my bunkmates were nice and I was doing OK, but when faced with another week of imprisonment, I figured it might be easier to live among ten women rather than 104, especially given the telephone situation—phone access in the cellblocks was hard to come by and I needed more opportunities to call and communicate with my children.

When I returned to my bunk, I found that Verónica had opened a can of refried beans, so I made myself a refried bean sandwich for lunch, and later decided to walk over to our cellblock's mini-convenience store to see what was available for purchase, in the hope that I would no longer have to wait until someone brought me food.

There are several small convenience stores, or *tienditas,* that sell a variety of everyday things and are located in different cellblocks inside the prison. These include basic food items, such as instant soup, yogurt, milk, instant coffee, sugar, and salt, offering a welcome respite from the inedible meals provided by the prison. These small stores are owned and operated by inmates who have the permits to do so. The one at my cellblock had been owned and operated by the same inmate for more than eighteen years. How she managed to be in Santa Teresa for that long, I have no idea. Santa Teresa is a prison for inmates who are being held in preventive custody as they await trial, or inmates who have been convicted, but are still appealing their sentences. Once inmates have no more legal recourse available to them, they are transferred to other prisons to serve the remainder of their sentences. In any case, I managed to score a drinkable yogurt, several fruit juices, and some soup. Later that week, I bought milk, more yogurt, and some bread from the tiendita in Cellblock Seven. Part of learning the ropes in prison was figuring out where to get the necessary goods to survive.

———

The following morning, when I got up to use the restroom, Enma, the main phone-list organizer, told me I could place a call, so I jumped at the chance to call my dad. He was in Honduras and sounded upbeat. My cousin Yoli (Marta Yolanda Díaz-Durán) had dedicated part of her radio show to my case, and had interviewed my father live, presenting a very good defense on my behalf. All I could think was, *So, they have not forgotten about me!*

I hung up with my dad, got dressed, and headed to Serigrafía, only to find it was closed. I tried to access the area to read to the children at the school, but a guard stopped me and asked for my permit. I had no official permit yet, so I reluctantly went back to my bunk, wondering how I would fill my ninth day in prison. Thankfully, when I reached the cellblock, I was told I had a visitor. I was surprised to find a stranger waiting for me in the visiting area, a man who introduced himself as Gerardo Villamar from the Department of Human Rights, in charge of monitoring Guatemala's penitentiary system.

"I'm here to see about an anonymous complaint we received regarding your conditions in Santa Teresa," he explained.

I told him the same thing I had told the warden, "No one is denying me food, but ever since the newspaper printed the article about my case, I have become uneasy. Several inmates in the hallways referred to me by name the other day, and just as I was on my way to see you right now, a woman hanging out with her friends said to me, 'I need to talk to you.' I asked her if she was interested in taking my English class. She said yes, with an insincere smirk, and then added, 'But I want to talk to you later.' I have no desire to talk to her or to listen to anything she has to say. *That* makes me uneasy."

"I'll take it all into account," he said and gave me a telephone number I could call at any time.

Just as I settled into my bed back at the cellblock to rest for a while, my name was called again. This time it was Miranda. He told me about his meeting with the US Embassy, but he did not know who had brought my case to their attention. Miranda was under the impression that the embassy had paid close attention to what he had said. He filled them in on my case, and also told them about the meeting with GFP's Guatemalan attorneys from Mayora & Mayora, when they had asked him if I was ready to tell them where my husband and the money were, in exchange for dropping charges against me. Miranda was very optimistic about what this meeting might cause, and the fact that the judge was now completely up to speed with my case, having had the chance to read the case file, but I didn't want to get my hopes up. Every day was an emotional rollercoaster in prison and I knew my heart could not take the possible disappointment.

Ever since my husband's alleged actions had resulted in my life being turned upside down, I had started to ask God to allow me to learn the lessons I needed to learn and to give me the strength to get through it all. After I was taken to the carceleta on Thursday, September 17, 2015, I began to ask God to let this experience serve a bigger purpose, to let this be the catalyst for some big changes. And during my second week in jail, I realized those prayers were more alive than ever before. I did not know what the future held, but I was determined to do everything in my power to find God's purpose . . . *But dear God, please let me do it while I am home with my beloved Nina and Fabián.*

———

Meanwhile, in the outside world, Guatemala's new president, Jimmy Morales, took his oath of office and, during the ten-hour televised event, much was said about violence, murder, and extortion, referring to them as

Guatemala's biggest cancers. It was quite surreal to watch and listen to such statements from inside a prison, and later fall asleep in a shared bed in a facility, surrounded by murderers, extortionists, and thieves.

———

Friday came along, a good day for inmates lucky enough to have loved ones on the outside. Fridays are known as encomienda day because they are the day of the week when inmates are allowed to receive certain prison-approved items from anyone who wishes to bring them, along with a five-minute visit through the prison gates. I was enjoying my milk with coffee, sugar, and oatmeal cookies with Verónica, when my name was called. As I approached the gates, I saw my beloved Rodri waiting for me with my weekly delivery of Lipton Peach Iced Tea and cookies.

Once back at my bunk, it wasn't long before my name was called again. This time it was Tina and Juanfer holding a huge bag filled with avocados, shampoo, conditioner, toilet paper, cereal, powdered milk, another blanket, toothpaste, crayons, and money, along with a card and a mandala coloring book. They had also brought five boxes full of the donated books I had asked for.

Tina had already seen me in this place, but Juanfer hadn't, and it broke my heart to notice how he did his absolute best to hold back his tears during the five-minute visit. Those visits from my brother and friends, being able to look into their familiar and loving eyes, were my gift from God that day. As if that weren't enough, my father suddenly arrived with a huge box of Dunkin' Donuts and a smile on his face, seemingly filled with an optimism that was in deep contrast to my overwhelming fear and constant sadness.

After our encomienda day visit came to a close, and I reluctantly said my goodbyes, I started walking back to my bunk when I was approached by a woman who introduced herself as Corey, the masseuse. Leticia, an inmate in my cellblock who had become my prison information resource, had told her I was interested in her services. She said she charged three-and-half dollars for a thirty-minute massage, or five dollars for sixty minutes, and had an available slot for that afternoon at 2 p.m. I quickly booked it.

The beauty salon was quite a destination. I assume most inmates did not use its services, managing to do their own hair, color, and manicures, or they had a friend do it for them. But for other inmates, the salon offered a welcome respite where, even if just for a brief moment, we all felt normal. The area that held the salon, once an open patio between the communal hall and Cellblock One, was covered with a tin roof, decorated with several posters on the walls, and had three fully equipped salon chairs with a mirror each. There was even an original retro hair-washing chair. There was no running water that I know of, but a bucket with cold water did the trick. The salon also included an improvised waiting area with chairs and magazines, a table where manicures were performed, and Corey's massage parlor off to one corner. On windy days, a portion of the tin roof often blew open, letting sunshine peek through for a brief instant until another gust closed it back again—the universe does magic that way; it makes sure we all land back where we belong. Alexia seemed to be the inmate in charge of the salon, having managed salons on the outside, but never actually working in one until now. She cut and dyed hair, sold beauty products, and made many inmates happy. The beauty shack—what a discovery!

After my massage, and before heading to Serigrafía, I stopped by Marta's office and was ecstatic to find the five boxes full of books that my dear friends had sent per my request. I spent the next hour happily organizing them according to language, subject, and age group, in the hope that this would be the start of a new prison library. As I placed the books on the shelf, I set aside Alexandre Dumas's *The Count of Monte Cristo*, which was still wrapped in plastic, for Verónica. I took an English grammar book (which I knew had come from my own house) and a beautiful illustrated dictionary for the women to use at Serigrafía. As I was wrapping up, I came across one of my favorite children's books, *The Giving Tree* by Shel

Silverstein, and almost burst into tears . . . Nina and Fabián knew that it was my favorite. I pulled myself together, grabbed two more easy children's books, and walked over to the three children at the playground to sneak in a quick read—I technically couldn't read to them because I hadn't yet received my permit, but I couldn't help myself. I needed to share this joy with them, even if only for a few minutes.

I was making my way to Serigrafía, when I was stopped by a woman from encamamiento who introduced herself as Susana, a friend of my mother-in-law's cousin Virginia. Susana was a lady I had already heard about while in Santa Teresa. She is an attorney and an inmate who had moved from Cellblock Three, to Cellblock One, to Cellblock Six, and finally to encamamiento, because she was so particular, and she now had her own small room with a bunk bed, which she shared with her three cats. She had a table, chairs, TV, and DVD player. Ashley believed that she was a genius because she had become well-known for her directness and had managed to get just about everything she wanted. Susana showed me her private room, and then unlocked her private bathroom located in the hallway leading to encamamiento, commenting with a big smile, "Aren't you jealous?" I found her to be fabulous and I agreed with Ashley . . . pure genius!

When I finally made it to Serigrafía, I found the place bustling because, after two idle weeks, there was finally a work order to be filled. While the women worked away, I got busy and wrote the lesson on the board: short and long vowel sounds. The English spelling and grammar book was perfect for my new teaching job.

At noon I took a quick break, returned to my block, and managed to speak to my mother and children. Nothing gave me more strength than hearing their voices. By now I had come to an agreement with Enma, the phone list keeper. I would return to the block around noon every day, wait for an hour or so, and get my chance at the phone. So far, it had worked well for me.

By the time I got back to Serigrafía, I found Ashley busy watching

Scandal, our guilty pleasure in prison. I had missed three episodes while I was gone, but my massage and my chat with my family were more than worth it. Once the *Scandal* binge-watching came to a close, Ashley turned to me for help in drafting an important letter that would hopefully allow her to further her education.

A few days earlier, Ashley had told me about her desire to attend law school so that she could be more knowledgeable and effective with her plans to help Guatemala. Her idea was to start later that year at Universidad Rafael Landívar (URL), where she could take night classes that would allow her to continue working during the day. Since I had not attended college in Guatemala, I did not know the procedure, but I was quite sure one could not start law school halfway through the year. I told her to call Vania, who was not only an attorney but also worked at URL. However, when Ashley called the number I had given her and introduced herself as a friend of mine from prison, Vania panicked. She and Ed thought it was an extortionist calling and they immediately hung up on her. Realizing that she had scared them, Ashley called my brother Turi so that he could explain to Vania who she was and clear the panic-stricken air.

As I had suspected, enrolling halfway through the year was not an option. Vania explained that classes were starting in a week's time and if Ashley wanted to make it into school, she needed to interview and take the entrance exams, and then enroll as soon as possible if she was accepted. Ashley hopped to it, scheduling both her interview with the law school's dean and the exam, but there was a small problem. Even though, by American standards, private university fees at URL are quite low, Ashley could not afford them, given her current salary. She needed to find someone to sponsor her education, and she needed to find that person fast. I was able to help her put together a letter that clearly stated her situation and the reasons she needed sponsorship. I was very pleased with the outcome; we'd done a fabulous job, but now only time would tell.

That evening, at around 8:30 p.m., Mimi called all Cellblock One inmates out of their bunks for a meeting. The ten donated foam mattresses had finally arrived. Mimi said that I had donated them and everyone thanked me, but I corrected her, "I didn't make this donation, my family did." Mimi asked me to take what I needed first, so I grabbed two mattresses: one for Verónica and me to share, and another for Mariana, who slept on the floor. The rest of the mattresses were for Mimi to distribute as she saw fit.

Verónica and I immediately went to work using raffia string and a marker to measure the bed area and the mattress. We then marked and cut our mattresses down to size with an illegal serrated metal knife that appeared out of nowhere. The mattresses were standard twin size, but our shared bed was even smaller than that. Pillows were made or mended using the extra material, and, at her request, we gave one of our neighbors a long piece to fill in the gap between her narrow mattress and the edges of her bunk, which she and her bedmate usually filled with clothes. Nothing went to waste. And, thanks to my family, I was now able to look forward to waking up the following day to a rested and pampered gluteus maximus.

———

A few nights earlier, while I was reading on my part of the bunk bed, Verónica started chatting with a young woman, whom she knew from their old neighborhood. I couldn't help overhearing that this young woman was in Santa Teresa for killing a bus driver, which immediately made me stop reading and perk up my ears. She claimed she had already killed two bus drivers in the past, but that this time, the driver's assistant and several other witnesses had come forward and she had been caught. She also mentioned, very reassuringly, that the two witnesses had given contradicting statements as to where the gun had ended up after firing—one claimed it had landed inside the bus, while the other claimed it was out on the curb—which made her believe she would get out soon.

As I inconspicuously observed this young woman out of the corner of my eye, I realized I would never have pegged her as a cold-blooded killer. Three innocent hardworking men were murdered for not paying extortion, three families were now devastated by loss, and this woman didn't seem the least bit affected by the horror of her crimes. It suddenly dawned on me: I was living and sleeping among cold-blooded killers.

I'd recently heard of another woman who'd spent six months in Santa Teresa for her alleged involvement in killing and mutilating two teenage girls—crimes she had admitted to other inmates—and was released because her husband had come forth to take the blame for both of them. A chill went down my spine. While people like Verónica received ten-year sentences for their parts in extortion, those who were a real menace to society knew how to play the system to get out of prison quickly. While Verónica had shed tears and written unsent letters to her extortion victim, this friend of hers was likely to go free and murder yet again. This was the system that had my life in its hands.

Meanwhile, Mariana, my bunkmate who was accused of killing and burning her husband on January 1, finally got a visit from her attorney, who was collecting evidence from neighbors, acquaintances, and the doctor who had once stitched up Mariana's face, all in an effort to prove that her husband abused her. I wasn't quite sure how domestic violence would help her defense when she claimed to be innocent, but I was no attorney, just a woman who had probably watched too many American courtroom dramas on TV.

———

On Saturday, day eleven in prison, I sat outside writing in the shade, under a perfect blue sky, in one of the worst places I could imagine. Eventually, I realized it was 2 p.m. and, assuming I would likely have no visitors that day, I joined Ashley at Serigrafía to watch another episode of *Scandal* while the rest of the girls cleaned the shop.

However, halfway through the show, my name was called and I was taken to the communal hall to greet my unexpected visitors: my father and my sister, Gaby. They had been outside, waiting in line in the sun since 11 a.m., and were finally let into the prison at 2:20 p.m. It was great to see them and enjoy their precious company, and I appreciated their positivity regarding my next hearing . . . I only wished I could feel the same way. At some point, Ashley and Daniela came by to say hello and meet my sister. I liked it when my family and friends were able to meet some of the people I was spending my days with, especially Ashley. I truly don't know what would have happened to my sanity and safety in that place without her.

By 5:30 p.m. I was back in my bunk, but it was burning hot. Lately, I had been having a difficult time spending time on my bed because the neighbors had placed their electric burner right next to it, and when they switched it on, it made my mattress and sheets so hot that I felt as if my entire bed was about to catch on fire. It was a dangerous and delicate situation, and I wasn't sure how to handle it. I first approached Verónica, wondering if I should ask Mimi or Clara for help, or if I should deal with it on my own. The consensus was to ask Clara, and I did. However, since the burner was inside another bunk, Clara said there wasn't anything she could do. So, I decided to take matters into my own hands, and approached one of my neighbors myself, to which she replied, "The burner's very hot at the moment but we'll move it farther away from your bed later." I doubted that would be the case, but it was worth a try.

In the meantime, I grabbed my book and my notebook and headed toward the locked cellblock entrance gates in the hope of catching some of the cool breeze. The small area was full of women smoking, waiting to use the telephone, and in line to shower. As I settled in a corner with my book, Enma, the telephone keeper, told me I could make a five-minute phone call. Some doors close and others open. I jumped at the opportunity, trying my mother's number five times, to no avail. I called my father and asked him to contact my children through my mother or my brother Turi, and tell them

I had been trying to speak to them. I asked him to tell them I loved them and would try again the next day.

———

During my first twelve days in prison, I did my best to be courteous, straightforward, and clear with my actions and my words; I shared what I had while keeping in mind that giving things for free often results in resentment instead of gratitude. So, when Mariana needed money, I hired her to wash my clothes and do my bunk cleaning, and when I gave away extra candy, cookies, or soap bars, I tried to give one to each of my three bunkmates. But of course, human nature is not that simple and fair.

One day, as I walked into my bunk area, Verónica quickly came over to tell me that my toiletry bag had fallen, so she had opened it to make sure nothing had broken. My toiletry bag closes with a zipper, so I did not appreciate this invasion of privacy, but nothing had gone missing, not from my bag that is . . . what was missing were two of the nineteen avocados that were left in the bucket earlier that morning; Verónica was quick to add that she did not trust Clara. Truth be told, I didn't trust anybody at that point, and the longer I was locked up listening to those women's conversations, the more I realized I could not judge them by my own standards on absolutely anything. Most of them had lived under completely different circumstances than me, and they were used to surviving at any cost. Two avocados I could live without, but the constant reminder that I was living among thieves, extortionists, and murderers was a nightmare.

As if that wasn't enough, Verónica also mentioned that Mimi had told her that Clara had mentioned that I did not shower and that I only used a wet cloth on certain body parts. (I did use a wipe on my neck one day because it was very hot, so maybe her small brain concluded that I used this in place of a daily shower.) Clara also told Mimi that she did not accept anything from me (which was simply not true), and that I had paid for

Verónica's full month of cellblock fees. Verónica allegedly told Mimi the truth, and now Mimi pegged Clara as the likely avocado thief; however, Mimi's main concern was that no one take advantage of me because I could easily complain to the Human Rights people. The inevitable prison soap opera was now unfolding before my eyes, yet I continued to do all I could to steer clear of the drama, hoping that the truth would eventually set me free from this devastating telenovela.

———

Sunday arrived. Mariana was up and out of the bunk early, Clara eventually left, and when Verónica got up later, I decided to do the same and go to the restroom. It was just like every other morning, until I walked out of the bathroom stall and started feeling terribly weak and dizzy. I managed to splash some water on my face and reach the entrance hall; however, by then, I was sweating profusely and knew I had to lie on the floor ASAP because I was about to faint. An inmate noticed me on the ground, trying to breathe deeply, and asked if I was OK, to which I quickly said, "No." She immediately rushed over to Lola, a sweet inmate in our cellblock who had been a nurse, and they quickly reached my side. Lola took my pulse and blood pressure and asked if I or anyone in my family suffered from diabetes. "No," I managed to say. My blood pressure was very low (85/62) and the tips of my fingers were tingling terribly. After drinking a glass of water they'd brought me, I slowly but surely started to feel better, thanked them for their help, and edged back to my bunk. A health scare in general is frightening, but one in prison makes you feel utterly helpless.

The rest of the day went by as usual, with a visit to Serigrafía, and a chat with Ashley, who told me that she had met with my brother Turi the previous day because he was going to help her create a webpage where customers could design printed products, like T-shirts, caps, bags, etc., and place their orders from their own computers. I knew then that meeting Ashley was one of the reasons I had ended up in that place.

At 5:30 p.m. I was back at my cellblock, trying to reach my children, but they weren't home, so I showered early and went to bed, thinking, *Tomorrow will be my children's first day of school for the year and I will not be there to see them off.* The following day was also my hearing day.

———

Monday, January 18, 2016, 4 a.m.: We were registered at the warden's office and then led outside, where we had to wait in the outdoor holding cell for over an hour before the perrera came to pick us up. It was already daylight when we boarded the truck. Only eight of us were going to the courthouse, one of whom was a very young, perky, and sweet-looking woman, who once again quickly taught me that appearances could be deceiving. Up until then, she'd been held in solitary confinement, and she spent the entire twenty-five-minute ride peering through the upper opening of the truck and yelling out profanity and stupidity beyond belief. My last trip to the courthouse had been amusing because the girls yelled out inappropriate but funny things to the outside world; however, this was just repulsive and devoid of any humor at all. It was a very cold morning and most of us tried to keep warm inside that bare metal truck, but as soon as we arrived at the courthouse, just before the guards opened the truck door, this woman took off her sweatshirt and stood there wearing nothing but her turquoise tights and a thin white tank top. She was aching to flirt with the men outside. Then, to my surprise, she pulled out three small bags of marijuana from her bra and quickly hid them—one in her hair bun, one back in her bra, and one in her crotch. And to think I usually have a hard time bringing in my lip balm! In all honesty, I was hoping the guards would catch her, but they did not, and I ended up learning a new trick. I remembered what my friend J. P. once told me, "We do not necessarily get what we deserve in life, but that which we manage to get for ourselves." And with that, I undid my hair and redid the bun with the lip balm carefully tucked inside.

I spent the next eight hours in the carceleta, not knowing what was happening outside. Miranda didn't come to see me, and I avoided the Rancho food the prison system brought for us at all costs. There were only so many ways one could sit on a concrete bench, and only so long one could hold positive thoughts while listening to the fellow inmates speak. I don't know what I expected; after all, I was in prison.

Finally, at 2:30 p.m., the guard called my name, handcuffed me, took me to be searched, and walked me up the stairs, where I found Manolo (Miranda's partner), my father, and my mother, along with a large group of my loved ones coming down the stairs to the basement. I was glad to see them, but a second later, after seeing their somber and serious expressions, I realized the news was not good. Manolo asked me to follow him to the elevator lobby. My hearing had been canceled because the judge was a no-show. Astounded by the latest blow, I burst into tears. My father insisted that I should stay strong, but I had just spent thirteen days being strong, making the best out of my horrible circumstances, missing my children and family, with barely a lucky five-minute phone call per day, wondering what was going on outside and whether people were starting to forget about me, feeling as if I had been buried alive in that awful place, while living among strangers, extortionists, and killers. I couldn't hold it in any longer; I needed to cry freely among my loved ones.

It was a very low emotional point for me, but I was grateful that I was able to break down among friends and family rather than in prison. I felt their support and love and was once again reminded that, no matter how desolate I felt, I was not alone. As tears kept rolling down my cheeks and onto my handcuffed hands, my loved ones formed a circle around me and prayed and cried with me and for me, and once again, amid the pain and helplessness, I felt blessed.

Eventually, after allowing me to have a bite to eat with my friends and family on the second floor, my guard said it was time to return to the carceleta. Before saying goodbye to everyone, I managed to ask Manolo where Miranda was, and he replied, "At another emergency."

I was furious. "If my being in prison isn't emergency enough for my attorney, then it may be time for a serious talk," I said, among other things, which I don't remember clearly, but I know were not very nice. Manolo was a gentleman and let me vent. I felt desolate.

My next hearing was scheduled for Wednesday, January 27. Nina and Fabián would turn six on January 26. I tried to tell myself that it was just another day on the calendar, but the truth is that it completely broke my heart.

CHAPTER 8

It's My Children's Birthday
...and I'm Not There

WEEK THREE

Hearing days are tough on the body, the mind, and the soul. It is incredible that more of us inmates didn't faint, despair, or die. The following day or two I went into recovery mode, sleeping in, allowing my mind to heal from the trauma, and doing my best to accept that I now had yet another week in prison to deal with, and no clear end in sight. I would've preferred to get up and do something, but there wasn't much to do. I could've called someone, I suppose, but I didn't have much to say.

I sometimes dreamed that all the people who cared about me, about my situation, and claimed they wanted a better Guatemala, would get together to tell the world that what was happening was unacceptable and that they wouldn't stand to be a part of that system. But I couldn't expect people to act as I would have if I'd been on the outside, or feel what I was feeling. I constantly reminded myself, *I must be grateful for all the love and support I do get,* because being locked up in that place was demoralizing. It made me feel powerless and helpless; all I could do was hope that someone out there was fighting to get things resolved. One piece of good news: Ashley was accepted into URL Law School! At least some things were still right in the world.

———

A chilly cold front swept through our region that week, which meant many inmates were sneezing and coughing. I too had a stuffy nose that made it difficult for me to breathe at night. Washing my hair before bedtime worked well when the weather was warm, but now that the cold had come in, it was a recipe for disaster. So, on my fifteenth day in prison, I once again had to alter my routine. At 10 a.m., I headed to the beauty shack for my first full body, one-hour massage, which at five dollars and in my present living conditions, was absolutely fabulous. I then went back to my cellblock to take a shower and finally wash my hair, and as I was getting dressed, someone stopped by to tell me I had a visitor. It was Manolo.

Since the prison warden was not available, no one was able to authorize my exit to the warden's office area, so our meeting took place in public, through the prison bars. I was disappointed with the legal process and visibly upset, and I let him know it. "I feel as if we are constantly three steps behind instead of three steps ahead," I complained, "and I'm tired of hearing 'unfortunately' this and 'unfortunately' that." Manolo was a gentleman and let me fire away, so I kept going. "I want to know if you are able to do more than a free court-appointed attorney or not, because so far, other than the death penalty, this is the worst-case scenario for me. I'm in prison without having had a trial, without a conviction, and without any concrete evidence against me." I was furious. And when I asked him about several issues they should be focusing on and why they weren't, his response was, "I don't know, Miranda is in charge." I have been told that not trusting one's attorney becomes normal under these circumstances.

As I looked at him in disbelief, not knowing what else to say, I noticed my father approaching the gates. He gave me a kiss through the bars, and we locked hands and spoke for a while. "I would give my life to change places with you," he said, and I had no doubt that was true. As we neared the end of our visit, my father handed me water, alfajores, and some other goodies he'd brought for me from San Martín Bakery, and pleaded that I eat something. "You can't lose any more weight!" he said. Meanwhile, Manolo had gotten to work and managed to obtain a special permit to allow my father to bring me lunch *every* day! I finally felt like my attorneys got me something.

Saying goodbye to my father was never easy, but that day I was especially riled up, so when he left, I cried. Wiping away the tears, I made my way to Serigrafía, and as usual, as soon as I stepped through that door, my outlook changed. Without that place to escape to, I don't think I could have survived. I later went back to my cellblock to wait for my turn on the phone. I spoke to Nina and Fabián and began to feel as if we were all bored with our now usual conversation. Holding their attention had become progressively more difficult as the days went by. I was beginning to feel like a fading memory and it hurt me, so I decided it was important that I share with them some of the activities I had been doing while "away at work." I told them about my English teaching job and about the preschoolers, which they reacted to with great enthusiasm, especially when they heard I was reading to children. But I knew all they really wanted was for their mommy to come home . . . and all I really wanted was to be with them.

———

The following day, at 9:30 a.m., I headed out to Serigrafía, but to my horror my sanctuary was closed. Thankfully, I had a 10 a.m. meeting with Marta, the social worker, so after our chat, I chose some children's books and a memory game and walked over to the preschool. Now, even though my preschool permit was still in the works, the guards gave me no trouble coming in and out of this area, since Ashley had gotten me a permit to be at

Serigrafía, and the guards knew I was setting up a library at Social Services.

The prison preschool is comprised of three separate areas: a small room with murals on the walls, a rug, a small TV with a DVD player, two tables, and small chairs; another area with cribs; and the last one with an adult-size table and chairs, children's games, and potty-training potties. There were six children under three years of age at the preschool that morning, so I decided to read to them. They loved it, but they had short attention spans, so I quickly moved on to a memory game, only to find out that they had a hard time following simple instructions. They clamored for another book, so I went back to reading until they started playing something else . . . it was tough work! After thirty minutes, I was done. The children wanted me to stay longer, but I had to go. I was exhausted. The woman in charge asked for my full name and cellblock number to include me in the report. I was turning out to be a model prisoner—one more thing I never knew about myself.

Later that day, my name was called and I found Gerardo Villamar, from the Department of Human Rights, waiting for me by the gates. He stopped by to check up on me since I had expressed concerns regarding my safety as a result of the newspaper article about my case. "I'm lying low," I said, "spending most of my time at Serigrafía or with the social worker and the children. The worst violation of my rights has to do with me not having a stable judge." He took notes. I did not know if there was anything he could do, but I needed to try.

"I've been worried about you," he replied. "My office has received several calls from people regarding your case." Those words were a huge relief. The outside world had not forgotten about me. All hope was not lost. After Gerardo left, my father came with water, a salad, and half a grilled chicken. He wanted me to eat and I did. I was in better spirits, so our visit was a good one.

Back at Serigrafía, I continued with the day's English lesson: colors. Then, Ashley came in with T-shirts that needed attention, so the women went to work while I finally got to watch Ashley's TEDx Talk. It was amazing.

When I returned to my cellblock for the night, I was offered an extra quick phone call and I spoke to my kids. By now, I had managed to get my name on my cellblock's permanent five-minute phone call list. From 7 to 9 p.m., there was a set calling list, so when my scheduled 7:30 p.m. call came around, I dialed my lifelong friend and Nina's godmother, Christie. It was so nice to hear her voice.

"I have a good feeling that you will be home soon," she said, "and my mom has arranged a mass for you on the day of your next hearing. Everything is set for Nina and Fabi's birthday celebration this coming Sunday. It will be held at Turi's house and will have a Ninja Turtles theme, just like Nina and Fabián had hoped for. Don't worry about anything, it is all taken care of."

———

On Friday at 8:30 a.m., I was still in my pajamas when my name was called . . . encomienda day! It was my brother Rodrigo with goodies in hand. It is always nice to see him, his smile, and his beautiful blue eyes. Right after Rodri left, I was called again. This time it was Karla and Stephanie. I was so happy to see them that I cried. Emotions run high when you're behind bars. They also gave me a huge bag of goodies, including many books to donate to the new prison library, a Sudoku workbook, and a word puzzle book to keep my mind busy during those endless days. They even brought the electric kettle I had hoped for, but it was not allowed in because I didn't have the necessary permit yet. Luckily, Ashley, who was just arriving, managed to grab the kettle and put it in her car until the permit was approved. (The kettle was to remain in Ashley's car throughout my stay in Santa Teresa because the permit never came through.)

That's how Karla and Stephanie met Ashley. I mentioned to Karla that Ashley needed a sponsor to pay for her university tuition and she said they would figure something out. My friends also brought a huge poster that my school buddies had handwritten and drawn for me, like in our school days. They said they had had a wonderful time putting it together for me, but it could not have been as much fun as I had reading it.

By the time my father came to see me at noon, I had just about everything on my wish list: towel, pillow cover, pizza, nude-color bra, four black thongs, a *guacalito* (plastic wash basin or bowl), tank tops, and a sweat suit. After our goodbyes, I took the bags to my bunk so that I could figure out what to do with it all. It felt good to have the tools to start making a difference in that place. With what I had at hand, I taught Verónica how to play cards and Sudoku, and she was quickly hooked. After I managed to organize everything, I shared what I could with my bunkmates and put together a bag of items to return home. Figuring out how to keep exactly what you need, and are able to fit in a tiny space is a complicated balancing act . . . another basic yet essential lesson learned in prison.

At 1:30 p.m. I went back to my cellblock to wait for my turn to make a phone call, then I spoke to my children. "I am putting together a library for the people here because they have no books. The books are being donated by our friends," I told them.

Nina got excited and asked, "Can I come help you?"

"That's not possible," I said, "but maybe we can put together a plan to build a library in another place when I come home."

"Yes!" she exclaimed.

When I spoke to Fabi, he wanted to know how many days were left until I came home. I could not give him a number because I truly did not know the answer, and also because he was smart enough to count down the days. All I could do was say, "I don't know, many days, until my work here is done," and my heart broke all over again.

—

My third weekend in prison started with what was now becoming my new familiar routine. I woke up, went to the restroom, came back, shared a Swiss Miss hot chocolate with Verónica (courtesy of my clever and generous friends), and received my daily five-minute visit from my father with goodies from San Martín Bakery—if I managed to gain back even a little bit of the weight I had lost while in prison, it was most definitely courtesy of my father and San Martin Bakery! Then, at noon, I taught an English lesson at Serigrafía, and by 1:30 p.m. I had my visitor of the day—my Rodri.

During this visit, I realized that I did not cry as much anymore. In a strange way, this new life was becoming somewhat "normal." We sat at a table with two chairs and a tablecloth, which cost us two-and-a-half dollars, and enjoyed our time together. At one point, I quickly ducked back into my cellblock to leave the gallon of water Rodri had brought for me and to use the restroom. When I was about to head back, I asked Verónica to join us. She combed her hair, put on her makeup, and came out to the communal hall. Together, the three of us made a wish list for Rodri to fill, which included avocados, lemons, toothbrushes, a small tablecloth, and some series on DVD. Before Rodri left, he put the list in his pocket and insisted that Verónica take his last five-and-a-half dollars. At first, she refused to accept it, but after a little convincing, she finally agreed. Meanwhile, Ashley had also stopped by during this visit, which now meant she had officially met my entire family.

Rodri, Verónica, and I were among the last to leave the communal hall that day. Leslie, the table and chair renter, picked our set up before we had even finished saying our goodbyes, and was quick to point out we had broken one of the chairs. Now, these chairs are made from very cheap plastic, they are old and have been endlessly used and reused. This particular one was already broken and its backrest had been stitched up with raffia string. It was not only already partially cracked, but was on the brink of breaking completely. And that's exactly what I said to Leslie before heading over to Serigrafía. However, soon thereafter, Leslie came looking for me to tell me that Teresa was the owner of the chair and she wanted fourteen dollars or a new chair. Leslie only worked for Teresa, but she was responsible for the merchandise, so if I didn't pay up, she'd have to replace the chair herself.

Teresa lived in my cellblock and sold phone cards, tortillas, and had the table and chair rental business, and who knew what else. She wore indigenous clothing and looked pleasant enough, but fellow inmates were scared of her because of her quick temper. And now it looked like we had a problem: I can be calm and generous, but that should never be misunderstood for weakness on my part. I knew that Teresa probably bought each chair for eight dollars, rented it out five hundred times at seventy cents for three hours at a time, and then when the old thing finally broke, she charged the poor victim fourteen dollars.

"I may be known as 'the millionaire' around here, but I am not one, and even if I were, I will not be taken advantage of in this way. But I do understand your predicament, so I will give you three-and-a-half dollars," I told Leslie.

"I'll pay seven dollars if you pay the other seven dollars," Leslie bartered.

"You have a deal," I said, "but from now on I don't want you to service my visitors. It's nothing personal against you, but I refuse to give Teresa one more penny of mine." And so, my first real prison confrontation was resolved.

Verónica later mentioned that there was another lady from Cellblock Two who also rented tables and chairs, so I had another option to figure out before Rodri came back at 8:30 a.m. the following Monday. Having principles can be difficult on any given day, and sometimes in prison, it is almost impossible.

———

I slept with a fleece sweatshirt, socks, and covered by my blanket that Saturday, but it was so cold in the middle of the night, that I had to grab the extra sheet I kept stowed under my pillow, and place it on top of my blanket for extra warmth. The following morning, Verónica and I slept in and eventually had our breakfast: *champurradas* (traditional Guatemalan flat, crunchy cookies), blackberry jam, and hot milk with coffee. Later on, my name was called, announcing that I had a visitor. It was my father bringing part of our wish list along with some delicious chicken from Pinulito, a classic fried chicken restaurant in Guatemala. I asked my father if he was going to my children's birthday party later that afternoon at Turi's house, but he told me the party had been postponed until the following weekend in the hope that I might be able to celebrate with them.

My friends and family were wonderful for doing this, for keeping such high hopes, but I could not allow myself to expect or wish for much. My father also mentioned that he and Rodrigo had spoken to a friend of theirs from the US Embassy regarding my case. This person was head of an unrelated department at the Embassy, and would find out whom they should contact. I knew it would take only one key person to believe in me and the injustice that was being done to get the ball rolling in my favor.

By 1:30 p.m. I had said goodbye to my father and was back at Serigrafía. Ashley was not there yet, so I held an English lesson on plurals and nouns, while the women waited for their next job order. Meanwhile, Andrea, who managed Serigrafía and was also her cellblock's voice, had been called to a special cellblock leader's meeting and came back with the news that the prison had lost, or no longer had, a special water seal to stamp visitors, so it had been decided that from then on, at the end of our weekly visits (usually from 1:30 to 3:30 p.m.) all prisoners would have to rush back to their cellblocks, and visitors would only be let out of the prison once all inmates were locked up and accounted for. This would cut afternoon visits by at least thirty precious minutes and require visitors to stay an hour longer after the visit was over. As the news spread, most inmates were very upset and some were concerned that inmate unhappiness could result in riots. As if we didn't have enough to worry about already.

The next morning, at 8:30 a.m., my name was called and I was told that the blue-eyed *canche* was waiting for me. The girl who came to get me, Leslie's rental business partner, buttered me up the entire way to the communal hall, and of course, when I got there, Leslie quickly stepped in and led me straight to my brother, who was happily seated at Teresa's rental table and chairs. So much for respecting my wishes. But the truth was that I still did not know from whom I was going to rent that day, so I guess it all worked out. These girls were very efficient at their jobs, but I still would rather have not given Teresa any of our money.

Rodri brought hot coffee and bagels with cream cheese for Verónica and me. He also brought the divider sheet we had asked for, cucumbers, two sweatshirts (one for Verónica and one for Mariana), and several other wish-list items, including twenty brooms and a dozen ropes for hanging laundry out to dry in the sun. These last items were a special request from Mimi from when I had asked her if I could help the cellblock in any way. She never asked me for anything personal.

———

On Tuesday, January 26, 2016, instead of waking up at home next to my children on their sixth birthday, I woke up in Santa Teresa, in Cellblock One, went to the restroom, and noticed it was 7 a.m.—too late to call my kids and wish them a happy birthday, because by then they were off to school. At 9:02 a.m. I thought about how, exactly six years earlier, God had given me the most precious gift of all, and I thanked Him, even though in some strange and unfair twist of fate, I could not be by their side to celebrate with them. I wondered if the people responsible for my imprisonment ever thought about the irreparable damage they were inflicting on my family and me. And then I remembered, I was not human to them; I was only a pawn to be used as part of a legal strategy against my husband.

———

My day rolled on as usual. I walked over to Serigrafía and found Ashley busy telling the women about her first day of law school. She was excited and so were the rest of us. I then taught the women an English lesson, and later accompanied Daniela to Social Services so she could check out a novel. The library was still not officially open, but Marta allowed me to take books out for some inmates and myself. Meanwhile, María, Santa Teresa's Educational Programs manager, noted that I should make sure to make all of my inmate activities "official" so that they count as positive points on my behalf in front of my judge. I decided that, if I was still an inmate after my court hearing the following day, I would do so.

Meanwhile, one of the inmates in my cellblock, the one who had kindly given me a small packet of shampoo and conditioner and lent me a small towel when I first arrived in Santa Teresa, had been telling me for the last couple of days that she needed to talk to me. She had been quite sick, bending over as she walked, due to terrible abdominal pain, so I stopped by her bunk to ask her how she was feeling and if I could help her in any way. It turned out she had cervical cancer and was currently battling an infection, but the doctor wasn't scheduled to visit our prison until the following week. She told me that her home was abandoned and nobody could go in to get her medical paperwork, and that her young children lived far away with their father. She had finally decided to reach out to me after the nurse had given her some special medication that had to be injected that day with a 10cc syringe, but she only had a 5cc syringe.

I immediately called my father, asking him to buy one on his way to see me. By 11:30 a.m., she had her 10cc syringe and I had my chicken Caesar salad along with my daily hug and kiss. At 1:30 p.m. I eagerly walked back to my cellblock, got in line to use the telephone, and called Vania's cell phone to talk to my babies. Their beloved Tía Vania and Tío Ed had taken them to celebrate their birthday at a pizza place and they sounded like they were a having a blast. My two children may not have had their mother with them that day, but they were not lacking in love, which gave me great comfort and relief.

Later that evening, I managed to make another phone call, this time to my mother, who said hello and quickly passed the phone to my son. He was so excited that he barely spoke to me and handed the phone over to his sister, who then passed me on to Vania, who finally filled me in on their afternoon. They had gone to eat pizza and then to a huge toy store so that my children could choose their birthday gifts for themselves. Fabi had chosen a truck pulling a two-deck car transporter. I knew exactly which one it was because he had wanted it since Christmas. Nina chose a Doc McStuffins Doctor Kit. I also knew exactly which one it was because it was one of my options for her at Christmastime. And now, they were all at my house. Belo, their paternal grandfather, was also there celebrating his grandchildren's birthdays. Vania congratulated me on bringing those two wonderful children into this world. She always has such beautiful things to say! I hung up and suddenly felt numb.

I then called my father and told him Miranda had not shown up that day, and I was tired of feeling as if I did not have an attorney. He told me that Miranda had contracted the chikungunya virus and was feeling terrible, but he had promised to be at my hearing the following day. Can you imagine your attorney not showing up at your court hearing? But then again, at my first hearing the public prosecutor was a no-show, at my second hearing the judge was a no-show, so I now felt like anything was possible.

———

As I've previously mentioned, prison stories abounded in Santa Teresa, and I was always interested in understanding how these women had ended up in this place. That night, while standing in line waiting for the shower, it was Leticia's turn to open up to me.

According to Leticia, after she got a divorce, lost custody of her children, survived a kidnapping, and lost her business, she decided to move to El Salvador, where she opened several businesses which did not thrive. She loved spending time at the beach and on one occasion overheard a man say that buying fish bait was very difficult to do during fishing season in El Salvador because the supply was controlled in Guatemala. She investigated the matter and decided to invest in a bait shipment container from China. The first shipment sold very well, so she ordered another one. By around the fourth container, inventory suddenly became difficult to sell, and a man called Manuel approached her and offered to help sell her product. She accepted and Manuel became her salesman.

Eventually, in 2014, she left everything behind and moved back to Guatemala. Approximately two months ago, in December 2015, while at a local shopping mall, she bumped into Manuel. He was accompanied by what seemed to be his family. After greeting each other, he mentioned in passing that he was looking for a place to leave one of their two cars because parking was expensive in Guatemala. They had driven to Guatemala City from El Salvador in two vehicles, but they could all fit in one while in the city because their luggage was left at the hotel. So, Leticia offered to keep one of his cars at her house and he accepted.

The next day, after he parked his vehicle at her place, Leticia had to run an errand in the city and decided to take Manuel's car, which she explained was something she did all the time back in El Salvador because their parking assignments were one behind the other. She said it was now obvious to her that she should not have taken it, but it had not seemed unusual to her at the time.

While she was driving Manuel's car, two of Leticia's girlfriends were following in another car behind her, when suddenly, Leticia was ambushed and stopped by the authorities. Although her girlfriends weren't included in the roundup, they decided to stop as well to make sure that Leticia was OK, which led them to be caught in this unforeseen situation. The authorities told all of them to get out of the vehicles and questioned them, and explained that they had been looking for this particular car. Up until then, Leticia was nervous but had faith that this was all a big misunderstanding that would soon be resolved. However, when the police searched the car, they found a weapon and close to a million dollars in cash hidden inside. Leticia and her two girlfriends were taken into custody and have been in preventive detention ever since.

She also told me that after landing in prison, she had been stunned to find newspaper articles claiming that she was a former beauty queen, or that she was a mafia queen linked to the Mexican cartel and La Reina del Pacífico, one of its leaders. She felt as if she'd suddenly been thrown into a twilight zone, and I understood exactly what she meant.

———

By 8:30 p.m. I was in bed, trying to fall asleep so I could get some rest before my big day. It took me a while, due to the noise, the early hour, and my nerves, but I must have dozed off at some point, because at around 11 p.m. I woke up startled by someone calling my name. It was the guards at the cellblock gates officially informing me about my court hearing the next day. Another useless interruption, so I turned around and went back to sleep. However, sometime later, I was startled awake once again.

This time it was Abuela. I had already heard about this woman's crazy late-night tirades. When I first arrived in Santa, the talk was still going on about how upset inmates in Cellblock One were because Abuela would pray out loud in the middle of the night, usually talking about the devil, but up until last night, the only thing I had witnessed was a quiet, thin, dirty, disheveled old woman who always wore the same clothes, walked around carrying all of her belongings in two torn bags, slept anywhere at any time, and sat on the floor with her head resting on her knees. I had tried giving her a bag of cookies once, just to have them reappear on my bed later. Verónica told me to let it be because Abuela did not accept anything from anybody.

That night, while I was trying to get some rest before my anxiously anticipated hearing the next day, Abuela went off on one of her infamous loud ranting prayers. "Come here ye demons! Why do you laugh? Come tell me to my face. Hit me then!" Other inmates began making fun of her, making rude or silly comments, but Abuela kept going. Eventually, the lights were turned on, the guards were called, and they had to physically remove her from our cellblock. I was afraid they would take her to solitary confinement, but was relieved to find out the next day that she had been transferred to Cellblock Eight—a block known for housing many lesbian couples, so I assumed poor Abuela would be invoking the devil often in her new home. I was also glad that the four bullies who got her riled up by bothering her the night before were punished with a plancha each.

Rumor had it that Abuela's child, who was born a hermaphrodite, had been convicted for child molestation, a crime considered heinous by every standard. Although Abuela's offspring considered herself female, the court had decided that since she had a penis, she was legally male, and was sent to a men's prison because no inmate with a male part was allowed to live among female inmates. Once in jail, it was said that she had been severely raped and beaten, and Abuela continually suffered for her child. I didn't know if any of this was true, but as I was quickly learning, anything was possible, and some people's suffering had no end in sight. As I pondered her predicament, I realized now that my own fate was hanging in the balance. *Will I be set free tomorrow?*

CHAPTER 9

Justicia para Anaité

WEEK FOUR

On Wednesday, January 27, 2016, as with previous hearing days, I got ready in a flash, while the guards finished up the 4 a.m. head count. It was the start of my fourth week in prison and my freedom was riding on that day's hearing. Would the judge show up? Would I get to go home to my children? Would justice be served? These thoughts were buzzing around in my mind, as we walked through the cellblock gates, which the guards opened for the inmates taking out the trash and those of us going to the courthouse, when suddenly I noticed some inmates out and about who belonged to neither group. Two of them were obviously smoking pot. I also saw a group of guards enter the communal hall followed by another group of inmates. They closed the door and remained in the dark. I have no idea what they did at 4:15 a.m., during the ten minutes I saw them enter and then exit together, but they must have noticed the strong smell of pot since the couple was smoking it right outside the hall and there are no window panes in the window openings. *What a surreal place; a true underworld*, I thought, as I observed them all in the twilight before dawn.

Eventually, the main gates were opened and inmates were called for booking. I knew the drill by now. After registering, we waited in the outdoor holding area, in the cold, for forty-five to seventy-five minutes, for the perrera to arrive. We were then lined up in pairs and taken to our vehicle, which would drive us to the place that is as close to hell as I can possibly imagine. However, I was in good spirits that day, not because I was as positive as everyone else about the possibility of going home, but because I knew I would get to see my loved ones . . . those precious moments with them meant the world to me.

My court hearing was scheduled for 9 a.m., so only a few hours after being locked up in the carceleta, I was handcuffed and taken upstairs to the second floor, where, just as I had hoped for, my loved ones were waiting. They were all so happy, so supportive, and so sure that I would be going home that it was almost contagious. Almost.

The court hearing began at 10:07 a.m. My loved ones prayed around me before I went in. Although I loved it when they did that, I had stopped pleading to God because I felt He was either not listening or He was not ready to set me free. I realized that all I could do was continue to have faith that He had a positive plan for me that, in all that darkness, I still could not see.

As I walked into the courtroom, I noticed that both my primary accuser, Juan Pablo Olyslager Muñoz, and his attorney were no-shows once again. I couldn't believe that my whole prison nightmare had started with one person's accusations, and now that person had managed to resolve his issue, get his money back through the sale of the farm he held as a guarantee, and no longer felt the need to show his face in court, while I struggled to stay afloat under the soul-crushing circumstances he had thrown me into. All this, while the Mayora & Mayora attorneys representing GFP sat shoulder-to-shoulder with the public prosecutor, possessing no real proof of my involvement, yet insisting on keeping me in prison.

After Miranda presented a wealth of evidence, indicating that I had never had any capacity or any involvement in my husband's business dealings, the judge decided that nothing had changed and that her original decision to keep me behind bars would stand. My next court hearing for pretrial motions was set for February 18, 2016. That meant twenty-one more days in prison . . . twenty-one more days without my children. I was so stunned by the outcome that I wasn't even able to shed a tear in court. My grief came pouring out when I broke the news to my loved ones in the hallway. I didn't realize my heart could shatter into more pieces until that day. In handcuffs, I received a hug from everyone, said my goodbyes, and walked back to the carceleta. *If this is what justice looks like in a Guatemalan court, I am going to need a miracle.*

———

Silver linings take on a whole new meaning in prison, and the day after my horrendous court hearing, I was granted one, though not without a fight. A few days earlier, I had come across a fellow inmate who was selling a light bulb fixture. Verónica and I were ecstatic with the prospect of finally having light in our bottom bunk—the only light in our bunk area came from a light fixture glued to the wall above the top bunk, which made it very difficult to read and write, and it belonged to our bunkmate Clara—however, our enthusiasm was short-lived.

When we asked Clara if it would be OK to make this purchase, she became fussy, and told us to ask Mimi. As it turned out, Mimi was sleeping at the time, so we returned to our plancha where Clara added, "The electric plug in the wall is mine. If you want electricity, you have to contact the prison handyman to see if he can come up with a separate electric connection for you." It became so complicated, that we decided to shelve the idea. A few days later, the day after my hearing to be exact, I brought the subject up with Clara again.

"If I decide to purchase the light fixture, how would an electrician cable it?"

Flustered once again, Clara said, "I paid the electrician twenty-seven dollars to get this electrical connection and you will have to do the same. And by the way, I have already sold this electric outlet to another inmate, so you will not be able to plug your light into it."

"Did you sell the light fixture as well, because in that case, I'll get us all another one," I said.

I'm not sure what she understood, but her response to me was, "Stop being disrespectful!"

"It is not my intention to be disrespectful, I just want to understand what your plans are so that the rest of us can resolve our lighting problem." I was now angry and before it got out of hand, I decided to go back to my part of the lower bunk bed in the hope that soon her small brain might manage to organize itself. And sure enough, ten minutes later she came down from her bunk, light plug and electric switch in hand, and simply said as she handed it all to me, "Buy a bar of silicone."

"What for?" I asked.

"To glue the fixture down here in your bunk."

"It was never my intention to take yours, but simply to add another," I insisted.

"Go ahead, glue this one down below and give it a try," she replied.

So, my theory was right. She wasn't a terrible person; it just took her a little while to come to her senses. Verónica and I glued the hardware on the wall next to where I lay my head. It was amazing to suddenly have enough light to read and write without feeling that I was going blind, a great accomplishment indeed. But, since I usually went to sleep before my other roommates, from that moment on, I not only needed to sleep through the bunk area's noise, but also with a bright light shining over my head, while my bunkmates read or sewed to their heart's content and Clara worked on her school homework on our bed. *Be careful what you wish for!*

———

Later that day, during my father's precious visit, he mentioned that my cousin Christian Wahl had started a Facebook page called "Justicia para Anaité." So, there I was, in the confines of prison, with no Internet access, wondering what this was all about and what kind of response, if any, this page would have. It had become clear to me from the start, especially after the reactions to my Facebook post before being thrown in jail, that social pressure would likely be the only weapon I had against my opponents and their "justice" system. During my last hearing, one of the opposing attorneys mentioned on several occasions that "it was being said" that it was their law firm who was stalling my process. The public's perception of them and their firm seemed to be very important to them. This Facebook page was likely the only chance I had to let the truth come out, while I was unable to fend for myself in any other way.

Once my father left, I headed to the Social Services office and managed to take two children's books before Marta locked the door on her way out. I then headed to the pergola where I found the children from preschool whom I had started reading to a few days earlier. Their excitement was contagious when they saw me come by with books in hand.

After the children and I wrapped up our reading session, I noticed Carmen sitting on a bench, observing me. I approached her, said hello, and she asked me to sit with her.

"Are you going to move into encamamiento?" she asked.

"I've been fine in Cellblock One, but now that my stay has been getting longer and longer, I am planning on looking into that option. I know encamamiento is full and that a judge's order is required to transfer there," I said, and then added, "I also realize that at the cellblocks one seems to be subjected to physical pain and discomfort, while in encamamiento one suffers emotionally among such strong-willed alpha women."

"That is exactly right," she replied. "Imprisonment in general is very tough, but my experience in encamamiento has been psychologically drain-ing. I'm impressed you noticed this so quickly because I've been here for five months and I'm just starting to make sense of it all."

But then again, how could Carmen see it clearly when she had never been in a cellblock? All inmates suffer in prison, being away from their chil-dren and their loved ones. But Carmen's pain seemed to be ever-present.

"What has your best and worst experience been so far?" asked Carmen.

"Best, the unconditional love and support I have received. Worst, the anger and impotence I feel from the injustice."

Later at Serigrafía, Daniela told me she had seen a picture of me with a horse in a publication called *Nuestro Diario*. I was officially famous now. Funny how that works: people who want to be famous often have a difficult time obtaining media coverage, and those of us who aren't interested some-how find the spotlight.

———

By the fourth week of my prison stay I had learned a great deal about the inner workings of our prison—all information was obtained through stories shared with me by my fellow inmates along the way, such as the sweet-looking young woman who had spent seven months in solitary confinement in 2015. As she explained to me one day, since I had the good fortune of not experiencing them myself, these specific cells in Santa Teresa are 5 x 11 feet, and have one cement bunk bed and one bathroom, with a shower spout coming out of the wall above the toilet. There are eight solitary confinement cells and at that time only numbers three and four had a light bulb that worked. The rest remained dark throughout the night. The young woman claimed that the reason she spent so much time there was because she had the habit of talking back to the guards. At first, she spent a full month alone, with no visitors, but said she enjoyed the solitude. I later heard from another inmate that the reason this girl enjoyed solitary confinement was because she loved to smoke pot, and that was the perfect place to do so. However, actual solitude was not guaranteed. With only eight cells available for a prison population of over one thousand women, there were times when inmates had to bunk with each other and share their "solitary" punishment.

Another inmate later told me another frightful story, which again reminded me that I was being held captive in a very dangerous place. One night, at around 3 a.m., she heard a fight break out through her bunk window, which faced solitary confinement. It was four women against one. The guards took them all out of the confinement cell they shared and asked if they wanted to fight it out. If so, they would give the women ten minutes to do so. The inmate at her bunk heard one woman state clearly that she did not want to fight, but the guards gave them ten minutes anyway. And so ensued the clear sound of commotion and punches as the four women hit the other woman's head and body.

The inmate next to the window, listening to this violence, strongly considered saying something but was afraid of guard retaliation against her. She recalled the feeling of impotence as she remained quietly on the sidelines while the assault continued outside. She considered filing a personal report on the incident, or calling the human rights organization, but she would have had to place the call from the public telephone in her cellblock and the guards would most likely find out about it. Furthermore, it was also likely that, when interviewed by the guards or human rights personnel, those same inmates from solitary confinement would choose not to speak up, in order to avoid further trouble with the guards. There seemed to be so many options for inmates to report abuses, but none of them were good if you wanted to remain safe within prison walls.

It was common knowledge that many of the prison guards smoked pot while on duty, and that some male lieutenants had sexual relations with inmates. But not all guards were terrible; many were nice and professional in spite of their work conditions. Prison guards work in seven-day shifts, which means that for seven straight days, they live at the prison, and the following seven days, they are off work. This basically creates two prison personnel shifts. While I was there, one group was clearly nicer than the other. I cannot imagine what it must be like to work as a guard in a prison, under those conditions, living among inmates of all kinds who may harm you at any moment.

Inmates are afraid of guards for obvious reasons, but I am sure guards are also afraid of inmates. When riots break out, guards are often taken hostage by dangerous inmates, many of whom are the women of dangerous and powerful gang members freely roaming the streets of Guatemala, easily able to harm a guard or their loved ones on the outside. Nevertheless, there are also guards who enjoy their position of power and pathetically use it to unnecessarily dehumanize inmates. I can only imagine what these guards have seen, what they have witnessed, and the miserable existence they have chosen to endure. Some may have chosen this dreadful life, but several have confessed that it was not so much their choice, but rather the lack of opportunities elsewhere which led them down this career path.

———

It's a very good thing that when I went to prison at forty-seven, I was old and wise enough to understand human nature in a mature way. As inmates, we were all going through tough moments in our lives. Some had it worse than others, and some even seemed to like life within these walls, since they managed to be set free and were back in Santa Teresa a month later. With all its failings, prison did provide a roof, three meals per day, water, electricity, and a safe haven from oppressors on the outside. Many commented on how they thought God had protected them by sending them to that place. In any event, conditions were harsh for most women, so I understood why women I barely knew or didn't know at all approached me with their stories and needs. I understood that many inmates had no visitors, no means, and no help from the outside; however, I also knew that I couldn't become everybody's savior.

First and foremost, I too was doing my best to survive inside those walls. And yes, I was blessed with the support and generosity of my loved ones, but I also made sure to share everything they so kindly brought me during my stay in prison. And yet, I was also incredibly aware that in a place like that, where need abounds, doing favors and being generous could also easily end up being more of a cause for envy and resentment than gratitude. There was a fine line that was very difficult to navigate. Those you did not help resented you immediately, and those you did help resented you later, when you were no longer capable or willing to give them another hand.

Therefore, when I shared my stuff with others, I always made it extra clear that it was my pleasure to do so, no strings attached, so it didn't seem like anyone should owe me a favor in return; owing favors can be dangerous in prison. Furthermore, when paying for something, I always indicated it was in exchange for a job well done or an actual item that I needed. But all of this and the fact that I didn't just freely give things away didn't stop some people from seeking me out constantly. When I heard, "Chhhht, hey, canchita . . . Anaité, come over here!" I knew that they wanted something from me. Sometimes I would wave and continue on and other times I would stop, listen to their concerns, and say, "How terrible! I am so sorry to hear that" or "We are all going through a difficult time." I did my best, but I refused to be manipulated, blackmailed, intimidated or made to feel guilty. That was my resolution and that's one of the ways I managed to survive those unimaginable days.

———

Friday came along and with it another encomienda day, along with several five-minute visits through the metal bars. Once back at the cellblock, my name was called again; this time it was the warden. On my way to her office,

I passed the entrance gates, saw my father, and signaled him to wait. The warden told me that, once again she had received a phone call from Human Rights regarding my health and needed to ask me how I was feeling. I gave her the usual update, "My blood pressure has been very low and, aside from the obvious dire circumstances that this place provides, I am doing OK."

What else could I say? No one had told me what the plan was, what I should say or ask or do. Miranda hadn't stopped by to see me or update me in any way, so if that chat with the warden helped me get to encamamiento, I needed to do my best to make it happen . . . although I still wondered if encamamiento was the place for me. There were ten beds and eleven women currently living there. Where would I even fit?

I left the warden's office and managed to stay with my father outside the gates. Soon after, Rodri arrived followed by my friends Karla and Tuffy, carrying books, cookies, sandwiches, brownies, granola bars, tank tops, and letters from my girlfriends who were far away or had not been able to visit me. And just when I thought the party couldn't get any better, my father-in-law showed up. He looked very thin. As is usual with him, he managed to keep up his good spirits for me, but I felt that he was heartbroken. His son may have angered several people, but the reason I found myself behind bars was that two of those people and their legal counsel somehow found it appropriate to use me as collateral to get back at him. Apparently, there were other people who also had claims against my husband, but none of them were willing to claim that I had been involved in any way.

As I gathered all the goodies my loved ones had showered me with, my friend Tuffy handed me a scapular. She was fully aware I would never have worn one under different circumstances, but she had faith it would keep me safe, so I obliged. As she was about to tie it around my wrist, Tuffy noticed the priest walk by and quickly grabbed the scapular, ran over to him, and asked him to bless it. He did, but not without first glancing over my way and asking me what my name was, how long I'd been in Santa Teresa, and ending with, "I will be expecting you at mass next Friday." He only came to the prison on Fridays. My dear Tuffy has tried to get me to attend mass for over thirty years, and she may have finally managed to succeed.

Before leaving my loved ones, I handed Karla my diary, the notebook I had started writing on January 6 during my first day in prison. Now, twenty-four days later, I was ready to share my story with my lifelong friends. I needed them to better understand what this episode of my life was like from my standpoint. My life story would not be complete without them in it. Along with my notebook, I included a note for them:

JANUARY 2016

My Dearest Friends,

I share with you today and trust you all with my experiences, perceptions, emotions, etc. of my Santa Teresita Adventure. I hope these words will one day be part of a book I wish to write about this difficult chapter in my life.

Sharing it with you, my lifelong companions, lightens the weight I now carry in my soul, and it does my heart, which currently seems to be eternally broken, some good.

I try to remain positive every day, yet every moment feels like a roller coaster ride.

I also try to keep my heart, my mind, and my eyes open to God's purposes and lessons for my life, but I regret to tell you that I am not always successful.

Knowing that my children are loved, protected, and taken care of by all of you is the most wonderful gift that you could ever bestow upon me, and I know you have gone "above and beyond," as you always do in your own lives. I love you.

And for pleasing my every whim and desire, I remain eternally grateful. I thank you for praying with me and for me, crying with me and for me, never abandoning me, for keeping the faith and being my strength and my voice when I do not have them for myself.

I wish I had a camera to send you pictures of the children playing memory games or listening to my voice as I read them books, and to show you the women reading the books you and your children have so generously donated. You have allowed me the small satisfaction of doing something beautiful in this unhappy place. Please keep sending your donations. You cannot imagine the treasure those books are in this place.

And please, write to me! It is my only means of communication with many of you and it makes me smile.

I can already imagine you together, reading this handwritten notebook. Please take good care of it because it is very important to me.

Thank you, thank you, thank you for being exactly the way you are!

Anaité

After saying goodbye, I headed back to my cellblock to wait for my turn on the phone to speak to my children, and for the first time in twenty-four days behind bars, I lost my temper. After waiting respectfully in line and finally dialing my home number, I got an answer from Olga, only to have the call suddenly dropped. I tried again, heard Olga's voice, then it went silent again. I dialed a third time, began speaking to Nina, and the line went dead once more. And then it hit me: Olga was probably answering my calls on a telephone that was likely low on battery power, but hadn't realized it. I got so frustrated that I slammed the receiver down, held in a violent scream, marched back to my shared bed, lay down in a fetal position, and burst into angry tears. Noticing my uncharacteristic outburst, Verónica and her friend Meche boiled water and we had some hot chocolate and biscotti.

Eventually, I calmed down and managed to get another chance to call my house and finally speak to my children. I asked Nina and Fabi to remember to pray before bed and thank God for all the things for which they were happy and grateful that day.

Since I do not follow an organized religion, I have been faced with the challenge of coming up with ways for my children to know the God I love. One of our nightly routines includes reciting the Lord's Prayer, because, having been brought up Catholic, I believe it is a beautiful prayer. We also make sure to tell God all the reasons why we are happy and grateful that day. It is something we do out loud, the three of us together, because I believe giving thanks is the most important reason for us to communicate with God. Being thankful is the only way to feel joyful.

Fabi wanted me to call later so we could pray together over the phone. I took a deep breath, my heart aching, and explained that I had no cell phone and since we all shared only one telephone, it was sometimes difficult to call him right before bed. I wanted my children to continue to practice this ritual even when I wasn't by their side, emphasizing that we must trust that He knows best. To this, my practical genius of a son responded, "Well then, let's pray together now!" And that we did. *Please God, let me go home to them soon.*

———

Every weekday the women in Cellblock One watched soap operas on TV all afternoon and after the 8 p.m. episode ended, I got to hear the beginning of the theme song of the series *El Señor de los Cielos*. I had seen seasons one and two on Netflix at home and they were now broadcasting season three on our local TV channel. Every time I heard the theme song, I wished they would leave it on, but it aired at the same time as the local news, which was religiously watched, so the channel on the TV close to my bunk was always changed and my wishful thinking ignored.

Inmates seemed to love the reports on crime, arrests, extortions, and so forth, especially because it was common to see a fellow inmate of ours flash by on-screen. This always caused a commotion at the cellblock, similar to the excitement of knowing a famous person even if that fame is only ten seconds long. Since I had never had the habit of watching local Guatemalan news, I quickly realized how violent and saddening it could be. The entire Guatemalan population is being fed with the notion that this is who we are and how we live, when in fact there are also many wonderful people and positive things happening in Guatemala . . . and even in here! For instance, with the help of my loved ones' amazing book donations, I was able to start a library and get inmates interested in reading, such a cherished pastime under the circumstances. Silver linings surround us, it's just a question of allowing ourselves to find them.

———

On Saturday, right after my visitors left, inmates were required to return to their cellblocks for the unpopular new 3:30 p.m. head count. As soon as the guards finished their rounds, I noticed there was no line to the bathroom so I gathered my toiletries and rushed to take a shower and wash my hair. When I returned to our bunk, looking forward to some reading time, I turned my new light on, but . . . no light! I did not know what to think. If the light bulb was dead, I had to go through the whole process of replacing it. If the hardware was dead, I could only imagine what kind of a small fortune I would have to pay to get it fixed. I found Verónica and she informed me that she had just left the bunk and turned the light off, so she unscrewed the light bulb, took it to another bunk, and asked if she could test it. To my relief, it was the light bulb! An hour and seven dollars later, the light was back on, dimmer than before, which turned out for the best. Amazing how what you take for granted on the outside becomes crucial under different circumstances.

While my light bulb drama played out and was resolved, the other inmates had been busy preparing for Disco Night. It was a hit: they blasted the music, mostly reggaeton, danced, laughed, and had fun. The first time I witnessed this, I saw no point in dressing up and dancing in a women's prison. But today, after twenty-five days in jail, I understood the need to have fun, to dance with the girls, to decompress. I still read most of the night, but I also took a break and went out into the hall to learn some dance moves from Meche, while the girls clapped and cheered us on. I later wrote in my journal: *There are thousands of places and people I would rather spend Saturday night with, but as long as I am here, I will dance!*

———

When I woke up on Sunday, my knee began bothering me. I assumed it was due to sleeping in my usual mummy-like position with that particular right leg curved toward the left, sometimes even crossed over my other foot—a position I adopted at night in the hope that I would not inadvertently kick Verónica in the face while I slept.

Verónica, Meche, and I were just beginning to enjoy our morning coffee with milk, sugar, and champurradas when my name was called. It was my dear father. The guards had mistakenly allowed him in along with the day's formal visitors to Cellblocks Three, Four, and Five, so he was waiting for me at a table in the communal hall. We chatted for a while, but we were both so nervous about holding an unscheduled visit in the hall, and worried that his special visiting permit might be revoked, that we could not relax, so we decided it was best for him to go. Before he left, he asked me about Carmen; since he was already inside the prison gates, we headed over to Serigrafía and found her outside chatting away with her friends. When she saw us, I said to her, "You have a visitor!" She smiled and said, "I know who it is!" The three of us spoke about her situation and about what it was like to be in this place. My father gave Carmen his phone number and asked her to call him any time because he would be happy to help her. I am a mother, so I know the infinite gratitude one feels when another human being goes above and beyond for one's child. Carmen never even noticed she had been generous to me once, but my father will probably never forget it.

By 11:15 a.m. my father and I headed toward the front gates and were told that visitors could not exit the prison until 11:30 a.m. The guard was nice, but rules are rules. So, my father and I sat down, side by side, on the dirty steps, and I had fifteen more precious minutes with him—another blessing in this dire situation.

Later, back at my cellblock, inmates were busy doing the weekly Sunday deep cleaning of their bunk area, which meant everybody's belongings were either on the top bunk or out in the main hallway. I noticed that the bunk to our right had the curtains wide open. I got curious, mainly because this was the bunk area that housed the electric burner, which was used several times per day, only inches away from my mattress and my body. As I strolled past the bunk in the hope of taking a peek inside, I watched as my neighbor María Elena plugged in her burner and it suddenly sparked and then popped. Almost simultaneously, there was an explosion and sparks inside another bunk, the one to our left, followed by screams, women running out of bunks, and general commotion. The lights went out in the entire cellblock and we were left trying to figure out what had happened.

After we calmed down, the buzz was all about María Elena's burner, and how she almost got the girls in our left bunk killed when the electrical explosion occurred. There was a huge black stain on the wall from the fire. I finished my coffee and left for Serigrafía. When I returned to my cellblock later in the day, I heard my neighbor's burner on once again. I had had enough; I was not going to compromise my safety any longer. I went to speak to Mimi.

"What are you planning to do about the malfunctioning burner that caused the commotion this morning? Do you realize that if the cellblock catches fire while we are locked in, we are as good as dead!?!"

"There's nothing I can do," Mimi insisted. "Feel free to call the warden and let her decide, but she'll most likely tell you the same thing."

"If that's the only way to resolve this situation, then that's what I will do," I honestly would've preferred to fix it among ourselves, but it seemed I had run out of options. We then walked over to María Elena's bunk and after a lot of back and forth, the women there finally, reluctantly agreed to move the burner away from our bunk bed as soon as it cooled down.

María Elena had not been present for this latest discussion and when she returned, she said, "What she is saying is not true because the burner has been working fine."

I told her that I had heard her on several occasions gasp when her burner sparked, which I knew was on a daily basis. She had even commented on how her burner was most likely on its last legs. Since we could not see each other because of the partition sheet, I went around and asked if I could come inside. I peeked in and the burner was now located toward the center of the floor area, eight inches farther away from me, and there was now a plastic box between the burner and my bed.

"I cannot believe we had to go through all this drama when *this* was all I had been asking for all along," I said and left again for Serigrafía. As soon as I got there, I let the pent-up tears fall down my cheeks again. The women comforted me, sharing their own confrontations. I had tried to remain positive under my dangerous circumstances, but I did have my low moments. It was then that I gave Ashley the following note for my father:

Dear Papi,

I had a problem today with my bunk neighbor. I am no longer OK.
Please see about moving me into encamamiento.

I love you,

Anaité

Before I headed back to my cellblock, Andrea said to me, "You are right about this. Don't let anyone make you feel bad." Back at my bunk area, I was surprised to find that everything seemed fine, but I knew it was not, and I was now ready to face living among ten tigers rather than 103 snakes. *God help me either way.*

———

On Monday, February 1, I was out of bed by 8:15 a.m. and ready for my name to be called. Rodri had said he would come and have breakfast with me; however, when I went out to meet him, I was happy to also find my classmates Nando and Tula in the communal hall. As we chatted, they told me that another classmate of ours had volunteered to take my rescue dogs, Annika and Alex, to his house. This was music to my ears because I had needed to find homes for them, and now my dear friends had even solved this issue for me. I got emotional when I asked Nando and Tula to thank Andrés on my behalf, because I would have loved to thank him myself, but even that small pleasure had been taken away from me.

I quickly quelled that feeling and replaced it with one of gratitude toward this amazing group of lifelong friends. Then Rodri gave me the details about my children's sixth birthday party, which had taken place at my brother Turi's house the previous day and had been a total success. I was happy for my children, but I couldn't help but think, *I missed my children's sixth birthday party. Who could ever repay me for that?*

In the afternoon, my cousins came to see me. We had such a pleasant and normal time, that for a couple of hours I almost forgot I was locked up in a prison. They brought me a quinoa salad and a huge box full of donated books. As was my usual routine now, I chose the ones I already had a reader for, set them aside, and gave the rest to Marta for the library. To my delight, that night during the soap opera hours, six of us were reading instead of watching TV.

After the 6 p.m. head count, I called my children. I spoke to my mother and told her she could stop avoiding me now because my friends had let me know that Andrés had taken Annika and Alex to his home, and that I thought it was a good solution. Unlike me, my mother has never been much of an animal lover, and taking care of my two children and four dogs had proved to be too much for her. She said she had not been avoiding me, she simply knew that phone time was precious and it was best utilized by me speaking to my children.

The next day, during my father's morning visit, while he was telling me he was doing everything in his power to get me out, he handed me a folder. When I opened it and found printed photos of my children during their birthday party, I couldn't help but cry. I had not seen my children physically since January 5, four entire weeks ago, and had only seen photos of them on Christie's cell phone during my January 27 court hearing, which was also the day I had learned that my friends had created a WhatsApp group called "Nina and Fabián" where they kept informed and made sure my mother and my children had everything they needed. My children looked very happy, but I knew they could not be fully happy without their parents. I knew this to be true because I had spent one year of my life without my father when I was Nina and Fabi's exact age, and I can still recall that pain. And that's when it dawned on me: my father understood my current pain because he had experienced this same sadness of not being able to hug and kiss his children many years ago. It felt good to realize someone truly understood me.

Along with the photos, I found prints of "Justicia para Anaité," the Facebook page my loved ones had created for me. I read every word on those pages and wished I could click everywhere and read more. I also found a printout of an article my cousin Marta Yolanda Diaz-Durán Alvarado had written in *Siglo 21* about my case. Meanwhile, my father proceeded to tell me the news regarding the US Embassy. As I had suspected, it had been my friends who originally contacted them. In turn, the embassy had contacted

Miranda for a meeting because they wanted to know if I had legal representation. Miranda told them about my case and confirmed that he was my defense attorney. I could only hope that soon I would be able to write about their pivotal and crucial involvement in setting me free. An American girl could dream, I supposed, especially when unjustly imprisoned abroad.

At 11:30 a.m., my father headed out with the rest of the visitors, and I walked over to Serigrafía. On my way there, I said hello to Carmen and she offered me some yogurt. At that same moment, the prison nurse came by and asked if my name was Anaité. She told me that I had to go see the doctor. Apparently, some other doctor was requesting a medical report. The prison doctor looked at me, then remembered that he already had a medical report on me, and said he would forward it to the new doctor. He asked me if I had been feeling well, because he remembered that the last time he saw me I was crying and going through the normal depression all new inmates experience. I decided to tell him that I had been feeling weak, that my blood pressure had dropped several weeks ago, and that I had never suffered from blood pressure problems before. I told him that although I had always been a thin person, losing a few pounds was a lot for me. I asked him to weigh me but there was no scale . . . no scale at an infirmary! He decided to take my blood pressure, and to my surprise, it was very low once again: 80/70. He wrote down a prescription for me and I was dismissed.

On my way out of the infirmary, I bumped into Susana and she invited me into her room. She offered me coffee and cake and I declined, telling her I was going to eat my yogurt. She asked me to sit with her and I finally met her three cats: Maximiliano, Emilio, and John Freddy. People said Susana was a bit off and way too straightforward, but I happened to like her very much. Eventually I said my goodbyes and headed over to Leticia's bunk in Cellblock One for my card game appointment. Her bunkmate had seen me with a deck of cards and had invited me over to play. Her game of choice was Conquián, a rummy game.

I remembered playing that game when I was younger, but this woman's rules were quite different from ours. Then again, when you play card games with your same friends long enough, you somehow end up with your own unique set of rules. I would later learn that cards were prohibited in prison because they were used to play games of chance. A friend had tried to send me a deck, but it had been confiscated. The only reason I had my own deck in prison, I concluded, was because my deck was a promotional one, decorated with M&M's chocolate characters, and had likely been mistaken for candy at the prison entrance. So, there I was, owning an illegal deck of playing cards in prison. All I knew was that those games meant a break from our depressing reality; it meant we actually had a little fun, which was one of the key tools needed to survive jail time with no end in sight.

Chapter 10

No End in Sight

Week Five

Wednesday, February 3, 2016, was the start of my fifth week in prison. Four entire weeks had already gone by, and I still had no idea what fate had in store for me. At 9 a.m., Mariana woke me up and told me I was requested at the infirmary, and I was asked to bring along any medications I had been taking. When I met with the doctor, he asked me several more questions about my health and the reason I was in Santa Teresa. I wondered if this was all about my possible change in living quarters. Since the burner incident, everything had been fine in my cellblock; I liked my bunkmates, I was used to my schedule (or lack thereof), and I was as settled as I could be. Moving to the VIP section could bring some comforts, but I knew it would also bring a whole new set of challenges. I had to live moment by moment to survive in that place, both emotionally and physically. I had to maintain an open mind and be willing to adapt to whatever the experience threw my way. All my crying aside, I had survived four entire weeks already!

After meeting with the doctor, I returned to my cellblock, had my morning coffee and biscotti, and then headed to Serigrafía, where Ashley handed me the entire *El Señor de los Cielos* series on DVD, courtesy of Rodri. Just then, Susana walked in and invited me over for coffee in her room. She shared stories about her work, the two children's homes she once managed where she took care of 150 kids at a time, until they were adopted by families, and how she herself had adopted two children. She showed me their pictures, which were hanging on the wall, while I petted one of her cats. I felt sad for Susana, for her children, and for all the orphaned and abandoned children in Guatemala who would never be adopted, all because international adoptions had become illegal under the premise that there were too many irregularities and illegalities going on. Once again, the most vulnerable and innocent Guatemalans were being sacrificed because of our government's ineptitude.

Meanwhile, back in my bunk area, Clara had been in a terrible mood for the past few days and had been lashing out mostly against Mariana. We all concluded she was most likely a bit loony. Not that I completely blamed her; it was easy to lose it and become grumpy in there, but she was so poorly educated that even by prison standards she was hard to digest. Clara was fifty-three years old, studying to pass first grade for the umpteenth time, sold vegetables and eggs from our bunk, and expected Verónica to take care of her customers when she was not around. She had the entire top bunk to herself, plus three-fourths of the small storage space beneath the beds, yet she fussed while the rest of us struggled to stow our belongings anywhere we could. To top it off, each time she sat on her top bunk, she would let her foot hang off the edge, which meant Verónica and me saw it right in front of our faces. Imagine the pirate's hairy foot hanging down from the bridge in Pirates of the Caribbean at Disney World! And to make living conditions worse, her customers barged into our bunk area at all hours. It took plenty of self-control to be patient. Mariana, who still slept on the floor, was only allowed to lay her mattress down from 9 p.m. to 9 a.m., which meant she had no place to relax during the day. Clara was rudest to her, and since Mariana could be feisty, things often got tense. I did my best to stay positive in that place, but believe me, it was a daily challenge.

———

That afternoon, while sitting in the shade outside of Serigrafía, Carmen joined me, and as we chatted away, Leticia walked by on her way from the infirmary back to Cellblock One. She stopped to say hello, I introduced them, and invited her to take a seat on the step beside us. That's when Leticia told us how she and her friends landed in solitary confinement as new arrivals in Santa Teresa. In the hope of protecting them somehow, their families had requested that they be kept separate from the general prison population. Since there was no such place in Santa Teresa, except for ex-vice president Baldetti's current special living quarters, these girls were placed in solitary confinement during their first week in prison, which coincided with Christmas. Thankfully, they had been placed together in one cell; unfortunately, sometimes the guards forgot to feed them, and they were not allowed visitors. Eventually, they were moved into regular cellblocks, but what an introduction to confinement.

Later on, while I waited in line behind Leticia to take a shower, she told me that she already had a plan in place in case there was a prison riot. According to her, we should take our towels, wet them, and place them over our faces to protect us from the gas bombs. We'd wait for the rioters to capture the guards and come open our gates, then exit the premises, and pretend that we were going along with the riot so that we did not make enemies. She said that she already had people who would protect her and her two friends if this were ever to happen. She said I should join them. I told her I would, and if all else failed, my plan B was to grab my wet towel and pretend to faint outside. We laughed!

Later, when I told Andrea about the riot plan, she laughed and said that we had it all wrong. She had experienced riots and gas bombs before, and wet towels only made your face burn even more. According to her, the best solution would be to put Vicks VapoRub—which was not allowed in prison because it could be used to pleasure oneself—under your nose, get out of the cellblock as soon as possible and lie on the floor, because gas rises. In addition, she assured me that everyone went crazy during riots so no one would protect us. So much for Leticia's plan.

As the evening came to a close, the women who had gone to their court hearings returned to Santa Teresa and we found out that María Elena, our infamous neighbor, was going home that night. In spite of our incident, I was happy for her. I had listened to her through our sheet partition for almost a month and discovered that she was funny, straightforward, and a good friend to her bunkmates. I also overheard her once admit that she was "human scum" on the outside, and that if she were ever given a second chance, she wouldn't waste it. Her release reminded me that prisoners did leave that place.

Later on, Mimi called a cellblock meeting and informed us that one of our fellow inmates had donated a microwave oven to our block—there would be a tight schedule to use it, but we now had a microwave. The other reason the meeting was called was because the warden had convened all cellblock voices to ask them to compile a list of inmates who were currently in Santa Teresa even though they had completed their sentences. I later asked Andrea if this was something they did often, or if it had something to do with the news articles currently in the media regarding this situation. She said it was the latter. I could not believe my ears. The system could not even make sure that inmates were freed in a timely and humane matter unless the media was involved! Thank God my Facebook page, "Justicia para Anaité," was getting attention—15,000 views and counting. With the media on my side, there was likely still hope for me, but I didn't want to make too much of it.

———

After lights out, we tried to fall asleep, but to no avail, because Mariana, Verónica, and I felt awful. We were tossing and turning with fever, headache, and nasal congestion. Mariana felt so bad that she went to the infirmary at 1 a.m., only to be told by the nurse to come back in the morning. I never even noticed she was gone.

At 8 a.m., I went to the bathroom and still felt terrible. Nurse Lola took my blood pressure and informed me that it was very low: 83/60. Since she did not have a thermometer, she assumed I had a 101.5°F temperature. She used her personal glucometer and told me that my glucose was within normal range. I felt nauseous and she thought I was most likely dehydrated. I called my father and asked him not to head over until I called him back with the list of medicines that we all needed. Then, Verónica, Meche, Mariana, and I headed straight to the infirmary, but the guard let only me through. I informed the doctor that four of us needed attention and medication. He filled one prescription form for all of us, for thirty tablets and four bottles of cough syrup. Back at the cellblock, I called my father and read him the list. I then headed to the front gates so that a guard could send the authorized prescription to the main prison entrance for approval. So much protocol to get cold medication, but if instead I had wanted to smoke some weed, well, that would have been readily available.

My father arrived at 11:30 a.m. with some goodies from my wish list, my lunch, and the medicine I had requested. Well, some of it. Since I had read the list to him over the phone, he had misunderstood the name and brought heart medication—he sent the right medicine the following day with Rodri—but he did bring enough cough syrup for all of us. Being sick in prison is no joke.

At 2 p.m. I was so tired that I decided to head back to my bunk, but not before stopping by the beauty salon and asking Alexia if she could color my hair. She said that now was a good time, so thirty days into my stay in

Santa Teresa, I dyed my hair. The rest of the afternoon I spent on my bunk, blowing my nose every minute or so. I called my house to thank Olga for sending exactly what I had asked for. I also spoke to Nina. Fabi was out with my mother, their beloved Yaya. I then called my father to remind him of the medicine for the next day. He said someone from INACIF would be coming by the following day to speak with me. I was still nervous and undecided about possibly moving into encamamiento, but every time I went to the infirmary or to visit Susana, I noticed that the public phone in encamamiento was available, so I could not help thinking that moving in there would be nice.

I managed to fall asleep that night, but had a terribly hard time getting out of my bed the next morning at 4 a.m. for our head count. As soon as the guards left, I started heaving to vomit and quickly lay down on the cold floor, afraid that I would otherwise faint and fall flat on my face. Mariana and Verónica immediately rushed to my side, put a coverlet on the floor, and moved me onto it. My hands were tingling all over and my finger joints were stiff. Aware of the gravity of the situation, Mariana massaged my stiff hands, while Verónica and two other inmates grabbed the coverlet edges and carried me to the cellblock gates, calling the guards to unlock the door. I blacked out and lost track of time, but I did hear Mimi complain to the nurse later that the guards had taken their sweet time and refused to open up.

The nurse, whom no one liked but had always been sweet to me, took my blood pressure: 80/50. Mimi stayed with me in the infirmary until I felt better. It was decided that I would stay in the infirmary the rest of the predawn hours, so that the doctor could see me as soon as he came in that morning. Verónica brought my handbag over and I took my first dose of blood pressure medication. The nurse then took me to a room in the back of the infirmary containing *three empty beds*. I lay down on one, she covered me, and all I could think was, *A bed all to myself for at least four hours!*

As I dozed off, I couldn't help imagining the headlines: an accused swindler faints in prison and is carried to the infirmary by an extortionist, a child kidnapper, and a murderer. All I knew was that when I was unable to fend for myself, at my lowest point during my prison days so far, these women—accused, and some even convicted, of terrible crimes—took it upon themselves to be my saviors. It suddenly dawned on me: There is light and darkness in each of us.

By 8:30 a.m., the doctor came in, asked the usual questions, and I was dismissed to go back to my cellblock, where my cellmates asked me if I was feeling better. Mariana was already up from her bed on the floor because Clara had been coming and going all morning, trampling all over her. I understood that we were living in very tight quarters, but Clara's rudeness was uncalled for and it bothered me. I tried to relax for a while in my tiny part of the bed, since Verónica was still sleeping and looked terrible. It was clear that many of us were sick from some type of flu going around, but while some of us were getting better, Verónica seemed to be getting worse.

At 9 a.m. my name was called. I had an encomienda. I went to the gates and found my Rodri, who was later joined by my sister, Gaby, and her mother, Anamaría. I was so happy to see them. I still had no clear idea where Santa Teresa was located on the map, but I was sure that it was not in the nicest or most accessible part of Guatemala City. This alone made it an even greater show of their love for me. As if that weren't enough, Gaby had brought a special gift: new Velcro sneakers! I tried them on immediately and they fit perfectly. I was ecstatic! Shoelaces are not allowed in prison, although you would never know this, since most inmates use them anyway, finding clever ways to get them past security unnoticed (in one case, they had been weaved into a knitted top). However, once the shoelaces and shoes were inside the prison, the guards would not bother inmates about them.

I didn't think this visit could get any better, until my friends Karla and Mariela showed up. They came carrying a bag full of treats for me, and other bags, which included magazines for the women, new educational toys of all kinds for the children, and handwritten letters that I had requested from my friends. And last but not least, Karla brought me a new notebook and pens to continue writing about my Santa Teresa adventure, because the notebook I had been writing in was running out of empty pages.

Eventually, a guard came to tell us that our time was up. She reminded us that encomienda through the prison gates had a strict five-minute limit, and that we had gotten away with a lot more that day, so I quickly said my goodbyes and returned to my cellblock, full of the love and hope that my family and friends always inspire in me.

After organizing the library and preschool donations with the help of some inmates, I returned to Serigrafía in spite of my fever, because I did not wish to be in my cellblock all day. I took with me the most precious of the gift bags I was given that day: a ziplock bag containing my new notebook, this month's book club book, and the letters from my friends. I sat on a step outside and opened each one of the letters, as I used to do in the days before e-mail, and the contents did not disappoint me. I tried to not see the signature before I read each letter, so that I could guess whom the sender was through his or her writing. And, in my feverish state, I laughed, I cried, and I enjoyed every second of those precious moments.

While I was busy on my usual sunny step, immersed in my reading, Daniela came over and handed me a folded piece of notebook paper with my name on it. It contained a beautiful, simple note thanking me for sharing my books, my salads, my stories, and our daily lives. The light and the darkness. At some point, Susana came by and asked if she could read my notebook. I do not know exactly how it happened, but I agreed, and she disappeared with it. I must have been so immersed in reading my letters, that I was caught off guard. By the time I finished going through my prison mail, I was really worried, wondering what I may have written in that notebook that Susana was now reading.

I like to think I am not a mean-spirited person who writes terrible things about others, but on those pages, I freely wrote my feelings, my perceptions, my truth, and I could see how that might offend someone.

Before I met Susana, I had heard that she was difficult and brutally honest with her remarks, but I had come to know a very intelligent, funny, sweet, and loyal person. She was always good to me, and the last thing I wanted was to offend her in any way. What made me even more concerned was that Daniela, who had observed the entire scene, turned to me and said, "You just made your first big mistake. You do not let anyone see your personal things in prison!" Aaahhh! And Susana was nowhere to be found.

Eventually, I caught up with her back in her room.

"Did you enjoy the reading?" I asked.

"Yes," she responded, "I have got to start writing my own book. I probably will as soon as I get out of this place."

I told her she should not wait, and then Susana wanted to know what "being too straightforward" meant. By then she had already asked Ashley about that remark of mine, and Ashley had told her that it was a good thing. Thank God that was all I wrote, because we had become so much closer since I wrote that remark a while back, when I had only heard rumors about her.

Feeling more relaxed about the notebook incident, I decided to go find the kids and read them one of the two books Gaby had brought for them. They were perfect choices because they had extremely thick pages, one sentence per page, and big, simple pictures. As I read the story, I asked them to count certain things, and asked them about the color of others. Hortencia, who was almost three years old, managed to count up to eight apples on a tree, but Alejandro, who was already five and whose mother claimed to be a secretary, had a very difficult time. It was tragic, innocent children growing up in this place, with mothers facing huge problems and with no resources or opportunities to help them help themselves. Not to mention the children these women already had on the outside. By now, I had come to believe that so many of these women were in this situation because of men, and I felt for their children and loved ones. And then I remembered I was one of them myself.

By 5 p.m., I headed back to my cellblock. I needed to shower and relax. My fever was still high and I was exhausted from the long day. Meche boiled water and made Verónica and me some lemon ginger tea with extra lemon, and tortilla soup with avocado. I eventually managed to fall asleep, only to be abruptly awakened at 10 p.m. The prison warden, accompanied by her lieutenants, was by the cellblock gate, calling my name, and when I arrived, she told me she'd received a judge's order to transfer me to the infirmary until a doctor came to see me. What did this mean? No one could explain, but the order had to be obeyed word for word, so Mariana and Verónica helped me pack some essentials . . . What am I talking about? We lived on essentials in that place! . . . underwear, bra, two changes of clothes, some yogurt, Special K bars, toothpaste, toothbrush, my medicine, water bottle, coverlet, bag with books, and other everyday things. I said goodbye to my bunkmates and was escorted out of my cellblock.

At the infirmary, nurse Rosita welcomed me and took me back to the room with the three empty beds. She placed a sheet on one of the beds and told me to settle in. I put my belongings on the bed, covered myself, and fell fast asleep. As I enjoyed the stars in the sky and some faraway lights through the clear window that faced the open fields outside the prison, I thought, *In this moment, I am safe. Tomorrow will be another day.*

———

I woke up on Saturday, February 6, realizing that for the first time in a full month my sleep hadn't been interrupted by a 4 a.m. head count or another body in my bed. I now had not only one, but three whole beds and an entire room all to myself! There were no radios or TVs blaring, no hot stoves crackling, and I soon discovered I even had a very basic bathroom with a disgustingly dirty and tiny sink . . . *all to myself.* A sink! There was no such thing in the cellblock. I thought, *Well, this certainly qualifies as an upgrade in accommodations.*

I finally got up when nurse Rosita came into my quarters accompanied by a guard. I decided to start getting ready for whatever this new day would bring. I washed my face with water from my water bottle; enjoyed some yogurt, orange juice, and a cereal bar. Then I used the sink to brush my teeth, changed into my clothes and began writing.

My first visitor of the day was my father. I was let out to the prison gates for our usual five-minute visit and was able to tell him that I had been moved to the infirmary due to a judge's order and had no idea when the doctor would arrive to see me. He told me not to worry because everything was OK, and he handed me a couple of "Justicia para Anaité" printouts. I felt supported and loved when I read the comments, and I still believed that this could be my only way out of jail, to see justice prevail.

Yet, what did *justice* even mean? Best-case scenario, I would soon be released, but who would give me back my time, my tears, my good name, my life? Who would take away the hurt and harm done to my children and to my family? Who would reimburse the resources spent on attorney fees? *Justicia* . . . it does not really exist. It is simply something we pretend may be accomplished to make things right once again, when we fully know that it is impossible to do so.

On my way back to my new, luxurious, and spacious, but temporary, accommodations, I looked into Serigrafía to let the women know that I would not be coming in that day.

Later on, I was told I had visitors and I was allowed to go outside again. As the sunshine started warming my face, I saw Ashley coming my way, accompanied by my brother Turi and his wife, Telma. We went back into my new suite and had a nice private visit. Telma told me she had chosen comfortable platform shoes for this special outing, but had been informed as she waited outside the prison that the guards would not let her through with them on. Apparently, drugs and other illicit items can be hidden in platform shoes, so they are forbidden. So, she had to rent a pair of prison-approved shoes from a stand on the street, which cost her seventy cents. She said she had come all the way to see me and that nothing was going to stop her from coming in. She was my hero of the day!

We each took a seat on a different bed, and they updated me on my Facebook page, my children's birthday party, and how my children were spending that night at their home for a fun sleepover. They assured me that I should not worry about the children because they were well taken care of by everyone, for which I will remain eternally grateful. After I filled them in on how I ended up in the infirmary, they mentioned that I looked very, very thin. I had not been eating much since I last fainted, and I was ordered to eat, but the mere thought of food made me nauseous. Since not eating made me nauseous as well, I finally decided to start eating small portions many times throughout the day.

Once my guests left, Ashley continued coming by every couple of hours to see how I was doing and to cheer me up. I asked her if one of the women from Serigrafía could ask Verónica to bring me the rest of my things. So, I wrote a note addressed to Mimi and soon after, Verónica and Meche came in carrying a huge bag with my food. Thank God! It is difficult to pack when you don't know where you are going or how long you will be there.

Nurse Rosita, a small, thin woman in her thirties, very pleasant and quick to giggle, also came in to see me every once in a while, to make sure I was OK and had not escaped, I suppose. She often sat on another bed and chatted with me, which is how I came to learn that she had been a nurse in Santa Teresa for almost two years, spending an entire week on duty, living on the premises, and then getting the following week off, just like the guards. The small private hospital where she had worked prior to this job had closed down. She liked working at that hospital because she was able to perform her job, and patients usually left happy and thankful.

For that reason, it had taken her a long time to finally find her new job in prison bearable. Given the deplorable conditions, she was rarely able to help the patients who sought her care, and she could feel their hate and despair. I advised her to try to not take it personally because the hate and frustration was not against her, but against that place, which not only failed to help inmates but also made it almost impossible for them to help themselves. There was no medicine, no equipment, no specialists, no accommodation for paying for one's own healthcare, and no doctors available to promptly take care of emergencies. Inmates considered the infirmary useless, except for the fact that it sometimes issued prescriptions, so that medications could be brought into the prison by a loved one. I agreed with my fellow inmates and I did not envy Rosita one bit.

At some point that afternoon, I took a shower. Well, sponge bathe was more like it, but I did not have to wait in line, I was clean, and I had survived another day under totally new circumstances. Later that night, a woman from Cellblock One came to the infirmary, so I asked her to deliver a note to Mimi, letting her know that the doctor had not yet come by to see me, and I needed more clothes, books, and so forth. I told her that Verónica knew where everything was. By 10 p.m. my eyes were very tired, but my brain was not. I felt as if I had been resting in my bed all day; luckily, when I turned off the lights, I was able to escape prison and enter my dreams.

———

As Sunday began, my second day at the infirmary, and my thirty-third day in prison, I was once again part of the inevitable head count, but I did not hear the bell ring and I did not have to stand up in line to be counted. The prison warden and some of her lieutenants simply came into the infirmary, made sure that I was still there, politely greeted me, and were on their way, while I comfortably stayed in bed and smiled. I realized I had slept intermittently as locks were constantly opened and closed throughout the night. The sound of metal on metal was so violent and disturbing that it was impossible to ignore it completely. Back at the cellblock, once the gates were locked for the night, they were seldom opened again until morning, but in this area, there were so many gates, all leading into one small common hallway, that the racket seemed constant.

I had no reason to get out of bed that morning, so I continued sleeping until nurse Rosita came by at 8:30 a.m. to say good morning. It was a very cold day. My first visitor was Ashley, who came right in, made herself comfortable on another bed, and chatted away telling me she had e-mailed my notes to Karla. After my girlfriends read my first notebook, they had many questions for me, so they had written them down and I had answered them. Knowing they were expecting my second notebook made writing much more fun for me. Ashley scolded me and pleaded that I start eating more, because I was beginning to look like I belonged in a concentration camp. She was probably right. I had not been hungry, I did not brush my hair, and the only mirror I owned was in the compact I had bought in prison. I kept it in a tiny bag along with the rest of my makeup, which I never used. I often went days without looking in the mirror.

Soon after, Carmen came in and said that she was making breakfast. She wanted to bring me an egg sandwich and coffee. I told her not to worry about it, all I needed was some boiling water with sugar for my powdered milk and decaf coffee. Ten minutes later, my hot water arrived and I enjoyed my coffee with alfajores. If I had to gain some weight, I would do so joyfully, and alfajores have always brought me joy.

It seems like inmates visited me all day. Lili told me that one of the inmates in encamamiento had been transferred to COF so now was a good time for me to transfer to that VIP section of the prison, but I had no idea what was going on. At some point, Mayra, the inmate who helped clean the infirmary, came in to chat with me. I had just met her, but I already knew she was a chatterbox.

"I really need to wash my hair," I said at one point, "but since it has been so cold, I've been putting it off."

"I could boil water for you so that you can wash it with warm water, if you'd like," she offered.

I knew by now that some inmates did this, or had someone do it for them, but I didn't want to owe anybody any favors; however, at the infirmary it was just us. I did not have to wait in line for anyone, the burners were not being used to cook, and so I said, "Are you kidding? I would love that!"

Mayra left and came back later to let me know that my bucket of very hot water was in the tiny shower waiting for me. I mixed it with some cold water to make it warm and enjoyed the feel of the water as it dripped from the guacalito onto my head and down my body. I washed my hair slowly and peacefully—I cannot explain how wonderful that all felt. Thank you, sweet Mayra.

I spent the rest of the day reading and writing, determined to stay awake so as to sleep soundly through the night, but my plan failed. I fell asleep some time during the afternoon, and heard people come and go, but never bothered to open my eyes until Leticia was brought in.

Leticia was incredibly resourceful, managing to get permits for a burner and blender and pay the senior member of the bunk a weekly fee to get a bed all to herself. She had also arranged to get her bunkmate to boil bath water for her and stand in line on her behalf to shower. Well, that day, while sitting on her top bunk, she suddenly stretched out to keep something from falling, lost her balance, and fell down, knocking over a pot of boiling water onto the neighboring bunk and landing naked on the hot burner. She had come to the infirmary with the stove top coil imprinted on her buttocks.

While she recounted this story, we laughed nonstop. However, this episode also confirmed that my complaining about the burner in my neighbor's bunk was not pointless. In any event, she was to spend the night at the infirmary: slumber party for two! We spoke for hours about everything. She shared more details of her story, her failed marriage, her clothing business, and her kidnapping. I told her she needed to write her own book. We laughed. And to think I was worried about the possibility of being bored and lonely that night.

—

I was living in a twilight zone. After spending three nights in the relative comforts and privacy of the infirmary, Monday morning came as a complete change once again. At 8:30 a.m. the doctor arrived and immediately told Leticia and me to go back to our cellblock. He said I must leave the room because he needed it to perform inmate examinations. I got ready, put my stuff away, and left the infirmary to start my day at Serigrafía, my current status in limbo. My belongings were now both in Cellblock One and the infirmary; however, due to the judge's order, which stated that I had to remain in the infirmary until the doctor came to see me, I technically couldn't reside in Cellblock One.

So far, I hadn't had much interaction with the infirmary: a prescription for powdered milk, the taking of my blood pressure, and a prescription for flu medications. They did not seem to have much of anything available for inmates, and no matter what ailed the inmate, the doctor's diagnosis seemed to always be the same, "It is due to all the stress and changes you are going through." And, since there is no actual doctor available on Saturdays or Sundays, my first days living at the infirmary were quite uneventful. But on Monday morning, I was reminded of an obvious fact that my brain had been most likely trying to suppress: I was living among women with AIDS and all types of other contagious and potentially life-threatening diseases.

The judge, who so casually sent me to prison without proper evidence or a conviction, was truly putting my life in danger. Even if the violent convicted felons, who were numerous in Santa Teresa, had not yet decided to harm me, there were still plenty of other death-causing possibilities that could take me down.

Later on, after enjoying precious visits from family and friends, I went back to the infirmary and noticed the doctors were gone for the day. I settled back into my room, thoroughly cleaned it, and then sat on the bed expecting the 6 p.m. head count. The rest of the afternoon went by in a flash. Before I knew it, the warden and two lieutenants were telling me I was temporarily being moved into encamamiento. The day had finally come. I grabbed all my belongings from the infirmary, as instructed, and followed the group to the encamamiento entrance gates.

The warden called the encamamiento inmates together to inform them that a judge had issued a court order and that I was moving in. The women complained that there were ten inmates and ten beds, so I'd have nowhere to sleep, even though everyone knew that one inmate had left on Friday, and two inmates shared a bed, but the truth remained that there were officially ten inmates and ten beds. Their complaints were ignored. I was instructed to leave my belongings in the encamamiento entrance hall and follow the warden and guards to Cellblock One to pick up the rest of my stuff, which Verónica had already packed for me. The warden told Mimi that the court order required that I take two foam mattresses with me to encamamiento, and I immediately felt terrible about this. Verónica quickly took the one from our bunk and gave it to me. She would now go back to sleeping on her old, thin mattress. I told the warden that one of them would suffice, that I did not need two, which would mean also taking the one I'd given Mariana, but the warden insisted that orders were orders, and I had to follow them.

I had never been inside encamamiento before and when I walked in, all I could see were curtains everywhere. There were three rooms and a bathroom so tiny it would most likely fit in a jetliner. However, this small bathroom served only ten women, which was an upgrade for me. I was told to settle in the room at the end of the hall, past the restroom, where Martina and Alina lived.

Alina was a tall blonde woman who always seemed quite serious. In the month that I had been in Santa Teresa, I had passed by her many times, but had never received a smile, a good morning, not even a nod. The other woman I did not remember at all. There were so many of us in that place that some people I managed to distinguish, and the rest I simply could not register. I had heard other inmates say very bad things about these two, so now the time had come for me to see for myself. I was exhausted; the drama was never-ending.

The room was quite big considering the living arrangements I had been accustomed to for the past four weeks. There were two beds by the window, a plastic shelf with a small flat-screen TV and DVD player on top of it, a small refrigerator, an electric kettle, and a one-burner artisan stove. They even had a plastic table and chairs in the middle of the room. As I returned from my second trip to fetch my things from the encamamiento entrance hall, I found these two women putting the table and chairs away to make room for my mattresses on the floor. Martina even made room for my belongings underneath her bed and they both welcomed me nicely. They were very patient with me as I made a mess on the floor trying to organize my belongings properly. They even made room in the kitchen area and took a bag down from the wall so that I could have a nail to hang something on.

As I put my things away, they mentioned that they kept to themselves as much as possible, didn't visit the other rooms, and did not allow visitors in their room. They expressed anger at the other inmates for not taking me in, especially since one of the rooms had an empty bed; instead of using that, I would have to sleep on the floor. I listened and all I could say was that I was grateful that they had welcomed me and that I planned to stay out of everybody's way.

By 8 p.m. I was so physically and emotionally exhausted from my day, that I spread my mattresses on the floor and got ready for bed. Since it was early, Martina and Alina mentioned that they usually turned off the lights between 10 p.m. and 11 p.m., but I didn't care. I needed to rest. As the women watched TV, I put on a fleece top and slipped on socks to warm my feet—it was one of the coldest nights in prison so far. "Good night," I said and then heard Alina quietly say to Martina, "Maybe we should turn off the light." I told them not to worry, to do what they normally did. I was not expecting so much courtesy on my behalf. I managed to fall asleep, but it was very cold and I was so frozen that I woke up several times throughout the night. I curled up in a ball and threw the coverlet over my head in the hope that the warm air I exhaled would warm me.

The next morning, I discovered that head counts in encamamiento were very different from those in the general population cellblocks. Instead of the guards coming into our private areas, we simply stepped out of our draped rooms so that we could be counted. The women here had a much closer relationship with the guards, knowing them by name and joking with them through the locked gates.

At 8:45 a.m., I got up, picked up my mattresses from the floor, curled them up like yoga mats, chose my clothes for the day, and headed to the bathroom. Although the sink was tiny, it was still too big for the space—the door could only close because part of the sink passed through a hole in it. Instead of a lock, there was a sign that one used, which read "FREE" on one side and "OCCUPIED" on the other. I stepped into the shower and noticed there was a showerhead, normally a good thing, but instead of getting a full stream of water like I did in Cellblock One, I got a cold light mist, which did not do the job fast enough for me. I am far from being a big woman, yet I had trouble maneuvering in that tiny space, and I wondered, *How do the rest do it?*

Eventually I left encamamiento for the day and reached the safety of Serigrafía. Lili came by and brought me up to speed on the latest encamamiento drama. Then Susana came in to ask how my new situation was working out for me. And last, but not least, Carmen came to assess the situation, and plan how I could move into her room. The three of them agreed that I was in the worst possible room, and I listened because they had been in encamamiento longer than I had. But so far, it seemed to me as if each of these three VIP rooms had their own problems. Lili warned me that she had once sold a boat and an all-terrain vehicle to one of my current roommates and never got paid for them, adding that I should be careful with my belongings. But what did being careful mean? Was I supposed to carry my belongings with me all day long like poor Abuela?

Their advice was overwhelming, but I decided to not let the encama-miento drama affect me. I appreciated their concern, but what little energy I did have I planned to spend wisely, so I did my best to stay clear of it all.

When my father came for his daily visit, I asked him to let everyone know that, given my new accommodations, my new visiting days were now Wednesdays and Sundays. Later that day, the doctor finally came by to see me. No examination, just a quick interview, where I filled him in on every-thing that had happened, which he said would be presented in a report on my case to the judge.

Serigrafía closed a bit early that day, so under my new circumstances, I was left homeless. Yes, I had a room, but since my mattresses were stowed away during the day, I was left with no place to sit, lie down, or relax. Although it was an extremely cold afternoon, I went outside and found a sunny spot on a bench, where I continued my writing. A moment later, someone came up from behind and playfully touched my back. It was my former bunkmate Mariana! I hugged her. I missed my cellblock mates, especially the playfulness in the evenings between Meche, Jenny, and Verónica. They were funny, they protected one another, and in spite of their sadness and troubles, they continued to have light hearts. I was still torn about which side of prison was less terrible for me.

By 5 p.m., we were locked in for the night. It was at this time of day, when it was still light out and nightfall was looming, that a dreadful feeling of another day lost came over me, together with a sadness that could no longer be ignored. I called Nina and Fabi and my mother told me that they were outside riding their bicycles. I called them again later and we got to talk for a bit. They told me that my mother did not let them take a shower together anymore because they were getting older. They wanted to know if the three of us could take a bubble bath together when I returned home. I told them that I thought that was a fabulous idea and that a bubble bath would be the first thing we did when I got back. I hung up and cried.

Alina, Martina, and I stayed in our room the rest of the night. There was no place to go, no common hallway or shared TV once the gates were locked for the night. We were only separated by curtains, but they were more than enough to create separate, warring worlds. My new roommates offered to share some of their dinner with me, but I politely declined. It was now even colder inside, so Martina asked me to hop on her bed so that I could watch TV properly. I grabbed my pillow and got comfortable sitting with my back against the wall. I watched two drug cartel soap opera episodes and was done for the evening. I made my bed on the floor and fell asleep. I could only hope that I was better equipped this time to survive yet another cold night.

CHAPTER 11

Life in Encamamiento

WEEK SIX

At 7 a.m. I glanced at my watch. It was too early and too cold to go anywhere, although the encamamiento gates opened at 6 a.m., so I kept warm under the covers. By 8 a.m., I started getting ready for the day. I showered, got dressed, and wrote for a while as I sipped my hot coffee. It was visiting day and I was not sure anyone would come to see me, but I wanted to be ready just in case. Eventually, my name was called and I found Rodri and my father outside under the pergola, so we headed to Serigrafía, where Andrea allowed us to visit inside.

They told me they were all moving heaven and earth to get me out of this place. Hearing this was comforting; I was so isolated that it sometimes felt like nothing was getting done. When my father heard my frustration, he reminded me that this was exactly what *faith* was all about: believing without seeing. He also filled me in on the latest events.

Apparently, Olyslager's attorney had contacted Miranda to negotiate, saying he was willing to desist his legal proceedings against me, if in exchange I agreed to sign an agreement to cease and desist any and all verbal and written "aggressions" against him. What Olyslager's attorney referred to as aggression, I like to call the truth. However, from what I understood, even if he desisted his legal actions against me, the public prosecutor would proceed. I needed Olyslager to confess that he had lied regarding my involvement, which would completely obliterate his gang's legal strategy. If he didn't agree to my terms, his offer was useless to me. His actions resulted in the worst possible damage that could be inflicted on another human being other than violence: I was in prison, away from my children, I had lost my job, and my name had been tarnished in the media by being linked to these terrible accusations. I had little to lose now and was determined to stand by the truth, and I still had faith that it would set me free. So my answer was a resounding *no*.

As I sat outside by the children's play area later that morning, a young woman with her six-month-old baby girl in her arms and her three-year-old daughter by her side, decided to come sit close to me on the bench. She said hello, we started to chat, and she opened up and shared her chilling story. According to her, she was in prison for allegedly murdering her husband, but she claimed she didn't do it. She'd never married, but had been with her partner for twelve years; however, he had gone to the United States to find work and had ended up in prison. Recovering from a C-section, and having to fend for herself and her children, she had decided to sublet one of her home's bedrooms to earn extra money. Her tenant was a nice young man.

According to this young mother, the man met his end when he inadvertently touched a high-powered cable near the house's rooftop terrace. When the police arrived on the scene, they asked her if the deceased lived in her house, and when she said yes, they assumed that he was her husband and that she had killed him. Because she had never married, there was no way to prove that she was actually with the man who was in prison in the United States, so she was hauled off to court and sentenced to fifty years in prison. Now, there she was, twenty-six years old, sentenced to half a century in jail. Her partner had eventually returned to Guatemala, but illegally emigrated back to the United States in search of work, leaving her mother to take care of their eleven-year-old daughter, while she rotted away in prison with her two younger children. I sighed and couldn't stop thinking about everything that was wrong with our so-called justice system. And there I was, in prison myself, expected to continue hoping that truth and justice would prevail and set me free.

Thankfully, I was able to take my mind off of all this that afternoon when I received a visit from my dear friends. Visits for encamamiento inmates were held under the pergola. There were three long concrete benches around the perimeter and some of us sat on one. Suddenly, I saw Susana coming down the steps carrying two of her personal plastic chairs so my two standing friends could also sit. She thought to do this without even being asked. One more unexpected act of kindness.

My friends were all smiles as we began catching up, yet it felt so out of place in those surroundings. Once again, I could only imagine what they thought when they saw me, with my hair always in a messy bun (since I only combed it after I washed it), my makeup-free face, a body comparable to that of a skinny fifth grader, and a constant sadness on my face that was only temporarily removed by the sight of my family and friends. Lore tried her best to be her usual cheerful self during our visit, but eventually tears started rolling down her cheeks. I knew they were trying very hard to remain strong and positive and to infuse some sunshine and joy into my dire circumstances. . . . If the situation was reversed and I was visiting one of them, I am not sure my heart could take it.

They brought many gifts, including three new books. I considered choosing one and sending the other two back because of my storage prob-lem, but then I decided to keep them all. During my prison stay, I received many religious and self-help books, which I accepted joyfully along with the love that came from those who sent them my way, but lately all I wanted were books that would take my thoughts far away from that place and into other worlds, even if only for a couple of hours a day.

Prior to my visitors' arrival, Susana approached me and said that, if I wasn't comfortable in encamamiento, I could take the top bunk and move in with her. Susana is the inmate who lived with her three cats in her own private "suite" with a bathroom all to herself, so she certainly didn't need a roommate, which made her offer an incredible act of trust and kindness toward me, one especially appreciated after two nights of sleeping on a foam mattress on the cold floor. But, as it turned out, a woman from encamamiento was going home that day, and there would soon be a bed available for me, so I declined, but was filled with gratitude over her gesture.

Later that night, the warden came down to encamamiento and informed us all that the soon to be empty bed available in Lili's room would now be assigned to me. Everyone remained silent even though it was common knowledge that one of the women who slept in Carmen's room constantly spent her time in Lili's room and wanted to officially move in there. Finally, Alina pointed at the woman and blurted out, "We all know that *she* wants to move in *there* so why won't anyone speak up?" And that's when everyone else started chiming in and suggesting that the woman move in with Lili and I take her old bed in Carmen's room. The warden turned to me and asked if I was OK with that, and I said yes, so I entered Carmen's room, took the bunk above hers and finally, officially had my own little place, my "apartment" in Santa Teresa.

I went into Martina and Alina's room to pack my belongings. Despite the stories I had heard about them, these two women were good and generous roommates to me and nothing of mine ever went missing.

By 8:30 p.m. the guards had released the woman whose time at Santa Teresa was up, the other inmate had moved into Lili's room, and I had moved in with Carmen, who had already made extra room for my things under her bed and helped me get settled in and make my bed . . . *my own real bed!* The new room was a bit larger than my last one, but it had two hospital-type beds and a bunk bed. My other new roommates were Sandra and Rina. The three beds were placed along the sides of the room, leaving a large area of empty space in the middle. There was a wall-to-wall window on one side, with small opaque windowpanes that let in light and could be opened a bit, revealing a view of the wash basin and clotheslines outside. Carmen had a small refrigerator where I could store perishable food and Sandra had an electric burner, which she was also willing to share with me.

After putting my stuff away, I returned to Alina and Martina's room to watch TV with them for a while longer and noticed they had already put their plastic dining table and chairs back in their original place. It reminded me that their generosity in taking me in was huge. No one has to do anything for you ever, especially in prison, where we all have so little. And yet, I had been constantly reminded that human nature tends to be kind and generous, even among people who may have done terrible things, and people who are themselves suffering terrible injustices. That night, I was once again able to sleep in my very own bed with no bedmate, only this time it was outside of the infirmary and in a shared room.

———

At 8 a.m. the next morning, I woke up and observed my new roommates come and go as they got ready for the day. It was another cold day, there was a line to shower, and I was in no rush, so I enjoyed my warm bed a little while longer. Halfway through my breakfast, which I ate on my bed since we had no table or chairs, my name was called. I went to the front gates and found my favorite visitor waiting for me on the other side: my dear father. He'd brought me a bottle of water and a ham and egg sandwich, and when I told him I needed a jacket from my house, he immediately removed the one he was wearing and handed it to me. We were both freezing, so we decided to cut the visit short and say goodbye.

Later, I headed to Serigrafía, where I found three young women from an online news outlet called *Nómada* who had arrived to film interviews with Ashley and her workers. They had originally contacted Ashley to feature her on their monthly cover, and although Ashley was flattered by the invitation, she believed that the story should really focus on the imprisoned men and women working for her who were making the choice to change their lives. Agreeing with her angle, *Nómada* interviewed the men in Pavón prison and then interviewed the women in Santa Teresa. I walked in just as they were filming Ashley, and listening to her talk about her vision and goals brought tears to my eyes.

By 5 p.m. it was time for lockdown. I called home and spoke to Kali who was in my kitchen with my children making cupcakes. I had called the kids earlier but they had been out at the park playing with one of their older brothers from my husband's previous marriage. These four siblings love each other deeply and I am very happy that they have one another. When Nina and Fabi were born, I decided I would neither promote nor hinder their relationship with their two older brothers. I thought it would be best for their relationship to be true, whatever that may be, and to my amazement, despite their large age differences, two different mothers, and the awful situation that ensued with the father they shared, they love one another in a beautiful way, sharing a special bond that is theirs and theirs alone.

Back in my room, my new roommates Carmen and Sandra were making oatmeal with sugar and cinnamon. They shared some with me and I enjoyed its warmth in the cold weather. The three of us chatted away. Rina, the fourth woman in the room, who had not seemed very welcoming the day before, was now nicer to me. At 7 p.m. I heard Alina calling my name; it was time to watch the soap operas on local TV and the series *Dueños del Paraíso* on DVD. I was honored that they invited me over because they certainly did not have to, and because they did not usually allow anyone else into their room. So, I grabbed my pillow, walked the six steps to their room, and hopped onto Martina's bed.

Martina and Alina were from Jutiapa, a department of the southeastern part of Guatemala. I was not clear on why either one of them was in prison, but I did know Martina's nickname was La Patrona (the boss). From what

I learned, this was how the story went. Martina's sister had been running for mayor in their hometown, and the odds were in her favor, which did not please her opponent one bit. One day, during an event at a restaurant, gunmen barged in and shot up the place, leaving nine people dead, one of them Martina's sister. Her death left the political party with no candidate, so they approached Sandra—Martina's cousin who was now one of my new roommates—to run for office in her place. Sandra declined, so they moved on to Martina with the same offer, and she accepted. When the votes were in, the opponent came out victorious, and he made it his mission to kill Martina and Sandra.

Given these circumstances, both women decided to flee for their lives. Martina apparently crossed the border and Sandra went into hiding. While in hiding, she got married and had a baby, but her husband soon abandoned her and the newborn, leaving her no choice other than to leave her hiding place and return to her parents' home in Jutiapa. Because the newly elected mayor was still hunting for them, Sandra spent the first nine months of her baby's life hiding in a dark room during the day and barely leaving the room at night to get some fresh air. She was terribly depressed and eventually snapped.

She and Martina decided they could no longer live like fugitives. According to Sandra, they filed a report with the police regarding their situation but nothing was done to protect them. Left to their own devices, they decided to take matters into their own hands and rid themselves of their problem. The first three attempts failed, and on the fourth they were caught. They were sentenced to ninety-four years each in prison. I later learned that Martina's eighteen-year-old daughter had also been killed because of this mess.

So, there I was, watching a drug cartel series with Alina and Martina, when suddenly we all gasped as actress Kate del Castillo killed her violent drug lord husband on TV. What a shocker! And what's more, we all agreed that it was terrible. This made me wonder if what I had heard was true.

Then, in another scene, two men were being offered two thousand dollars for every kilo of cocaine they managed to bring into the United States. Martina and Alina both agreed that a kilo of cocaine went for ten thousand to twelve thousand dollars on the street so that was a good deal.

They then told me about the time, a while back, when a small airplane crashed near their town. Two of the Colombian passengers had escaped the wreckage before the police arrived at the scene, and the many kilos of cocaine left at the wreckage had been taken away by the townspeople. It was apparently the kind of thing that happens in certain parts of Guatemala. And here I was, on Martina's bed, curled up in my pajamas, underneath her coverlet, watching that TV series and learning about other people's reality. Apparently, I had been living in a bubble.

By 9:30 p.m. I said goodnight, deciding to leave their room before they kicked me out—wondering if I would receive another invitation—and walked back to my living quarters, and hopped into my bed . . . my bed! As my fellow inmates often say, "One more day in Santa Teresa, one day closer to returning home."

———

My visitors came early on Friday, encomienda day, so early that I didn't even have a chance to shower. First it was Picus, my godmother's son. Picus is an attorney, so the guards opened the gates and let me go out for an attorney visit. We chatted in the cold for about an hour before Rodri and my father joined us. As usual, they had brought whatever I needed. After Picus left, my father told me that things were moving along with the attorneys and that the interviews for the television special had been recorded.

Sylvia Gereda, a Guatemalan journalist, is one of the few investigative reporters with the ability and guts to expose reality in a country ripe with news to report, regardless of whose feathers it may ruffle. In a place where you may easily be murdered in order to steal your cell phone, Sylvia is fearless, and my situation had apparently inspired her to do a special report on women who landed in prison because of their husbands. So, Rodri, Gaby, my friend Tina, and my cousin-in-law Claudia had all been interviewed as part of this special program. I wasn't sure if I'd get to see the show because it would air on a local cable channel, and we certainly did not have cable in Santa Teresa, but I was sure it was a godsend.

As we wrapped up our visit, Anamaría and Gaby came down the steps. Papi and Rodri decided to leave so that the guards would not ask them all to go, and by 10 a.m. they were all gone.

On my way back to encamamiento, Mariana came to me and gave me some of my recently washed clothes. I thanked her and told her I would give her more clothes later. Back in my room, I started organizing the new things my family and friends had given me, and put together a bag of goodies for my girls in Cellblock One. I then headed over to deliver it, even though as a member of encamamiento I was no longer allowed to stray so far and into the general prison population. When I reached the cellblock, I asked to see Verónica; she walked over to me and we sat on a concrete step outside. After I gave her the goody bag, she mentioned she was glad that I had come to see her, and even more so that the women at the cellblock had seen me ask for her. Apparently, several inmates had been telling her that I was only nice to her while I needed her. "They even call you names," she said. To which I responded, "Oh, just let it be." The women in Cellblock One had been nice to me while I was there, and now some were happy that I was gone, most likely because they were jealous of Verónica and the way she might have benefitted while I was there. I could not care less if those women spoke badly about me. I reminded Verónica that some people were truly miserable and had no joy in their hearts and there was nothing we could do about that. Easy for me to say since I did not live there anymore, I know.

Back in encamamiento, I sat outside, on the same sunny bench as the day before. The children came and went as I wrote and asked me if I would read to them. But the social worker was gone for the day and all the books were locked in her office. After more than a month of waiting, on the following Monday I would finally receive the permit allowing me to read to them regularly from 10 a.m. to 12 p.m.

The rest of the day glided along as usual, with a visit to Serigrafía, a chat with Ashley, lockdown, a call to my children, and some socializing indoors. Alina and Martina didn't invite me over that night because Martina had been in bed with a terrible flu and fever, so I gave her some of the pills the doctor had prescribed when I had been ill, hoping that they would do the trick. Back in my room, after Rina and Sandra had fallen asleep, Carmen and I continued chatting a while longer and eventually started talking about my case.

I hardly spoke about my case with my fellow inmates, but something made me trust Carmen, so I told her that I was due in court on the following Thursday for a hearing regarding the pretrial motions. After telling her what little I understood about my case, she said she thought I might have a shot at getting the judge to side with me and might even go home to my children that same day. I liked hearing her optimistic take, and respected her point of view, since she was an attorney who had worked for the Attorney General's Office for fifteen years of her career. She had left that position after the office had been restructured and economics seemed to take priority over justice. That rang true with my experience so far, as I definitely felt more like a statistic where justice had no say in the matter.

Saturday came and went, but not without its surprises. It was the first time I experienced a water shortage in prison; yes, that day we had no running water for three hours. I do not need to explain to anyone how vital water is in any regular home, so imagine what no water is like in an overpopulated prison. My fellow inmates, who had been there much longer than me, told me that there had been no running water from April to October in 2014. For seven straight months, water was only available for one hour each day and each inmate received approximately one gallon per day, of which one liter was used to wash up, and the rest to drink, since most inmates could not afford to buy bottled water. The reason: the government had not paid the water bill. And to think it all happened under former vice president Roxana Baldetti's watch, who was now an inmate in Santa Teresa herself. So, suffice to say, when the water stopped flowing that Saturday, the inmates and I panicked. Thankfully it was just a three-hour scare.

Apparently, the same thing had happened with the electricity that same year. The government had also failed to pay the electric bill and Santa Teresa was left in the dark during a four-month period, with no televisions, no freezers, and no electric burners. An inmate uprising would've seemed appropriate in 2014, if you ask me.

———

The weekend came to a close on Sunday, February 14: Valentine's Day, which was also day forty in jail for me. Rodri came in to see me at 10:30 a.m., though he had been waiting outside since 8 a.m. The guards had taken their sweet time letting people in that morning, inspecting in detail the larger than usual Valentine's Day crowd. But he had made it and that was all that mattered, and as usual, he came bearing gifts: cleaning supplies, vegetables, a food supplement, and a book donation for the library, which included children's books and workbooks with CDs to learn English, all from Cawa, a young mother of one of Nina and Fabián's former classmates. Although I had taken my children out of that preschool when my husband's situation had surfaced and I could no longer afford it, some of these young mothers had remained present in my life, going above and beyond for us during that difficult time.

That morning I also received a Valentine's Day gift from Anamaría, which included nail files, colorful gel pens, and a beautiful blank notebook. I immediately decided I would use the new notebook to communicate with Nina and Fabián. I now had one more way, other than the telephone, to keep in touch with my children. I hoped they would write for me, draw for me, anything! Being away from them was devastating.

Meanwhile, Carmen came from encamamiento into the outdoor hall-way and joined us under the pergola. By then my father was also with us. That's when Carmen suddenly noticed that Judge Jisela Reinoso Trujillo was visiting the prison—I had not seen her because my back was facing the gates. She was the one who had heard my preliminary hearing back in September 2015, when the Attorney General's Office had so gallantly arrested me after I said goodbye to my children as they boarded their school bus. During that first hearing, Olyslager's attorney had requested that Reinoso step down from my case because he worked for her cousin Frank Trujillo's law firm, and she agreed, but not before hearing my first testimony as demanded by law. She let me plead my case, sending me home to my children on my own recognizance at the end of the day, and giving the Attorney General's Office a three-month period to investigate. On Monday, September 21, 2015, Judge Reinoso was taken into custody herself, accused of unlawful enrichment, and was at the time free on bond pending trial.

Rodri said I should approach her and say hello, but I refused. As I watched her, I wondered what my fate would have been had she stayed on as my judge. Accompanied by her children, she was welcomed to our area by people she knew from when she spent time in Santa Teresa, and it looked like she had brought some sort of donation. My father decided to go introduce himself and thank her for letting me go home to my children that day. He also made sure to tell her that another judge, Julia Rivera, had revoked her decision, and I was now locked up in Santa Teresa. As they spoke, they both turned in my direction, I waved, and she put her hands together in a prayer position and bowed my way.

———

When visiting hour concluded, I went back to my room to organize the new donations. I'm amazed at how much time we women spend organizing our possessions, especially when the space is tiny and multipurpose like in a crowded prison. I constantly try to "own" as little as possible, while other inmates become hoarders. I suppose it may have a direct correlation with how often one receives or how much access one has to supplies. My father had a special permit that meant he could come see me every day. Because of this, I did not need to keep many extra things. If that had not been the case, my strategy would certainly have been different.

After a visit from friends that afternoon, night came and I was once again locked inside with my roommates, discussing our dinner plans. Rina usually ate her own food because she had digestive problems. Carmen, Sandra, and I usually shared—Carmen and I provided the ingredients and Sandra cooked them for us. We did not have a table or stools because somehow, the woman who had left for Lili's room had decided to claim them as her own. Carmen had since requested another permit for a table, but as we waited for the paperwork to be approved, we ate on our own beds. It was far from ideal, but we each had a bed and we had access to good food, so there was no complaining from us.

That night, our dinner talk revolved around the meaning of a verse in the Bible. One of my roommates was Catholic and two were Protestants, and all three were very religious, so my belief in God-only rather than organized religion often threw them off. But we were all respectful about each other's beliefs and our conversations tended to be extremely interesting. That night we discussed how a few months back demons had come to Santa Teresa and started possessing inmates.

They told me it happened to six or seven women over a week's time. These women started screaming and growling in unheard-of ways; they'd throw things violently and became so strong that no one could restrain them. Priests and pastors were called in to try and resolve the situation, and the guards were so scared that, once inmates were locked in for the night, the warden had instructed them not to come back down to the prison. Some of the possessed women were thrown into solitary confinement for everyone's safety, including their own. Eventually, rumor had it that these women had been playing Ouija because they were part of a cult that worshipped the goddess of death, and that was the reason they had become possessed. My roommates told me that hearing those women scream and growl in the night was terrifying. They still shuddered at the thought. Frankly, it sounded very creepy to me, and I didn't even believe in demons.

As the evening rolled on, a loud thump interrupted our conversation. We hopped off our beds and ran out into the little common hallway, where we found Alina unconscious on the floor. Alina is diabetic and when her blood pressure drops, she faints. One of the women quickly revived her using acetone and she was taken back to her bed. She had hit her face on the wall as she fell, and her body felt cold to the touch. I think it was the first time since I had been there that I yelled at the top of my lungs, calling for the guards, yet by the time they arrived and opened the gates for the nurse to come in, Alina was already recuperating in her bed. Out of ten women in encamamiento, when one fainted, eight of us were concerned, while one simply said, "This is a show. She is fighting with Martina and wants attention." And that was how my 2016 Valentine's Day came to a close.

———

On Monday morning, when I woke up, I realized my back was hurting from spending so much time in bed, but I was still enjoying the luxury of having a bed all to myself, so I didn't care. Eventually, I got up, showered, and made sure to be at the preschool, as scheduled, at 10 a.m. It was the first day I officially started working with the children.

When I arrived, there were only two children at the school: three-year-old Adrian and a baby girl who was sleeping. Apparently, all the other children had gone to religious services with their mothers. I asked the other two women at the school why the mothers would take such small children with them instead of enjoying the services by themselves, and was told that the pastor usually brought food or candy for the children who attended. I hoped the children were learning something useful while they were there.

The two women—a young teacher who worked in the prison system and a woman I did not recognize—told me how difficult their jobs were because the mothers were not responsible, or educated, and many times, they favored sleep over their children's education. Since I was already at the school, I decided to make myself useful and focus on Adrian. We looked through an animal picture book, we played with a number puzzle, and tried several other games. While I was happily observing his strengths and weaknesses and thinking up ways to help him, I was oblivious to the fact that my father and everyone else had been looking for me everywhere.

Ashley was the one to finally find me and bring me to my father, whom I hugged and then led to a bench to sit and catch up with. Just then, I spotted Carmen coming back from religious services and asked her to join us. My father told us about the big news regarding SAT (Guatemala's IRS) and attorney Frank Trujillo. Apparently, a huge company had been accused of not paying its taxes properly, several SAT workers were arrested, and Olyslager's attorney, Frank Trujillo, who had been allegedly implicated in the case, was now a fugitive from justice with a warrant out for his arrest. Yes, the same Frank Trujillo whose law firm had asked the judge in January to keep me in prison, and yes, the same powerful man who was once a magistrate in Guatemala's Appeals Court. Frank Trujillo, brother of Hector Trujillo, with whom he worked in their law firm Trujillo, Gongora y Asociados and whose client list included former Guatemalan president Álvaro Colom, his wife Sandra Torres, and now former vice president Roxana Baldetti. Even the powerful justice system players were now being brought in to face the justice they themselves had once been responsible for imparting in this country. And I wondered, *When did all this happen to me? How did I end up in this mess, among these people?* Not long ago, I did not know any of these people existed, and now I found myself trapped in their claws.

When my father left, I saw Verónica, Meche, and Jenny by the gates.

They were anxiously waiting for Ashley to interview them for admission into Serigrafía. I approached them and reminded them that they were wonderful, smart, young women and that they should simply be themselves and stick to the truth because Ashley had zero tolerance for lies. They took turns going in and coming out. The interviewing panel included Ashley, Daniela, and Andrea, and by the end of the day, they had chosen fourteen women, among whom were my three girls. I was so happy; however, Ashley asked me not to say anything yet because she would be giving them the news personally on Wednesday. I could hardly wait!

Later that afternoon, Ashley showed us a movie she had produced with NADUS Films recounting the lives of several Guatemalan gang members. Unfortunately, it was not released in Guatemala, to safeguard the lives of several of the people featured in the documentary. It was difficult to see up close the lives and lack of values of some people who share our city. Quite a few of the women I had met in Santa Teresa, including some who had become dear to me, came from these places and these worlds, and I still had a very difficult time grasping it all.

I then decided to find María at the Education Department to tell her I wanted a DVD player as a teaching tool for the children and the women at Serigrafía, so that I could use the DVDs that came with many of the donated educational books. I asked her if she would sign my permission request and she readily agreed. I planned to ask Ashley and Marta to sign my request as well. Most requests in prison come with an almost guaranteed *no,* but I believed that my plan might actually work.

Back in encamamiento the biggest news was that Carmen had managed to score a permit to get a plastic table and three plastic bar stools for our room. Rina already owned a small wooden table, where she cooked and ate, while the other three of us cooked with Sandra's electric burner placed on the floor and nowhere to sit down and eat, so this was a huge gain for us. After a lot of back and forth we had finally scored a square plastic table on which we could cook, eat, and write . . . a real treasure!

———

I woke up on Tuesday, February 16, at 8:30 a.m. I had now spent six full weeks in prison, and I wasn't sure what the future held in store for me, so I simply focused on each day: getting up, drinking coffee, reading, and making sure to be at the preschool by 10 a.m. When I arrived that morning, the teacher was busy playing one of the donated lottery games with six children. I sat down to help her and was impressed at how well she handled them. I needed to pay attention and learn. Once the game was over, I read to the children until it was their snack time.

I then went outside and waited for my father's arrival. For some reason, he was not allowed into the prison, so we had our five-minute visit through the gates. He brought me one of the best items ever that day: my children's mail book (the notebook I had decided to use to communicate with my kids). I quickly opened it and discovered that Nina had written in very creative English that she was happy and grateful because God gave her a beautiful Mommy. And Fabi wrote, "I don't know what to write Mommy," but he did draw and color a beautiful flower for me. Nina also drew a picture of herself and me with a big heart that said, "I love you Mami linda." Seeing their handwriting and drawings brought tears to my eyes, but as I cried I also made sure to write back and draw a maze for each one of them because I knew they loved it when I did that.

———

It was so hot that Tuesday that Carmen and I decided to buy popsicles from Mimi. Because we were not allowed to go into the general prison population cellblocks where they were sold, we were forced to become creative. We could either pay someone to go get them for us, or better yet, have Sandra yell out our order through the alley, which was no longer accessible but had once led directly from the infirmary into Cellblock One. When

Sandra got a response, she placed our order for one green-mango-with-lemon-and-*pepitoria* and one jocote popsicle. Five minutes and $1.35 later, we were savoring our delicious and refreshing snacks.

Later that day, part of Mariana's story came to light, and I became privy to it through a fellow inmate. It seemed the night before, after her attorneys had left the prison, she opened up to one of the inmates and confessed that her husband had fallen from the second-floor balcony and died instantly. In a panic, she asked her son to help her move him to a far corner of the property, and they burned the body. Knowing now how the police act in situations like this one, instantly blaming and imprisoning the woman with no actual proof to back their actions, a part of me now understood her. After my own ordeal, and after having heard so many different inmate stories, I understood how citizens preferred to avoid calling the authorities even when they were innocent. In a country with an untrustworthy justice system created to accumulate convictions instead of search for the truth, being innocent certainly did not mean you had nothing to fear.

As I thought about this story back in my room, I was told there was a tall, bald man and a woman looking for me at the front gate. When I got there, I saw Vania and Ed. Because Vania is an attorney, I was allowed to go out of the main prison area to sit with them in the administrative office waiting area. Vania had brought me a book donation, and hummus with crackers. They told me that my children were doing very well. Ed added that, while we were all learning a great deal through this experience, one of the things that had impressed him the most had been the quality of friends that I had by my side. He had never seen anything like it, and I couldn't agree more. At some point, I turned to Ed and Vania and said, "I obviously can no longer be Roberto's wife, but I hope you'll be my family forever." To which they both responded in unison, "Of course!"

CHAPTER 12

Hearings, Hearings, and More Hearings

WEEK SEVEN

During my time in encamamiento, Sandra, Carmen, and I became very close friends, teasing each other constantly and even giving each other nicknames: Carmen called Sandra "Sister Amen," and Sandra called Carmen "Sister Hallelujah." I never expected I too would join the circle, but they eventually turned to me and baptized me as "Sister Glory to God"! The sum of those small human and simple moments helped us endure the endlessly long days in prison.

When I woke up on Wednesday, February 17, all I could think was, *Twenty-four hours until my next court hearing.* My night had been filled with bad dreams, where I expressed my anger about the hearings, spoke my mind, and was filled with nerves, fear, and rage. It was to be expected. How else could I possibly feel after forty-two days in jail with no end in sight for something I didn't do?!?

I realized I had been surviving in that place courtesy of the generosity of my loved ones and some strangers as well, and, thanks to them, I had not gone without or wanted for anything. On the contrary, everything and every single need had been met and multiplied . . . except my freedom and the justice everyone deserves.

That day went by like most others, with the cherished visit from my father, followed by a visit from friends, my usual visit to Serigrafía, and some time chatting with Susana in her room over tea—something I hoped one day we could recreate on the outside, at home, with tea or maybe even wine. *A girl can dream.*

As the evening came to a close, I showered and went to bed early in preparation for my early rising. I managed to fall asleep only to be awakened by the guards at 1 a.m. to let me know what I already knew all too well: that I had a hearing the next day and had to be ready by 4 a.m. It was hard to fall into a deep sleep after that interruption; my mind was racing and all I could think about was how I had yet to experience justice at the courthouse, how court hearing days were so horrible and detrimental, and how I strongly doubted I would find what I needed in that hellhole. *God, please let me be wrong.*

—

I had five minutes to get ready, to put on the clothes I had laid out the night before, wash my face, brush my teeth, and go. We were registered at the warden's office, one by one, and taken to the outdoor holding area, where we waited for over an hour in the predawn cold for the perrera to come get us. It was either not as chilly that morning or I was better prepared. There were approximately thirty women going to hearings on that day, Thursday, February 18, 2016—day forty-four of my imprisonment. After being loaded into the truck like cattle, and having to stand because there were more women than seats, the driver once again acted like he was driving a race car, whizzing through traffic, accelerating and stopping frantically, and most likely not once thinking about the lives he had locked in the back. Meanwhile I prayed that we would make it to the courthouse and our hearings alive.

When we finally arrived, I deliberately decided to be the last one out of the truck, buying myself an extra few minutes before being searched by the guards, even though that meant there might not be a place for me to sit once all thirty of us were inside the holding cell. I figured my hearing was scheduled for 8:15 a.m., so if I had to stand for a couple of hours, it would not kill me. After we all jumped off the truck and were thoroughly searched, we were handcuffed in pairs, and were followed down the ramp by the guard who held the key to the handcuffs. Once at the holding cell gates, the handcuffs were taken off, and we were locked inside.

That day, in addition to the thirty inmates from Santa Teresa, there were three women from COF and two overnight arrests. Thirty-five women and two babies with barely enough room to move: just another day in the nightmare that was the courthouse's holding cell. It was a place where time stood still, where a minute felt like an hour. I couldn't help but recall the first time I was thrown into the carceleta on September 17, 2015, and how shocked and surprised I was to hear that most inmates were actually looking forward to returning to prison. It sounded ridiculous to me. I would have thought that a day outside the prison would be a good thing—now I couldn't have agreed with them more.

Rancho food was delivered at some point in the early morning hours: black beans running like water, and two machine-made tortillas and half of a stiff boiled plantain per person. Although most of us had not had breakfast, the food was left untouched. All we got to drink was a small bag of purified water—the equivalent of an eight-ounce glass per person—from 4 a.m. to 8 p.m., when we finally were transported back to Santa Teresa. Yes, just one glass of water for a sixteen-hour day. The only chance to eat non-Rancho food or hydrate ourselves was that short period when we were taken up to our hearings, when, if you were lucky, your attorney or loved ones could purchase something from the courthouse cafeteria, and you had time to gulp it all down before going back to the basement. Most did not have this luxury.

At 8:15 a.m. I was handcuffed and taken up to the second floor. My loved ones were waiting for me and, as usual, they were the highlight of that terrible exhausting day. I approached each one of them to receive a hug—I was unable to hug them back because my hands were cuffed. When Miranda arrived, he pulled me aside and explained what was going to happen during that hearing and suddenly informed me that he wanted me to speak. I returned to my group of loved ones, visibly upset, while Miranda proceeded to check in. How was it possible that he could not let me know about this earlier, let me prepare in some way? I didn't want to go against his plan, so I took a deep breath, chatted with my family and friends, and asked to see photographs of my children on someone's cell phone. When I saw a picture of my children in their pajamas, on a couch watching TV, Fabi lying across Tina's son's lap, and Nina sitting right beside them wearing a ski hat, my eyes filled with tears. How happy it made me to see them happy, at peace, comfortable, and in loving company. I felt blessed a million times over knowing that they were in such good care, yet I also couldn't help but feel sad. I only wished I could've been in that picture-perfect moment with my kids rather than in handcuffs, at a courthouse, waiting to see what the judge had in store for me next, which turned out to be nothing.

In fact, no decisions related to my case would be made that day. Miranda came out from one of the rooms and informed us that the judge had been called by the magistrates and therefore my hearing had been postponed until the following Tuesday. Five more days that meant nothing to those free in the world but an eternity to someone who is locked up. I didn't even complain. I expected nothing but pain from this process and everyone involved, and so far, I had been proven right.

I couldn't help but think of a phrase commonly heard in prison, which inmates used to try to convey the horror of surviving that experience: "I do not wish imprisonment on even my worst enemy!" Yet I couldn't disagree more. To this day, I still believe that anyone in a position to request or order sentences of preventive detention (attorney generals, public prosecutors, attorneys, judges, and so forth) should be required to spend a minimum of five days in prison, undercover as an inmate, to truly understand what they are imposing on a fellow human being who has not had a trial and has not been convicted of a crime or sentenced for it. Five days of eating Rancho food, sharing a bed with a stranger, and living among killers, and I assure you that changes would begin to happen.

I still can't understand how Judge Julia Rivera so calmly sent me to prison, claiming that I could speak to or interfere with the other persons involved, or even falsify documents. Her decision left two five-year-old children without their mother and a family in despair, and this after another judge had granted my release on my own recognizance, and after the investigation time period had elapsed. How? Why? If she had spent five days of her life in that place, there was a chance her decision would have been different. Even Olyslager had originally stated that he did not request imprisonment for me, but the gang of attorneys and attorney general officials, who would stand in for one another, thought differently, and I have the audio to prove it.

As I refocused my attention, Miranda said he needed me to make a decision, and I wanted him to explain it to my loved ones so that they too could be involved. Olyslager was still insisting that he'd desist in his claims that I had *conned* him if we agreed to stop all media attacks on him. My initial reaction had been a resolute "No." Not only did I not trust him, I also had gone over this scenario with Susana back in prison, and she had explained to me that even if the accuser did desist, that wouldn't stop the Attorney General's Office from coming after me. "I will do whatever you see fit," Miranda said. However, he did clarify that I should keep in mind that if the accuser did indeed desist, at least one charge would be off the table. I turned to my father and asked him to weigh in. "I think you should accept this offer," he said, adding, "What we need right now is to get you out of prison." I wasn't ready to make a decision yet, so I asked Miranda to find out the complete details, get them in writing, share them with me, and then we would see.

Before saying my goodbyes, I was told that Sylvia Gereda, the prominent journalist, had spent two weeks trying to get a permit to interview me at the prison and that the interview had finally been approved for that day at 2 p.m. in Santa Teresa. Unfortunately, I wouldn't be there—hearing days rarely ended before 8 p.m.—so I mentioned that the only alternative would be to call her and let her know that she could interview me in the carceleta, where the media was allowed access at any time, and they sprang into action.

By 10:30 a.m., I had said my goodbyes, and was once again on my way to the land where time stands still. However, my idea worked, and at 1:30 p.m., there was a man at the holding cell gates asking for me. His name was Quique and he was accompanied by a cameraman. He told me that he worked with Canal Antigua and Sylvia Gereda and he was there to interview me. In the blink of an eye, I was being wired with a microphone, a huge light was turned on in front of my face, and Quique began asking me questions. I answered as best I could and eventually Sylvia arrived. We spoke, she explained the show's format to me, I told her about what had been happening on my side of the bars, and the camera started to roll. I was amazed at the way she captured the information, processed it, and went directly to shoot the scene. It was almost like improvising because of the speed of it all, but it seemed to come out perfect. It is always fabulous to see someone excel at what they do. I was given one chance to answer every question I was asked. I did not know the questions in advance, I didn't have a chance to fix my hair, apply makeup, and I didn't get any tips regarding how to play to the camera. Whatever came out was the raw reality. I only hoped the finished and edited product would portray my tragic circumstances and the reasons behind them.

During the interview, when she asked about my husband by name, I made sure to request that she not use his name and only refer to him as my "husband." When asked why, I explained that there was probably no person angrier with him than me. Yes, the other players involved might have lost their money, but I had lost my partner, my husband, my family unit, my trust, my good name, and now even my freedom. Nevertheless, he was still the father of my children and I vowed to protect them any way I could. Furthermore, he shared his name with two other family members, and there was no reason to harm them. Thankfully, she obliged. I know this request might sound trivial considering all that was happening, and I knew that keeping his name completely out of the picture would be impossible since his actions apparently instigated the situation, but this was my story, my truth, my experience, and it is important to me that my children be able to read and hear my words one day. Their father had allegedly made terrible decisions for which he would likely have to answer, but as prison and this experience has taught me, we are all so much more than our worst mistakes.

Once we were done, I suggested to Sylvia that she might want to take the opportunity in the carceleta to interview some of the other inmates, since part of the show aimed to expose inmate conditions in prison. I turned around and asked the women if any of them would like to be interviewed and several agreed. When they talked about Rancho food, the cameraman managed to zoom in on the actual food lying on the floor, untouched. We later realized that filming in the carceleta had been a great twist of fate because in Santa Teresa the interview would have most likely taken place in the warden's office area, with no bars, no Rancho food, no privacy to speak my mind, and no opportunity to interview other inmates. I started feeling like my day had not been a complete waste.

Before she left, Sylvia took my hands in hers and told me she would do everything she could to portray the truth and that if I needed absolutely anything, all I had to do was ask; for that I will remain eternally grateful.

Once back in Santa Teresa, I stopped for a moment before entering encamamiento to look at the moon, the stars, and the light clouds drifting quickly across the sky, and I let the tears roll freely down my face for a few brief seconds. Then I took a deep breath, walked inside, and heard the gates lock behind me.

By the time I woke up the next day, Sylvia had posted the spot advertising her upcoming show on women in prison, highlighting my story, and it had gone viral! The first bomb had been dropped and my retaliation had gained momentum. The social media attacks had caused a stir, but up until then I had basically been a silent victim. Now we were finally at war.

Later that Friday, after visits from my friends and family for encomienda day, my name was called once again. It was someone bearing a legal notice for me. As had been the norm during this experience, I found myself invaded by panic when legal papers bore my name. I returned to my room as fast as I could in the hope that Carmen would "translate" the document for me, but she was not there, so I read it for myself. We had filed a motion asking the magistrates to review Judge Rivera's decision to imprison me as a preventive measure and decide, instead, to set me free. It had been denied. Yet another devastating blow.

When Carmen later read the notice carefully, she said she was appalled by the reasoning, or lack thereof, of the magistrates. I called my father and asked him if we could publish the decision. I wanted it on "Justicia para Anaité," and I wanted to make sure a copy was sent to my cousin Yoli and another to Sylvia. I had been left with little to lose; there were advantages to this position, and I was ready to use them.

———

On Saturday, my father stopped by to fill me in on everything that was going on in the legal arena with my case. Mayora & Mayora had apparently contacted Miranda and wanted to meet. I felt frustrated because being imprisoned meant I did not get the timely, accurate information I needed in order to influence my own destiny. How was I supposed to defend myself behind bars? I felt so helpless.

Impotence is a word commonly used to describe the general feeling experienced in prison. I suppose it is one of the reasons almost all inmates own, carry, and constantly read the Bible. There are many times where one feels that one will be delivered from that place only through a miracle. "My Christ will perform a miracle on my behalf," "Our Lord has made me a promise," "God has put me here to safeguard me from other evils," "God has sent me word," "God has confirmed it."

But for me it was different. I trusted that God had a plan for me and I had faith that He knew best; however, that did not mean that I liked what was happening. It simply meant that I would remain open to finding His purpose. He knew I desperately wanted to return to my children and reclaim my freedom, so I had no need to ask Him every moment of the day, or expect any sort of confirmation, promise, letter, or fax, but I did hope His plan included my freedom in the near future and not as far away as it had started to feel it might be.

From what I gathered from my father, it now seemed as though the law firm wanted me to admit to some sort of wrongdoing, anything, so that they could claim that their actions against me were reasonable. They were now apparently claiming that they would desist and we would not have to worry about the attorney general or the judge. However, I was not willing to admit to anything but the truth, which was certainly not convenient for them. My answer, of course, was no. They had also asked my father to stop his media attacks, but I insisted that he continue communicating the truth until I was free, home with my children where I belonged, and until there was no possibility that the attorney general could come after me again. My next hearing was scheduled for Tuesday and the Sylvia Gereda show was scheduled to air on TV a couple of weeks later on Sunday, March 6, and there was nothing I could or was willing to do to stop that.

Later that afternoon, I called Ed and spoke to my babies. They were deliriously happy spending the weekend at the beach in Monterrico, on their way to play Rummikub. *How I wish I was there.*

—

Sunday came and went with a visit from Rodri and my father, but it was the first time during visiting hours in my forty-seven days in prison that I did not receive any female visitors. As sad as I felt, I knew it was bound to happen. Everyone had a life to live and better places to be, and my prison stay had now entered its second month. I don't think any of us thought it would last that long. Nevertheless, once again, I survived! I knew it didn't mean they loved and supported me any less. I knew I could count on them.

Monday rolled by, and I did my best to distract myself from thinking of my hearing the following day, until 7 p.m., when I received a visit I had been hoping to get for a while. It was Miranda. I had already complained to my family and his colleague Manolo that he had only visited me twice during my forty-seven days in prison, but he had finally shown up again, which likely meant it was important.

We got to talking and he asked me to explain several details regarding the purchase of my home. I did, and after, to my surprise, he once again took his time to apologize for not coming to see me sooner and more often. He explained that he'd been out of the country one week, sick and in the hospital another week, and busy with several other high-profile cases. He apologized several times and, with great relief, I gladly accepted them. Miranda had not been in constant contact as I would have hoped, but according to every lawyer who had become familiar with my case, he was doing his job well, was timely, and was playing by the book, even though none of that guaranteed my freedom.

Back at my room, I made sure that my clothes were laid out properly and that my father's jacket had tissues, reading glasses, and lip balm in the pockets. I made myself some Sweet Dreams tea and it worked like a charm. At some point, Sandra called my name and told me that the guards wanted to notify me about my hearing the next day. I must have seemed too drowsy to come down from my upper bunk, so Sandra let them know that I was aware and I quickly went back to my sweet dreams.

———

I was ready and waiting at 4 a.m. on Tuesday, February 23, 2016, for my sixth hearing that year. The new young guards took me out of my sector way too early, so I was the only one at the front gates waiting in the cold darkness. Eventually, the inmates in charge of taking out the trash started to arrive. They carried huge trash bags that seemed very heavy, and took them out the front gates and into an open area where the prison cats were waiting, knowing full well that those bags would be filled with the unwanted Rancho food from the day before. Minutes behind them came the guards accompanying the other women who had hearings at the courthouse that day.

While we all waited to be called by name, searched, photographed, and taken to the outside holding cell, I enjoyed the predawn sky and its fresh air. When my name was finally called, I went to the gate, but instead of being placed in the general holding area with the other inmates, I was led back inside the prison gates and told to wait. I decided to exercise while I waited, which involved going up and down the ten steps to the gate and walking around in a rectangle, almost in the dark. Each time I walked by the small area open to the sky, I took a second to look at the stars. It was not until later, when we had almost arrived at the courthouse, that I caught a glimpse of the beautiful full moon I had been missing.

Finally, when the guards called my name, I was informed that instead of the perrera, I had been scheduled to be transferred in a police pickup truck. As I climbed up the stairs to exit the prison, I was grouped with two nicely dressed inmates whom I had never seen before. When we got to the truck, I was surprised to see there were three other inmates who were on their way to another court (Mixco), already sitting in the back seat. I immediately recalled Susana's experience and started to complain, as I now knew what they had in store for us: sitting in the truck bed. "This is not possible," I said, "the prison system is in charge of our safety, we are older women, we are handcuffed," but it was as if I were talking to myself. There was no other vehicle in sight and my two well-dressed companions began to climb onto the open back of the vehicle. My grumbling was useless, so I followed suit and climbed into the truck's flatbed, sat down with my handcuffed hands in my lap, and watched as six fully armed guards climbed in and sat around us.

It was still dark and very cold out, there was traffic on the road, and the cars made way for us to pass by. As I observed the road that led to and from Santa Teresa for the first time since my incarceration, I couldn't help thinking about how annoyed I used to get when police cars or perreras carrying prisoners disrupted traffic, and how I now wished I was riding in the comfort of my own vehicle. We arrived at the courthouse and were taken to the basement, but instead of being locked up in the women's carceleta with the other inmates, my companions and I were left outside standing with the guards. Apparently, this was the procedure for inmates who had been deemed unable to be in contact with the general prison population. This was not officially my case, although I had been transferred to encamamiento, but it was the case for the other two inmates traveling with me because they were ex-PNC workers (National Civil Police). Their names were Mari Ro and Celeste.

A short while later, a courthouse officer came to inform our prison guards that we were not allowed to remain in that area. There was actually a sign on the wall that said so, but I was not going to be the one to let them know because I was quite happy standing there instead of being cooped up inside the infernal carceleta. We were then escorted to the Basement Headquarters located next to the men's holding cells. I took a seat on a chair, as did Celeste and Mari Ro to my left. Sitting patiently to my right was another nice-looking woman I had never seen before. We were all wearing the same accessory: shiny silver handcuff bracelets.

This new woman introduced herself as Alicia. She told me that until nine days before, when she was apprehended at SAT, she had been working as an attorney. She claimed she remembered me because in January, during one of my hearing dates, she had seen me in the waiting area surrounded by many of my loved ones. She said it was unforgettable to her because in all the years she had worked at the courthouse, she had never witnessed anything like it. We got to talking about our experiences on the "other side" of the legal system and both agreed that the Attorney General's Office was the worst evil you could ever have against you. In her case, the CICIG as well.

Alicia had spent the most recent nine days of her life at a military prison called Mariscal Zavala, where she was one of four women in a cell, sharing a common bathroom. As she pointed to a group of handcuffed men in elegant suits standing close by, she told me that the men had it a lot better. While the women were allowed to leave their cells for one hour each day, the men were out, free to roam around the prison all day, with access to exercise facilities and visitors. Meanwhile, she had yet to have her preliminary hearing and hoped that day would finally be the one where she could plead her case before a judge. She wanted to be heard—her hell was just beginning.

At 8 a.m. Mari Ro and Celeste were taken up to their respective hearings; by 8:15 a.m. it was my turn. I found Rodri, my mother, and my father waiting for me. When Miranda and I finally walked into the courtroom, I felt calm. After I had come to clearly understand that there would be no justice at this courthouse on my behalf, not with this judge, the Attorney General's Office, and especially not with the prosecutor and the relentless Mayora & Mayora attorneys, I had felt more at peace. I did not like it one bit, but having no expectations made me stronger somehow. I realized that I was not getting anything from them, regardless of what my attorney or I did. Everything about this case seemed to have been predetermined. I was already in prison for something I did not do, and since they could not send me to the gas chamber, the electric chair, or the firing squad, there was no reason to make a deal with them.

I'm aware that this thinking process made no sense, but that was what I felt. *Impotence.* There was nothing I could do to help myself because the outcome did not depend on me. If I had been required to run the fastest, jump the highest, or hit the hardest, I would fight with all I had, but there was nothing for me to do but sit and listen to all the terrible accusations against me and silently wait for the outcome.

The hearing began with its usual legal mumbo jumbo, and I zoned out for a few minutes until I heard the judge announce that of the forty reports she had requested through the different jurisdictions regarding other lawsuits against my husband, only twenty-four had arrived. There were still sixteen reports missing. She then looked at me and asked if I wanted to proceed with the hearing despite these missing reports, or if I would rather reschedule for another day. Miranda requested a moment to talk to me.

Since I was being accused of being part of a criminal structure to defraud "people" of their money, we needed those reports on other cases against my husband to prove my innocence, given that not a single one even mentioned me. In addition, since we were claiming that Olyslager already had a civil lawsuit pending against just my husband and his accountant, a criminal lawsuit would have to wait until the civil lawsuit was resolved. If we decided to continue with this hearing, we would forfeit those sixteen missing reports as evidence. I said to Miranda, "Please check to see if the most important and compelling lawsuits are included in the available twenty-four reports." He did, and his answer was, "No." So I made the heart-wrenching decision to postpone the hearing. There was no objection from the opposing parties. How could there be? More prison time for me probably made them feel as if they had won something. I wondered what that could be.

I then heard the judge say something like, "Due to the proximity of the hearings . . ." and as my blood reached its boiling point, I shot my hand up in the air requesting to speak, but the judge motioned for me to wait.

She continued to say something about finding another hearing date, so I raised my hand more forcibly. I was not about to sit back and watch her send me back to three more months of lock-up until they found an appropriate time to reconvene. Noticing my determination, the judge eventually stopped what she was saying and allowed me to speak. I reminded her that the system had had twenty-six days to get those reports and present them to the judge as ordered. I wanted to know who had failed at their job, and I wanted to know how many days the law allowed for those reports to be presented, because in the meantime, I was rotting away in prison. Yes, I actually said, "rotting away in prison" and not once did I say Your Honor, Your Excellency, Your Majesty . . . or anything similar. And to top off my performance, my attitude was a demanding one. So much for my attorney's advice regarding my showing the court a "humane side," even crying if possible. Well, not today.

The judge responded that my attorney would explain it to me, that it was not her responsibility to get the reports, and that each individual court was responsible for sending the requested documentation. To my surprise, she apologized to me. Yes, *apologized*, and my next hearing was scheduled for Thursday, March 3, nine days from that day.

It must have been 8:40 a.m. when we left the chamber. Outside waiting for me were my family and friends. When they heard my hearing had been postponed yet again, they were appalled, even though this time we were the ones who had requested it. Still, it was one more blow. I was allowed to remain with them for a short while, but my young guard was most likely new because he was very worried that his superiors would reprimand him for not returning me to the basement immediately. After I said my good-byes, I was once again led to that horrid place where the sun does not shine and time seems to stand still.

As the day slowly progressed, I chatted with people who came to sit beside me on those basement chairs. I heard many stories, mostly from guards who were waiting to take inmates to their scheduled hearings. My first interesting chat was with a pretty, young female guard from Jutiapa, where she told me men steal girls over thirteen years of age to give them a "try," and if they are virgins, they marry them. She was twenty years old, had a one-year-old baby, and was paying the mortgage for her home all by herself. Her younger brother was living with her so he could study and graduate high school, while she worked her seven-day prison shifts and spent Friday evenings as a law student at San Carlos University. Her older brother had left as an illegal emigrant to the United States, and although he called once in a while to check in, he never sent her any money to help out. Meanwhile, her parents were still furious at her because she was an unwed mother, giving them the perfect excuse to not support her in any way. Her baby's father did help with some of the baby's expenses, and despite all those strikes against her, she managed to not only survive, but to aim higher and hope for a better life once she graduated.

Some time later, another guard came over to sit beside me. He was very serious and carried a huge weapon. As we began to chat, a young boy in handcuffs, who did not look a day past fifteen, was brought in. Shocked, I asked him if minors were also brought into that courthouse.

He nodded and added, "He looks like a good-for-nothing thief."

"And how do you know? Did you see him steal something?" I asked.

"No, but it is obvious."

"If you did not see him steal, you should not assume such a thing. I hope you are never on the other side of justice, handcuffed and accused of something, just because you look like you did it."

"I have been on the other side," he responded.

"What do you mean? Imprisoned?" I asked.

"Yes. I was in prison for three months in Jutiapa because I broke someone's hands and legs. These teens deserve to be beaten so that they learn. I have a six-year-old nephew and I leave him black and blue. Once, his classmates told him to take a pen because it was very nice, even though it didn't belong to him. He took the pen home and when I asked him where he had gotten such a fancy pen, and he told me the story, I hit him hard because it is the only way he will learn not to steal."

"But he is only six years old! He does not know better. You must inspire him to be a good person."

"No! They must be taught by force," he exclaimed.

"But a child's hug is one of the most precious things in life. I have two six-year-olds and I cannot explain to you what I would give to hug them again."

"Yes, I know. He sometimes hugs me."

"And do you have children?"

"No, and I will not have any. I am not even getting married. I have two girlfriends and they are aware of each other."

Relieved that he did not intend to be a parent, I said, "Well, I congratulate you for being so honest."

"I am already broken. There is no fixing me. I have killed another human being."

"Do not say that, we can all be fixed."

"When I was fifteen years old, I joined the army. I wanted to join, but there you are taught to not think for yourself, you must obey orders and do as you are told. I have done terrible things and I no longer care about anything or anyone."

"May I tell you what I see? I see a man doing the impossible to protect his inner child. I assume that you suffered a lot when you were younger and at some point, you built a wall. I see a man good enough to still fully understand the gravity of his actions and who believes he is not deserving of love. You may never know if the affected parties have forgiven you for what you have done, but you need to forgive yourself. We all make mistakes. We all choose constantly between good and evil. If in the past you chose evil, there is nothing you can do about it now, but from this day forward please do your best to choose good. And regarding your nephew, every time you harm him physically or emotionally, you destroy a little bit of his soul. So please, do your best to inspire him and give him a good example. Please ...”

I wanted to continue talking to this man, but our conversation was cut short when my guard arrived and informed me that the police car was ready to take me back to Santa Teresa. My chariot awaited, but I didn't want to go. This man was so hurt inside, and so clearly needing to open up and talk to someone, that I wanted to stay and finish our talk. I also wanted to make sure the six-year-old boy would be safe. For once, I wasn't ready to leave that building when the time came, but, an order is an order, and I had to go.

By 2:30 p.m. I was out in the sunshine, where our transportation awaited. The women who had gone to Mixco in the morning were not there, but I was told to climb in the flatbed because there were already two other women and a guard sitting in the back seat. I realized that the women inside the cab were Celeste and Mari Ro. I did not want to go in the truck bed, so I asked Mari Ro to move over a bit. I said that I was very thin and we could manage. Mari Ro immediately agreed and helped me in. The guards closed the door, hopped in the flatbed, and decided not to argue with me. Poor Mari Ro could not sit properly, but she did not seem to mind. Some people are team players and Mari Ro was one that day.

Once inside the car, as we drove back to Santa Teresa, Mari Ro shared her story with me. In April 2008, she had been driving down a busy Guatemala City boulevard at 11 p.m., when men in a pickup truck ambushed her and her commissioner. She was his assistant and they were life partners. There were at least two firearms involved. The commissioner, who was driving Mari Ro's small sedan, died during the attack, while she managed to crash the car to a stop as the assailants sped away. Mari Ro was injured by a bullet that almost took her life. A month after this bloody attack, Mari Ro, fearing for her life, traveled to the United States where she worked and lived with her family. Eventually, our attorney general asked the US government to extradite her to face charges against her. The CICIG and the attorney general accused her of being involved in the criminal structure that assassinated the commissioner. According to Mari Ro, once she arrived in Guatemala, CICIG and the attorney general offered her the option of becoming a protected witness. If she agreed, she would have to corroborate everything the attorney general said. But Mari Ro refused on the grounds that she would rather rot in prison than become a liar like them.

During her first trial, she spent one year and five days in Santa Teresa. A three-judge panel absolved her of the crime. Not happy with the verdict, the attorney general appealed and the case was retried. Mari Ro spent another five and a half months in prison during the second trial, which is when I met her, and once again she was absolved and set free. Later that year, the Attorney General's Office appealed the latest decision, and in October 2016, the appellate court ruled in her favor once again. You would think that this would deter them once and for all, but it didn't. They went after her again, by appealing to a higher court, insisting on trying her for a third time. Why this interest in finding her guilty? Why couldn't they let it be, when two trials had absolved her and the judges had sent her home? What are they hiding, who are they protecting, and why are they so keen on getting a guilty verdict against her?

CHAPTER 13

Fasting, Encomiendas, and a Movie Marathon

WEEK EIGHT

At 8:30 a.m. on Wednesday, I jumped out of bed and got ready for visitors' day. Unlike other hearing days, when I had been transferred to the courthouse in the perrera and had to wait until the other inmates were done with their hearings before returning to Santa Teresa, yesterday's experience sitting all day in the basement headquarters in cuffs, but not inside the carceleta, was a welcome change for me. It left me less exhausted than usual.

The first visitor to arrive with my coffee and several bags full of donations for the children was my brother Rodri, accompanied by my brother-in-law Carlos. He could not tell me who the toys were from because he was only the delivery man.

I was so excited about the donation that I had to look quickly through the bags. The older children saw me and came closer to us. Alejandro greeted me with the usual request for me to read him a book, *"Seño, me lee un libro?"* I told him the books were still locked in Marta's office, so I couldn't read to him at that moment, but we could play with one of the new toy donations instead. He chose one of those plastic grids with holes that you can attach colorful pins to, to create art, pictures, and letters. By now, two more children had joined us and Rodri sat down on the floor and played with them. This was just one other touching moment during the past weeks when I wished I'd had a camera in prison. We had so much fun that I almost forgot where I was . . . almost. Eventually, my father joined us.

At 11:30 a.m. the bell rang, and my visitors had to go. I took everything back to my room so that I could organize it. Among the items was a one-thousand-piece jigsaw puzzle that was not suitable for small children, so I decided to find an adult who would enjoy it. Susana was so excited about it that I gave it to her. Nothing went to waste in Santa Teresa, well, except for Rancho food and many women's precious time.

Lunch was lonely for me that day because Carmen and Sandra had decided to fast for three consecutive days on a religious conviction, so there was no cooking going on. Even though I did not always eat what was cooked in our room, mealtimes were fun and I worried that while Carmen and Sandra fasted, I would be the one to lose weight since they usually made sure that I ate properly.

Carmen was really worried about the lack of TV/DVD in our room, so she arranged to rent a flat screen TV with a DVD, from Friday afternoon to Sunday morning for eleven dollars. We all agreed that it was a fabulous idea! By paying $2.75 apiece, we would get two full evenings and an entire Saturday to watch movies.

At around 2 p.m. my name was called again. Visitors! I came out into the sunshine and found my friends Karen and Katya waiting for me. They wanted to know how many children were in Santa Teresa and how they could help. I invited Marta over, and she told us about the prison procedures, the special permissions, the processes . . . trying to help was a difficult endeavor. She said there were thirty-five children over six months of age at the prison, and of those, an estimated twenty attended school in the morning. Although I had never seen that many children at the school at one time, I assumed this was the total number of children signed up for the program.

———

On Thursday, I awoke, as usual, by the sunlight and activity of my room-mates getting ready for the day. Sandra asked me if I wanted hot water because she was about to boil some to make coffee for the guards. I said yes. The young guards who had been in charge of us during the night had fallen asleep on the cold floor of the hallway right in front of our gates. Sandra had discovered them when she left the room a little earlier. When they noticed her, she asked them if they wanted some coffee, and they accepted. Several nights ago, when the weather had also been freezing cold, Carmen had given a guard one of her blankets. Despite of our circumstances, we are all human after all.

When I arrived at the preschool later that morning, the children were busy learning how to use scissors. Once they finished cutting their straws, they made necklaces for their mothers. As they worked, I read to them, and finished just in time for their school pickup and my precious five-minute visit with my father at the gates.

Day turned into night, and I found myself in my room, closely watch-ing over Carmen and Sandra to make sure they didn't faint or starve, but they were doing fine. Whenever I think of fasting, I automatically become famished. It's the intention in anything you do that makes the difference, I suppose.

———

I came to really enjoy encomienda day, and the element of surprise involved in who might show up at the gates, showering me with gifts as if it were

Christmas morning. Fridays in Santa Teresa were good for me.

The first call of the day brought my father, my warrior, my rock. Once we realized my stay in Santa Teresa would be longer than we had expected, we devised a routine: every Friday my father drove by my house to fetch clean sheets and a towel for me before he headed my way. Among the things my father brought for me that Friday were Nina and Fabi's school grades. To my surprise, they had received a 95 to100 percent (equivalent to grades of A) average in all their classes! And to think that all this time I had thought they had been doing great in school because of the fabulous mother they had! One less worry on my list.

Back in my room, I found Carmen and Sandra on their knees, with their foreheads touching the floor, praying. Carmen was silent, while Sandra prayed out loud. I stood still and observed them, listening to their prayers, feeling their pain, and waiting for them to finish while tears streamed down my face. I knew their suffering, I knew their stories, and I knew their hearts. Throughout this chapter of our individual journeys we had become a team. We saw one another as much more than our current circumstances dictated. It was not like this for many in prison, but so far, it had been for us.

They eventually finished praying, stood up, and it was finally time for them to break their fast. They prepared a simple soup and then enjoyed what was left of the Chinese rice my father had brought me the previous day, and Rodri's rib platter from that day. Not only was the fast over, we now had our TV/DVD combo and the movies we wanted: Let the movie marathon begin!

———

On Saturday, when I woke up at 9 a.m., Sandra and Carmen headed to their religious services, and after a full afternoon and evening of TV the day before, I was ready to take advantage of the two hours alone in my room to watch yet another movie; this time I chose *The Little Boy*. When the movie ended, I wrote in my diary until I was interrupted by Rina, who came into our room carrying an eight-month-old baby girl. I came down from my bunk and asked if I could hold her. After hugging and playing with her for a couple of minutes, I broke down and cried. I had two of these little miracles in my arms not long ago, but today, it felt like an eternity. They were my double gift from God, and now I could only communicate with them through the prison telephone and our special notebook, and I felt that with every passing day I was becoming more of a distant memory to them.

During my father's visit later on, when he noticed my distress, he assured me that everything was going well and moving forward with my case. Sylvia Gereda had interviewed the judge; according to my father, when Sylvia asked the judge about the postponed hearings in my case, she had responded that those had been my attorney's fault. So, Miranda was interviewed and was able to give his side of the story. Olyslager declined to be interviewed, and although it had been twelve days since he expressed interest in negotiating the terms of his desist, he had not yet presented or signed anything. GFP's legal counsel, Mayora & Mayora, apparently declined to be interviewed as well, and said they would instead issue some sort of written statement.

The following day, when Rodri came to see me, he asked me to be stronger around our father. Apparently, he left our visit distraught at having seen me so "broken." I knew exactly what he meant. The previous day, after he had filled me in on what was happening with my case and the Sylvia interviews, he looked at me and asked me to do a quick exercise.

"Visualize what it is you need to get done in prison, because it is very likely that you will be going home on Thursday," he said.

"I cannot do that, I can't even go there, because if I go to the hearing and it is postponed, or if the judge or the public prosecutor decides not to show up, or if the reports are not in, or if the judge sends me back to prison . . . if I imagine myself going home, hugging my children, and then I don't, *that* will break me. I prefer to expect the usual evil, and avoid unnecessary heartbreak. Who knows? Maybe I'll be proven wrong and be surprised this time around, but I cannot visualize it, I cannot expect it."

As I replayed our exchange, I realized I may have not been clear enough with my father. I tried to explain to Rodri what it was like to be imprisoned, to have no contact with the outside world for days, no cell phone, no computer, no Internet, not even a radio or an old TV. What he was asking of me was difficult. My father was my only daily contact with the outside world, and I needed to be able to talk to him, to express and share my feelings with him. But my brother insisted I put on a strong face next time, and I agreed. It was no use to argue. I could not have possibly understood what I was going through myself if I had not personally experienced it. I also realized that my father's feelings at the sight of his daughter's unjust imprisonment was unimaginable to me as well, so I decided I would try to be more positive around him from then on. It was a good reminder: this entire situation was not only happening to me, it was happening to all of us.

Eventually, my father arrived and I was once again in the company of my two fearless warriors. While we sat and talked, a woman from a town called Chiquimulilla passed by as she went from the infirmary back to her cellblock. She was an older woman whose daughter was friends with my friend Patty, and who during a cellblock visit weeks before, had recognized my cousin Magalí because my family had ties to Chiquimulilla. When she saw me, she came over to say hello to my father. She told us she was in Santa because her husband and his brother had been feuding over land for many years, and since the brother had died, his son, her nephew, had accused them of many things. Because of these accusations, her husband and she had been sent to preventive detention (the men's prison is next door to Santa Teresa). Her husband was very ill at the time, but a judge had ordered his imprisonment anyway. While getting out of the police car to enter the prisons, she noticed that her husband was very weak. She said something to the guards but she was quickly taken away. Once locked up in Santa Teresa, she was still very worried. Some days later, she finally managed to call her son and learned that her husband had passed away that day, when she last saw him, as they each entered prison. Not satisfied with this turn of events, the public prosecutor and the nephew were now accusing her son in lieu of her husband. I couldn't help but think, *And I'm supposed to visualize justice being served?*

There is an old adage that says, *"Quien nada debe, nada teme,"* which loosely translates into, "He who owes nothing should fear nothing." I believed in this adage; I was originally not fearful of being accused for my husband's actions because I had not done anything wrong, I had never been involved in his businesses, and I had always been very strict about not signing documents before reading them, a lesson my father had taught me while growing up. So, I was quite sure I had never even inadvertently signed anything, not even as a witness. I knew that my family and I would pay for many inevitable consequences regarding my husband's actions, but prison had never crossed my mind.

When people in Guatemala are accused of a crime, they usually flee the country, whether they are innocent or not. Several of my close friends suggested that I should do the same earlier on, but I truly believed this adage and stood my ground. I would gladly have helped the Attorney General's Office get at the truth and prove my innocence, so much so that I had even spent the first three months of the attorney general's investigation at home, compiling all the paperwork regarding the purchase of the only two properties I owned, all the information regarding my US tax returns, as well as all my bank account statements, which explained every transaction in detail, believing that my bank accounts would speak for themselves. However, the authorities never contacted me to see if I was willing to answer any questions, prior to being arrested in the house I had lived in for eight years, and my financial history was never requested as evidence because it would have only proven my innocence. So today, that old adage, which I once believed to be true, rings differently in my mind. Today, when others use that phrase to determine in a simplistic way whether someone is guilty or innocent of something, I can't help but think, *May you never learn what I have learned.*

Later that day, after lunch, I decided to go outside in the sunshine to write for a while and saw Susana down at the visitor's area. She had her table set up with a beautiful tablecloth, five chairs, her colorful plastic dishes, and plastic "silverware." She was sitting alone, with her cat Max in her arms, waiting for her four children to visit her. I sat with her and held Max until the children arrived. They were such an adorable bunch. Susana later told me that on their way out of the prison, the visitor mob had been so out of control that her twelve-year-old daughter had fallen and been trampled while one of her older daughters lost a shoe trying to make sure that her sister made it out alright. Unbelievable! A twelve-year-old girl comes to prison to visit her mother, spends hours outside under the sun waiting to get in, is searched, and is finally let in to visit for an hour, only to be trampled on by a mob on her way out. *May my children never have to come visit me in this place. Please God, send me home.*

———

By 6:15 p.m. that Sunday evening, we were locked in our blocks, and going about our business in our room when we heard someone wheezing loudly outside the infirmary in the corridor which ends at our gate. It sounded like someone was gasping for air, unable to breathe. Sandra and I rushed out to see if we could help. There were two young women sitting on the bench in front of the infirmary; one of them was having an asthma attack. They knocked on the infirmary door, but the nurse was not there. Sandra and I offered to help through the gates. The young woman asked for water and Sandra handed her a small plastic bag containing one serving, which she drank in a flash. Meanwhile, the other woman fanned her and tried to help, but what could any of us really do? Sandra and I were locked behind bars, the nurse was gone, the infirmary was locked, and there were no guards in sight.

This was one of the toughest issues for me to digest; we were prisoners who had temporarily lost our right to live freely within society, but that did not mean we should be deprived of our basic human rights. What's more, we were wards of the state; it was the state's responsibility to make sure that we were safe. We had no drinkable water, no safety, no medical treatment, no edible food, and if, God forbid, we should get ill in this place, the likelihood of dying seemed to be quite high—thankfully, no one died that night. Eventually, the nurse came back, took them in, and Sandra and I returned to our room.

As if this episode hadn't been enough, later that evening, we heard that a former inmate who suffered from renal failure, who been in Santa for two years, had been found dead in a ravine, after being set free the previous September. My roommate Rina was very sad because they had become good friends. The woman was twenty-two years old and the mother of a six-year-old child. While in Santa, she had been part of the ex-Mara 18 block, which held the women who had decided to quit this gang and had found the Lord; they were kept separate from the general prison population for their own safety. Apparently, while in prison, this woman had vowed to never go near gangs again, but she had not been free more than twenty days when it became known by many that she had been visiting gang members at the men's prison next door to Santa Teresa. No one can say for sure if she went back to the gang willingly or because she was threatened in some way. Either way, a twenty-two-year-old woman was murdered and another young boy would now grow up without a mother. The cycle of violence, poverty, and loss continued.

———

When Monday morning came around, I did not feel like getting up. The longer I slept, the less I was awake, and the less I felt like I was in that place. By 10 a.m. the sun was shining and I forced myself out of the room to start my day. As I headed to the pila to wash my dirty clothes, I sensed that the other inmates were looking at me funny. Women such as myself usually paid other inmates to wash their clothes and do their cleaning because there was always someone worse off who needed the job, but after I left Cellblock One and it became complicated for Mariana to continue washing for me, I discovered that I enjoyed washing them myself. On my way there, I saw my girls taking their course at Serigrafía. They looked well and happy. Verónica had also started studying ninth grade, so she went from not having anything to look forward to, while in prison, to having a full schedule, which was much to be desired under those circumstances. Verónica was a very bright and good-hearted young woman. I had no doubt that under the proper circumstances, she could have gone to college and become anything her heart desired.

By 11 a.m. I had finished up my washing and was reading books to the children. As usual, as I read, the children got so excited that they slowly started crawling closer and closer to me until they were all over me once again. I closed the book and asked them to sit properly before we continued. "Please remember that only Mommy touches the book," I said, and immediately corrected my statement to, "Only the teacher touches the book." My heart hurt.

Soon after, my father arrived for our five-minute visit. Meanwhile, Susana was desperately searching for her cat Milo, who had gone missing the previous day. Sad and not knowing what else to do, she offered a two dollar reward for any news leading to his safe return. The inmates complained that they wanted more money, to which Susana wittingly responded, "If I offer more money, it will no longer be a reward, it will be an express kidnapping!" She made me laugh. I reminded her that Milo was a cat and would most likely come home soon, but by the end of the day, he was still missing.

Later on, Daniela came looking for me. "I need to ask a favor of you, but I'm a little embarrassed."

"Ask honestly and I will answer honestly in return," I said, bracing myself for what might come next.

She wanted to borrow some money. I told her I was quite low on funds myself, and asked her how much she needed. I truly did not want this situation hanging between us, especially since I had been very careful so far about how I chose to be generous. She needed $1.50. I asked her when she planned on giving it back, and she said Wednesday. "OK," I said, "I can do that," and I gave her the money, hoping this would not become a pattern.

That afternoon, I called my home phone number, and to my surprise, Nina answered. She reminded me that she had a telephone in her room. I knew this, but she had never answered it before. I immediately freaked out thinking that she had probably heard the prison system recording, which played as soon as the telephone was answered, saying something like, "You are receiving a call from El Centro de Detención Preventiva para Mujeres Santa Teresa." I could not believe it, I could no longer call my children on our home line. I would have to call Olga's or my mother's cell phone numbers from then on.

Another day was coming to an end, and there I was, trying to make the best of it, trying to make sure my time in there was not a total waste of my life, trying to keep my chin up, trying to not let my heart break from missing my children, unable to hold them and tuck them in at night, while all the parties involved in causing my imprisonment enjoyed the luxury of going home to their families every night. *Where's my justice?*

———

By 9 a.m. on Tuesday, March 1, I began to stretch and wake up. My room-mates had gone to their religious services and had left hot water for my coffee. If I had to wake up in an overpopulated prison in a third world country, I was glad it was with these women. Problems were inevitable, but we all managed to get along quite well. I went along with my morning routine and at 11 a.m., I had a visit from Miranda. It turned out Olyslager had now decided to wait until the Sylvia Gereda show aired on Sunday to decide if he would desist from his accusations or not. In the meantime, Miranda wanted my father to hold off on his Facebook attacks until Monday. "This man has been claiming he wants to desist for fifteen days now," I said to Miranda, "but he has not done so yet, and I frankly have no faith in anything he says." I was glad that Miranda was working all the angles because that was his job; if Olyslager desisted, my case would become stronger. How could Olyslager sleep at night? If a person I knew to be innocent was in prison because of my statements, I could not live with myself. There had to be so much more at stake here than met the eye. I asked God that we all get what we deserve, multiplied.

Shortly thereafter, my father arrived, so Miranda asked him in person to hold off on his media attacks against Olyslager until midnight Monday. My father was not happy. He was obviously not fond of the man in question for what he had done to me, to his grandchildren, to his entire family. Any parent could understand that. So, my father responded, "That man is never going to desist." We were on the same page; we did not expect anything from him, but I asked my father to oblige anyway, even though I knew I was asking him to stop doing the only thing he felt he could to help me.

When Miranda left, I turned to my father and said, "I love you, and I know you have done everything humanly possible to get me out of this place. I could not have ever wished for a more wonderful father than you." I could tell he was distraught. If only I could take away his pain. I cried and he wiped away my tears with his trembling hands. As always, he was my rock.

My father left me with a delicious lunch consisting of two ham and cheese croissants, two mini pizzas, and two fabulous smelling cinnamon rolls. I asked Susana if she wanted to share, and she quickly said yes, so we had lunch in her room. She was happy because Milo had finally reappeared. A woman from maternity had come to tell her that he was hiding in the children's ward. Susana immediately went to look and, sure enough, there he was. She took out the fourteen dollars she had finally offered for his safe return, but the woman refused to take it, a move that was unheard of since everyone needs money in prison. To top it off, fourteen dollars was considered a small fortune; equivalent to washing one hundred pieces of clothing or doing bathroom cleaning duty three times a day for a whole week. Nevertheless, genuinely good people are everywhere, even in prison, as that woman reminded me that day.

While I was with Susana, Carmen came by looking for me. She said that her congregation was planning a little celebration to culminate the forty-day fast, and wanted to know if Rodri's restaurant could give them a quote to cater the event. I gave her Rodri's phone number and they decided on pulled pork sandwiches for sixty people.

I then called Olga at my house because I needed her to send me a purple sweatshirt and a black-and-white scarf to wear to my next hearing. I had been wearing the same pair of pants and shoes to every hearing so far, and frankly, I did not care. I tried to be as elegant and as comfortable as possible, but other than that, I was not going any further to attend this legal process.

Later on, another woman named Claudia, or El Seco, who was one of the inmate callers at the front gates, came looking for me. She needed to ask a favor. I said my usual, "If it is possible, it will be my pleasure."

"I am studying at the prison school, and last year I read and wrote two book reports. The school is now telling me that those two books are missing and that I must either bring them back or replace them with other books. I really need for you to give me two books, so that I may turn those in."

"All the books I get are donations for the new library at Social Services," I explained, "and once I turn them in, those books are no longer at my disposal."

And then I remembered that I still had several books at Serigrafía that the women had been reading, so we headed over there and she chose two. Apparently, Susana is known in prison as "the cat lady" and I'm known as "the book lady."

Later that day, when I called my children, they were not at home. Olga told me they were out with my friend Anabelle and had gone to the movies.

There was something uncomfortable about having six-year-olds and not knowing where they were every second of the day. I called again later and Olga told me the children were entering the house as we spoke. Fabi said that they had gone to the movies with Anabelle, Titan, and Mariela, and then they had gone to eat. He added that he was happy and grateful because he went to the movies, and because he loves Anabelle, and because he had not seen Titan in a long time. Nina was happy too. That was all that mattered: if they were happy, I was happy.

That night, at 10:30 p.m., about thirty minutes after lights-out, my name was called. Startled, I jumped out of my top bunk and went to the encamamiento gate where a guard informed me that I was to be ready at 4 a.m. *What?!* I thought my hearing was on Thursday at 8:10 a.m., and so did everyone else. I called my father and got no answer. I called Miranda and got no answer. I called Rodri and he did answer!

I told him what little I knew, asked him to contact someone, and said I'd call him back in five minutes. That was how long it took me to get everything ready for my newly scheduled hearing in the morning: my clothes, toilet paper, reading glasses, scarf, deodorant, and toothbrush. In the meantime, my roommates were trying to figure it all out as well; could it be an error, from whom, where? Carmen, my unofficial prison attorney, asked the guards to let us see the forms. Thankfully, they were young, nice guards who were happy to help us out. They came back with the list and next to my name it read "Cita Médica/Hospital Roosevelt/7 a.m." OK, so it had nothing to do with my hearing on Thursday. But, a doctor's appointment at the hospital? Why? Carmen said it probably had to do with the doctor from INACIF who had come to see me three weeks earlier. That was outrageous, if it was the case, because I could have died by then! And it was exactly how some inmates actually did die.

There are approximately twenty-two thousand inmates in Guatemala; however, there is no official penitentiary system hospital and the individual prison infirmaries are bare. Our infirmary had no scale, no thermometer, no medicine, not even Band-Aids. There was a nebulizer, a pressure gage, and an ultrasound machine but no paper to print from it. There wasn't even a glucometer to measure sugar levels. In Cellblock One, nurse Lola had her own glucometer and charged inmates $1.40 per measurement so that she could replace the strips and help others.

Furthermore, inmates were not allowed to go to a hospital unless they had a court order, which required a report from an INACIF doctor. It took from fifteen to thirty days for a doctor to arrive to visit a patient, so in case of an emergency, you can imagine the predicament. And to aggravate things further, there had been two recent events that had made it all even worse for inmates. The first involved a bomb thrown at the entrance of the San Juan de Dios Public Hospital, in an attempt to kill an inmate or help him escape (I do not know which). Several bystanders were killed by the bomb. The second event involved an inmate who escaped from the hospital while in police custody. This had resulted in the public hospitals turning away inmates, leaving them with no medical care options.

I understand that society in general is not fond of prisoners, but prisoners are still humans and have rights. Inmates were turned away from public hospitals because the police did not do their jobs properly; inmates escape when the state fails. How was this any other inmate's fault? It was like closing down schools for all children because the teacher failed to teach a couple of them properly. But in a country where not even hardworking, law-abiding citizens get proper healthcare, who could possibly care about getting it to prison inmates?

Suffice it to say, I didn't want to go. Thankfully, Carmen said I had one possible way of getting out of this visit. I could send the warden a note declining my "right" to go to the hospital, and that's exactly what I did. I called my brother and father back to update them on my decision. My father agreed with the plan, even though we weren't sure if it would help. All we could do was try. By 11 p.m. we were all back in our beds, and I could only hope the note would do the trick.

CHAPTER 14

One More Day, One Less Day

When I woke up at 8 a.m. on Wednesday, I realized the note had worked, because no one had come to fetch me to take me to the hospital. Relieved, I started getting ready for possible visitors, and when I was called and went outside, I was delighted to find my former classmates Eddie and Luis Fernando. Looking around, Eddie said, "This place is much worse than I'd imagined." And I reminded him, "And this is the VIP section!" They had all sorts of questions for me, but I was just happy to see and hug them. Spending thirteen years of your life learning and growing with the same classmates makes them your brothers. We have been witnesses to each other's lives; the good, the bad, and the ugly. It felt good to have them there.

Luis Fernando had brought me prayers for a novena. He strongly believes in Saint Jude Thaddeus, patron of difficult and lost causes. "You'll begin reading the novena prayers today and you will finish reading it at home," he said. He had faith that I was leaving this place soon. *May his prayers be answered*, was all I could think at the time, especially having already completed eight full weeks behind bars.

A short while later, Rodri and my father came in. Rodri was carrying pulled pork for my roommates. I helped him and took the food to my room. When I returned, J. P. had arrived—he'd forgotten his ID so he wasn't allowed in earlier—and I found myself surrounded by five wonderful men.

The guys had brought cash for me, in denominations of one, five, ten, and twenty quetzals, which seemed like a small fortune. In prison, even the most honest are forced to become creative, but being devious or sneaky did not come naturally to my loved ones or me, so whatever we tried to do turned into something comical. Since we were out in public, we tried to be cool and place the two ziplock bags stuffed with cash inside the book Luis Fernando had brought for me. However, the book was so small and the two bags were so full that they barely fit inside, and we burst out laughing.

At 11:30 a.m. the bell rang and they had to go. Before he left, Rodri called me aside to let me know that he was not charging my roommates for the food. He asked them to have the congregation say a prayer for our family and for me instead. Carmen confirmed this later, saying, "His beautiful blue eyes became teary as he asked me for the prayers."

Later in the day, as I was starting to give up hope of any female visitors, my name was called. I had a table and four chairs ready because I was expecting Christie and the girls. However, when I came out to the visiting area, I saw Patty waiting for me, all smiles. We hugged tight and sat down. She handed me my favorite ham and cheese croissants and told me our friend Ana Isabel couldn't enter the prison because she had forgotten her ID.

Patty had arrived much earlier, but when she had been searched, the guards told her that she could not bring in her credit cards. She walked out of the prison to give them to Ana Isabel, who was nowhere to be found. However, that wasn't about to stop Patty from seeing me that day. She walked back to the checkpoint and announced assertively that she had been to her car, even though she hadn't, and she walked in still carrying her wallet with the credit cards inside. Just when she thought she was in the clear, she came down the steps and realized there was another checkpoint. She managed to quickly throw her little wallet inside the goody bag after the bag had been searched, but before they searched her once again. And there we were! Meanwhile, Ana Isabel had taken a taxi back to Patty's house where she had left her car, and convinced Patty's housekeeper to let her into the complex so she could get her ID. She then got into her own car and drove back to the prison, joining us twenty minutes later.

Once my visitors were gone, Carmen and I decided to rent the TV and DVD for a full week. Rina also wanted in, and we decided to treat Sandra, since she was very generous and did so many things for us. So thirty-five dollars later, we had reserved our Saturday entertainment. Meanwhile, my roommates were fasting once again, but Sandra made sure that I ate. She served me a perfect, delicious *tamale* with lemon and by 8:30 p.m. I had my Sweet Dreams tea and was looking forward to a good night's sleep before my hearing.

Unfortunately, it was not meant to be. It was a very hot night and I was extremely uncomfortable. I tossed and turned for a long while and must have fallen asleep because at some point I, along with everybody else, was awakened by inmate Maggie from maternity who was screaming at the top of her lungs for the guards. Maggie is the mother of several children on the outside and had a one-year-old son living with her in the prison. I knew she was scheduled for a hearing the next day too. "Guard, guard, nurse!" This went on for quite some time until finally someone responded.

Later that night, we also heard what seemed like very loud drunk women in the infirmary. Since we did not know what was going on, we concluded that maybe Maggie had gotten drunk, or had taken some sort of anxiety pill that did not sit well with her. In the end, there was nothing the rest of us could do, so we turned over and went back to sleep. The following day, we found out that Maggie was fine but had been calling for help because an inmate in maternity had placed Clorox in another inmate's Coke and when she drank it, she started convulsing and throwing up blood. Thank

God that the victim did not share her Coke with her own child! As for the rowdy women, they were in fact drunk or drugged new arrivals, and since new arrivals came in late at night and had to be checked by the nurse, we had to listen to the ruckus. So much for Sweet Dreams.

———

In the early hours of Thursday morning, March 3, I jumped out of bed and rushed to get ready for my hearing. Tona, another inmate from encamamiento, was also going to the courthouse that day. During the three weeks or so that I had been in encamamiento, I had barely spoken to Lili's three roommates. As I said before, we did not socialize much because there was no common area in which to do so. In addition, I had been under the impression that these inmates did not welcome me when I was first transferred there, so I had stayed clear, being pleasant when we ran into each other in a hallway, or entering or leaving the restroom. That morning, when the guard opened our gate at 4:10 a.m., I walked by myself to the prison entrance. Tona arrived moments later and stood right next to me, and that's how our full day of chatting began. I went from assuming she wanted nothing to do with me to realizing we could have a lot of fun together, even during the worst possible day—a day at the courthouse and its carceleta.

There was no police pickup truck to take us separately to the courthouse. There were inmates going to Salamá, Villanueva, and Mixco; there was even an inmate with her ten-month-old baby boy. The perrera was late so we waited for over an hour in the outside holding cell, in the cold, in the dark, in fear of what this day and its judge might bring. Most inmates kept repeating the usual "My Christ will save me," "I trust God has heard my prayers," or "God is merciful." I expected nothing good from the humans involved in this process, and I trusted God would do what He considered best, His will. I did not have to like it, and I would not be angry with Him if today was not the day.

At 7 a.m. we finally reached the courthouse. The guards were ruthless that day. Tona and I were cuffed together on our way from the perrera to the carceleta and we sat together all day, except for when we were taken away for our hearings. By 8:05 a.m. my name was called and I was handcuffed, searched one more time, and then led up to the second floor.

Unfortunately for me, a guard I nicknamed Miss Congeniality found and took my pink lip balm. She looked me in the eye and said, "You cannot take this up. You are going to a hearing, not to put on your makeup." She also said I had to either leave my jacket behind in the carceleta or wear it properly, since I had taken it off and had it hanging over the handcuffs. I tried to put it on, but the sleeves were too narrow and the handcuffs would not go through. My prison guard tried to help me out, and also let me leave my lip gloss with an inmate I had never met before in the carceleta. It was the only solution I could find, other than throwing my coveted lip balm away in the trash can. As it was, the only other things I had brought with me to the courthouse were tissues, and mints. I have read about slaves, kidnappings, and about the Holocaust, so I was fully aware that there were worse situations to live through than mine, but in my personal journey through this life, I had never been treated with less dignity.

When I reached the second floor, I found my mother, sat with her, and quickly asked her to show me pictures of my children on her phone. As I cried at the sight of their beautiful faces, I spotted one of GFP's attorneys chatting away with some woman. I jumped out of my seat, telephone in my cuffed hands, marched over to him, placed the telephone in front of his face, and said, "These are the two wonderful children whom you are keeping away from their mother. You son of a bitch!" And with that, I turned around and walked back to my chair. My guard was so busy on her cell phone that she never noticed I was gone. My mother could not believe what she had just witnessed, and I was happy I had said my piece. I later regretted it just a little, but it had felt sooo good.

When we were called into the courtroom, Miranda told me that the public prosecutor was a no-show. Since I was steadfast with my no expectations rule, I remained calm after receiving this news. I thanked God that I had adopted this attitude of hopelessness because it had kept me sane, and then I thought to myself, *Good thing we rented that TV and DVR for a whole week.* The brain is funny that way!

The hearing proceeded in its official legal mode in which the judge stated the date, time, and case number, took attendance, and stated that the public prosecutor had sent an excuse for not showing up, claiming that he had to attend another hearing at 8:30 a.m. The judge then allowed the attorneys to speak. Miranda stated that having another hearing was not a valid excuse because the Attorney General's Office was *one and indivisible,* which apparently meant that they could and should have sent someone else in his place.

Then, I raised my hand. I think by now the judge found my behavior amusing in a way, so she stopped what she was saying and allowed me to speak. I asked if it would be appropriate to record that the main accuser Olyslager and his attorney were also not present, and had not been present since my first hearing on September 18, 2015. The judge explained to me that the only people required to be at the hearing were the defendant (me) and the public prosecutor. My accuser, his attorneys, the foresters, their attorneys, and so forth, could attend the hearings if they so wished, but none of them were required to be there by law. That was fine, I just wanted the audio to include these facts.

Juan Ignacio Gómez-Cuevas and Julio Roberto García-Merlos García from Mayora & Mayora, representing GFP, had not missed a single hearing; however, since Olyslager had by then been repaid through the sale of the farm he held as guarantee, he seemed to be done with me.

I hope that someday anyone who wants to know the truth about how the justice system works in Guatemala may be able to listen to the court recording themselves. I dream about my case being studied at the university as an example of how this system and a false statement can be used by powerful attorneys to keep an innocent person in prison.

In any event, minutes into the hearing, it was over. For me, that meant a twelve-hour plus ordeal in exchange for a couple of minutes that achieved absolutely nothing.

On our way out of the courtroom, Miranda said he was very upset because he had been negotiating with Olyslager and his attorneys regarding their withdrawal of the accusation, and they had suddenly cut off all communications with him. Miranda claimed it was because my father continued to attack them on Facebook. I told Miranda that I did not have access to the Internet, so I did not know what he was referring to. If he had a problem, he had to talk to my father. "You're stressing me out, my nerves are shot, and if anyone should be having any sort of fit it should be me, the one person who has spent more than fifty days locked up in a prison, the one person whose hearing was just canceled, *again,* the one person who has not seen her children in two months!"

When we reached the hallway, I gave my loved ones the news, and they were once again astounded and frustrated. Someone immediately messaged Sylvia Gereda to give her the update. The television program had already been edited, but they might still be able to include this last-minute information at the end of the show.

I remained with my loved ones for a while, courtesy of my guard, so Miranda took advantage of the opportunity to talk to all of us together. He wanted to know if we could give Olyslager a truce until Tuesday regarding the media attacks, so that he could try to get him to desist.

I asked Rodri to show me my father's posts on "Justicia para Anaité," since this issue kept coming up and I had not read them, and Miranda himself had no Facebook account. Frankly, what I read seemed accurate to me. What they considered attacks were simply the facts about the case. So, I reiterated my stance, "If Olyslager wanted to even try and do the right thing, he would have done so by now. He has been talking about it for weeks. Why is he so scared of the truth? I do not believe a word he says."

Rodri chimed in, saying he'd give Olyslager until Friday, but my mother quickly responded, "This is Anaité's decision," which silenced my brother and made him take a few steps back to gather himself. But that wasn't going to stop my father who said to my mother, "You may be able to reprimand Rodrigo, but you are not telling me what to do." The situation was out of control! It had gotten the best of all of us. Miranda then said he would do as we wished, but that his job was to get me out of this and he needed Olyslager to desist to give me a better chance with the judge. Miranda's frustration was evident, but he apologized for losing his cool. I understood; he was only human, just like the rest of us.

Once we had all calmed down, Miranda added that he had just had a meeting with the judge and she had asked him several questions regarding the case. Miranda answered accordingly and even showed her where the relevant information and evidence was. He claimed that the judge finally understood and there was a good possibility that I would be going home on Tuesday, which was the rescheduled hearing date. "I've heard this speech before, and I am still hopelessly in prison," I reminded Miranda. I could not believe anyone anymore.

By around 9 a.m., my guard informed me that it was time to go, so I said my goodbyes and was taken back to the carceleta. Miss Congeniality searched me again. Once inside, the woman I entrusted with my lip balm gave it back to me before I even asked, and I sat down next to Tona, hoping that our conversation would make the long ride back to the prison go by a little faster than usual.

Tona considered herself a devout Christian, so we talked for hours about how each of us viewed God and our relationship to Him, and the Bible. She would later tell me that that day was the best time she had ever spent in the carceleta, and I agreed.

As we continued chatting, she told me her husband had committed suicide while they were alone in their home. The ambulance arrived, along with law enforcement and a forensic doctor. It was determined that the official cause of death was suicide, a single gunshot to the right temple, and that he had been standing at the time the trigger was pulled. Nevertheless, nine months later, the Attorney General's Office and the deceased's family accused her of murdering her husband, and she had so far spent nine months in Santa Teresa. This was despite the fact that she had presented ballistics reports concluding that her husband had a ring on his temple consistent with the gun being shot at extremely close range and that the bullet's trajectory was consistent with a self-inflicted wound, indicating that he was standing at the time rather than lying down in a defenseless position (drunk, drugged, or sleeping), and her fingerprints were not on the weapon. The public prosecutor claimed she had murdered him, saying there were people who would attest that she was a very jealous woman, and that he was certainly not suicidal. That day, after her hearing, she told me that the judge had stuck to his original decision, which he'd made after her first hearing: she was going to trial.

I share these stories, although they reflect only one side of the picture, because they are omnipresent, and because something similar is happening to me. We all come up with a million reasons why this could never happen to us, and I suppose those thoughts make us feel safe, but are we sure that this could never happen to us, to our mothers, our sisters, our daughters? There are plenty of inmates in prison who accept that they are guilty, but not everyone in prison is. Judges, like inquisitors from the 1500s, judge according to their personal beliefs and their personal and political agendas. Are we capable of perceiving an injustice even when we do not know all the details? Are we at peace claiming that we are not attorneys and therefore we do not understand? Not all judges hold the same power, and I believe many would like to support the search for the truth, but are too afraid given the current political climate, which only means more innocent people thrown behind bars without any concrete evidence to prove they are guilty.

———

On Friday at 8 a.m., I called my father and reminded him that it was encomienda day and I wanted to change my bedsheets and towel. He hadn't planned on stopping by Santa Teresa because he had a meeting, but he promised he'd call Olga and go by my house. Meanwhile, my first encomienda was from Christie, Tina, and Karla María. My entire being changed when I saw them. Before our five minutes were up, they assured me that my children were well taken care of, and that they were already planning time at the beach, at the farm, and in Antigua, Guatemala, so that we could spend time together and recover as best we could from this experience once I was free. I had no doubt that I would survive this experience, but completely recover? Impossible. Being thrown in jail has taken so much away from me and taught me so much, that I know I will never be the same again. I can only hope that the Anaité that emerges from this storm is a much better one.

When my friends left, I went to the preschool to see the children. They were getting ready to use their scissors to cut magazines. As soon as they saw me, they jumped out of their seats and began pleading for a book to read, so I happily obliged.

The next encomienda came from Gaby. I saw her smiling face and a bouquet of beautiful yellow flowers in her hands. It never occurred to me that flowers would be so lovely in prison. Leave it to my generous, creative, wonderful sister to think of that, and leave it to my roommate Sandra to create a vase out of an empty iced tea bottle. The flowers brought joy and smelled fabulous in our room. As she handed me the flowers, I asked Gaby, "Did you hear about what I did and said yesterday?" I was referring to my emotional outburst with the GFP's attorney. "Yes," she said, "we all know what you did, and even Papa said he was glad you did it!"

After my sister left, I still expected my father, but he was nowhere to be found. He later explained that he had reached the prison at 11:40 a.m., but since encomienda had ended at 11:30 a.m. and he had forgotten his special pass, he wasn't allowed through. Thank God for that pass; it made a huge difference in our lives during such a troublesome time.

In the evening, I called my house and spoke to my children. My heart broke when Nina asked me in her tiny sweet voice when I was returning home. "It will probably be a while because I still have things to do here." Up until then, my children had been sheltered and still did not know where I was. All they knew was that I was away for work. Those two wonderful children have been champs through all this, and I thank God for my mother who has been with them every step of the way. As they say in Santa Teresa, "One more day at Santa Teresa, one day closer to going home."

———

My father arrived on Saturday with my bedsheets and my towel. He had received the agreement Olyslager wanted him to sign, in which my father would agree to stop his "media attacks" in exchange for Olyslager withdrawing his claims against me. I did not want him to sign it, but I understood that by doing so the game could begin to change, and with it, so could my opportunities to regain my freedom and start a new chapter in my life. As the saying goes, "Where there's a will, there's a way," I just wasn't sure what the right way was. Giving Olyslager anything at all turned my stomach upside down.

Back at our accommodations, we had been hit by the dreaded prison plague: bedbugs! My roommates were constantly cleaning and searching for these little creatures, whose small, annoying bites leave huge bumps on the skin that itch for weeks, and scar the skin forever. Carmen was cleaning through her belongings, which were stowed under the bed, when she found one there, and that's how I had the misfortune of finally seeing one. They look like small cockroaches with hard shells, and when squashed to death they stink like rancid peanuts. I had been spared their attacks so far and was very glad that my roommates were all phobic about bedbugs and were constantly vigilant.

Meanwhile, Susana had been worried about the safety of her three cats. A couple of days earlier, one of the inmate mothers reproached her because she claimed that one of Susana's cats had eaten two pounds of chicken that she had left on the kitchen counter. Another time, the woman claimed the cat had eaten her sour cream. Susana had told this woman that she had to be more careful with her food, because there were many cats in this prison. She refused to compensate the woman for her loss, not so much because of the monetary cost of the lost food, but because by compensating one woman, she would possibly set a precedent and constantly have to pay for alleged lost food. To top it off, that morning, I overheard someone say that another woman in the ex-Mara 18 sector (Susana's closest neighbors) was upset because one of Susana's cats had messed with her raffia yarn. Susana was right to fear for their lives.

By early afternoon, our TV/DVD combo had arrived and we decided to watch *Homeland*. I was worried that Sandra and Rina might not enjoy this series because it was only available in English with Spanish subtitles, but to my surprise, they loved it, so the rest of our day turned into a *Homeland* marathon.

I did not call my children that day, not only because I was lost in our series marathon, but every time I thought of Nina's voice asking me when I was coming home, sadness invaded my heart, and I just couldn't take it. I did not have the energy to pretend otherwise, not even for the few minutes it would take to hear their tiny voices. I needed to gather more strength.

Later that day, Verónica came to tell me that after days of having a premonition, her sister had unexpectedly broken both her legs. There had been no accident, no injury, and no other apparent reason. This was the sister who made a modest living by selling fruit to take care of her six children, including a two-month-old baby girl, and Verónica's two children. So now, with a cast on each leg, she had to figure out how to survive and look after the eight children in her care. The older kids helped her as much as they could, but when they went to school, she stayed home with the three little ones and dragged herself on the floor to use the bathroom. Tears rolled down Verónica's face as she told me that she needed to get out of this place. *Impotence.* All I could do was listen and hold her hands tightly through the barred window.

———

At 9:30 a.m. on Sunday, I walked out to meet Rodri, who was furious because he had been outside the prison since 7 a.m. waiting to be let in. The prison system steals at least one hour out of every cherished visit. My father came in next and we talked about the case and my options.

"Will you be signing the agreement with Olyslager?" I asked him.

"We are meeting Monday at 4:30 p.m." he responded.

"Will that allow his 'cease and desist' to be presented before my hearing Tuesday morning?"

"Yes," he said, "but the fact that the court already knows that he has been paid by the sale of the farm he held as guarantee, makes it all official anyway."

I asked him why the cease and desist agreement was even still relevant, and he said that it could make a big difference in the eyes of the judge. Evidence didn't seem to matter much to my judge, unless it came from the Attorney General's Office. *Maybe she will surprise me this time.* My father and brother also told me that my dear Koko would serve as my accuser's trusted liaison and witness to his signature of the document. Koko is Picus's older brother, his parents are my godparents, and my mother and father are his godparents. We grew up together and he is like a brother to me. He also knows Miranda and Olyslager, and this was how Koko found himself in the middle of this mess. My father and Rodrigo told me that they were unhappy with Koko because they had called him on several occasions, but had not been able to reach him. This broke my heart because they were feeling this way about one of the most wonderful people I know. I asked them to reserve judgment until we knew the facts.

On Monday morning, Miranda confirmed my suspicions. It seemed that Olyslager did not want to meet face-to-face with my father, so Koko would act as liaison. I could not blame Olyslager. Coming face-to-face with the father of the woman he had harmed in this way had to pose a problem. Olyslager and his accusations were the reason why I had spent two months and counting in prison, and the reason why my children were without their mother. Olyslager did not do this to me alone; he had done this to my entire family and my beloved friends.

My father and brother left, and since I wasn't expecting any other visitors that afternoon, I was surprised to hear my name called again. When I went out, I found Tita and Auri waiting for me. Tita was my children's nanny for four years and she loved and took care of them as if they were her own. When I was no longer able to pay her, she had stayed with us for another full month without pay. She claimed she wanted to stay because she was not ready to leave my children. The day she left, my home became one of the saddest places I can remember. She had been a constant part of our family and my children did not know life without their Tita.

Auri was my cook for eight years. She did not live with us, but was another angel in our daily lives. When the financial bomb exploded in our household, I was forced to let her go. She had found work with my neighbor and I felt lucky to still have her close by.

We gave one another a long and tight group hug. I knew that my predicament had hurt them and that I had been in their prayers, but seeing them there in the flesh filled me with joy. I could only imagine what it had taken for them to come to Santa Teresa that day, on a Sunday, their rest day, their family day, with the financial cost the travel presented and the time involved in coming from their homes, which were so far away. But there they were, making sure, once again, that I was alright. I had always known these two women were precious beings, and that day those thoughts were confirmed.

Once we were locked in our room for the night, Carmen chose her outfit, flat-ironed her hair, and started preparing for the following day's hearing. The rest of us supported her, got our "no wine/yes cheese" party rolling, and finished watching the rest of *Homeland*. When the clock struck 8 p.m., I thought about my loved ones and how they were all likely glued to the TV watching the Sylvia Gereda show on Canal Antigua. I could only hope the program would help the truth come to light.

———

Carmen was up at 3 a.m. and went about getting ready for her hearing. By 4:20 a.m. we blessed her and prayed that God be with her. She had been very nervous and afraid, but as of last night, her demeanor had changed. After being locked up for months, it was now time for war. The waiting was over and she was ready.

At 8 a.m. I abruptly opened my eyes, and Rina and I turned on the TV to Channel 7. We tuned the signal as best we could with the wire antenna we had been given, which gave us 60 percent visibility on the screen, but we could listen clearly. We watched Carmen's case take its course while we drank our coffee and had breakfast. The hearing was still on live while we deep-cleaned our room; Sandra found several more bedbugs. We continued watching through lunch.

I interrupted our viewing when my father arrived bearing pork chops. He was very positive about my hearing the following day. Truth be told, for the first time, I was quite positive about it too. Then Miranda came to see me and explained what the process would be the next day. Although none of the logical evidence or explanations we had presented so far had made any difference to the judge, some things had changed: social and media pressures were on, the Sylvia Gereda show had aired, and my original accuser was somewhat out of the equation since he had been paid by GFP when they bought the farm back from him. There seemed to be a glimmer of hope on the horizon.

At 7 p.m. I called my mother and Fabi got on the phone and told me that he had gone to tennis class that day, but that Nina had not gone because she had been taken to the hospital. I asked Fabi to put my mother on the phone again, and she told me that Nina and Fabi had been fighting in the car, using the middle seatbelt. At some point, Fabi had hit Nina on the forehead with the seatbelt buckle and her head had started bleeding. They rushed her to the hospital, and twelve stitches later, she was sent home. I asked my mother if she had used the medical insurance and she told me that my friends Dr. Eddie and Dr. Pepe had taken care of everything. Angels, angels, and more angels. I had been quite calm regarding my children's well-being, but this news made me more anxious than ever to go home. How could my child be hurt and I not be there with her? In that moment, I could not help feeling hate for those who put me there. To top it off, Fabi asked me when I would be coming home, to which I answered, "I'll be coming home as soon as I finish what I am doing here."

"But what are you doing there?" he asked.

"I am teaching English, and reading to the children, and starting a new library," I said.

"Well, maybe you can come home during the school vacation," he said.

"That sounds like a wonderful idea. I will let you know as soon as I know, my love," I said, my heart shattering into a million pieces.

———

On Tuesday, March 8, I hopped out of my bed and did my five-minute get-ready routine, while Carmen wrapped up her hour of prep time. It was hearing day for both of us. By 4:30 a.m. we were taken through the process to exit the prison, but that morning it all seemed particularly chaotic.

Apparently, the guards had failed to notify some inmates the night before about their hearings, which meant they were left scrambling to get ready for one of the most important meetings of their lives with only a moment's notice. This likely happened because their attorneys never showed up or rarely contacted them. For some inmates, months and even years go by without news about their legal situations and progress. At one point, a guard at the prison gates kept calling an inmate's name, while her friends kept telling him that she was ready to go, but was still locked inside her cellblock. This was an indication of the IQ level of many of the people in charge of our lives and our process to become free.

Finally, the women who would be traveling in the perrera were called and taken to the holding cell. Carmen, Celeste, another young woman, and I were handcuffed, taken up the stairs separately from the other inmates, and ultimately told to sit in the wet, muddy flatbed of a pickup truck. Sitting on the sides of the flatbed were eight fully armed guards. I covered my head with my scarf for the ride to the courthouse. We arrived so early that there were no courthouse guards there to welcome us, so we had to wait for almost twenty minutes before they arrived for their shift and proceeded to search us. We walked down the ramp, filed past the men's carceletas, and waited another twenty minutes before another guard unlocked the carceleta gate. By then, the other inmates had arrived as well. I sat on the now familiar concrete bench and this time met Miriam, a young woman sitting next to me who began to tell me her story.

Miriam was twenty-two years old and had a five-year-old girl and a one-year-old son. When she was fourteen, she killed two people and was never caught. She'd never been involved in gangs before, but knew about them. It was not until her mother was being evicted from their rental home for failing to pay rent that Miriam went to the gangs, asking for a quick, good paying job to help her mother. She got the job, continued doing jobs for this gang, and eventually joined them. The official welcome into the gang involved eighteen members beating her half to death. Eventually, she got pregnant, but she was no longer with the father of her children because he beat her too much. She currently had another boyfriend and a girlfriend. She preferred the girlfriend, but the boyfriend provided for her. She claimed that the gang members respected her because she had been the woman of one of the gang leaders.

As I heard her story, I continued to be amazed at how nice a murderer could seem. My mind battled between anger and sadness when I thought of the victims and their families, and then shock at finding out that a murderer had a good side as well. But what about the damage caused by our decisions? How can that ever be fixed? Justice seems to be nothing but a meager best-case scenario, the best humanity can do to fix the unfixable.

At 8 a.m. I was handcuffed and taken up to my hearing. The court-house guards seemed to get worse with every visit. This time, I even had to put my bra back in its proper place after they searched me. Once up on the second floor, I barely got to see my mother and my friend Stephie. The attorneys and I were called into the courtroom, and once again, we were informed that the public prosecutor was a no-show. Eventually, he came in late, claiming that he had another hearing at 9 a.m. and asking the judge to postpone my hearing because the Attorney General's Office was short on personnel. The judge told him that there would be no postponing this hearing, so he then requested a fifteen-minute recess to make arrangements, and the judge gave him until 10:30 a.m. I was led out of the courtroom, passed my enquiring loved ones, and was taken back to the carceleta to wait another couple of hours. That was when I met Isabella, another inmate anxious to share her prison story.

Isabella was thirty-four years old, and lived in Guatemala City's Zone 7 but her family was from a faraway place called Quiché. Her broken Spanish confirmed her indigenous background. She had twenty siblings and nine children of her own, including three sets of twins. Her first husband had been murdered. The man she recently lived with, the father of her youngest child, hid drugs in her home and when the police came and searched the premises, they arrested them both. She was pregnant with triplets when her sisters-in-law beat her severely. And so, when she landed in prison, five months pregnant and black and blue, she was rushed to the hospital, where she miscarried. Her own family had warned her and asked her not to be with that man, and now they wanted nothing to do with her. She had no idea where her children were or how they were doing.

As I digested this new story, I was called back to my hearing. The public prosecutor spent the better part of the next three hours reading the entire list of accusations against me. I had yet to get used to hearing my name followed by all sorts of terrible statements. It was almost impossible to listen and not jump out of my seat to immediately defend myself. My best option was to try and go numb. At 1:30 p.m. the judge announced a one-hour lunch break, and I immediately chimed in and asked the judge to grant my family permission to send down some food for me, which she did.

At 2:30 p.m. the hearing began once again. It was now time for Miranda to counter and defend me. He was very thorough and proceeded point by point, making it clear every step of the way that I had had nothing to do with the purported actions of my husband or his accountant. It could not have been made any clearer, but it was already 4 p.m., so the judge ended the hearing. She stated that she needed twenty-four hours to review the entire case because, according to her, it was very complicated and extensive. We were to reconvene the next day at 1:30 p.m., at which time she would give us her decision.

By the time we came out to the waiting area, only my mother, father, Rodri, Gaby, and her two girlfriends were still there—the group had been larger earlier in the day and I will never forget all the people who showed up to every one of those hearings. They were there to support me during one of the lowest points of my life. I said my quick goodbyes and was once again escorted away.

The police car was waiting outside the courthouse. I got in the flatbed and the guard told me to hop inside on the back seat instead. Celeste was already there and we were only waiting for Carmen to finish up her hearing. The perrera with the other inmates was loaded, locked, and ready to go. When Carmen came down, I moved over and the four of us (three inmates and one guard) sat in the back seat. It was terribly uncomfortable, but it was much better than the flatbed.

Carmen informed us that her hearing had been cut short because a public prosecutor had accused the defense attorney of tampering with an evidence seal. Enraged, the defense attorney began defending himself, but then suddenly repeated several times for all to hear, that he was not feeling well, and he was therefore excusing himself. On his way out of the courtroom, he fainted and fell to the floor. As we were preparing to exit the courthouse's outdoor parking lot, we saw the ambulance drive by.

That whole fainting incident got me thinking about how easily attorneys ask clients to remain calm while they are being accused of terrible crimes, being lied about, misconstrued, and destroyed in court. However, when the tables were turned and this attorney was the one on the receiving end of an accusation, he couldn't handle it and fainted!

Back in Santa Teresa, Sandra was waiting for us. She had prepared iced tea and spaghetti with capers, tomatoes, and chicken. I ate, showered, and got ready for bed. I wanted to lose myself in a DVD series, but all my roommates could talk about was Carmen's case, because they had watched the proceedings live on TV all day. I just wanted to rest, so I could be ready for the following day. Before going to sleep, I went by Susana's room to tell her the news. "I truly hope that you go home soon, but I've become very fond of you and will miss you," she said.

"I feel the same way about you," I replied, and added, "While I wonder if I will go home soon, I keep thinking of my worst-case scenario, and thanks to wonderful people like you, this place has not been as bad as it could have been." We hugged and cried.

Chapter 15

Freedom

Week 10

On Wednesday, March 9, 2016, at 4:30 a.m., I was at the front gates ready and waiting. However, by the time all the inmates were in the outdoor holding cell, waiting to go to the courthouse, a guard informed us that nobody would be taken that day because the prison system had no support from the PNC. I told the guard that I did not have to travel in a police car, that I was perfectly fine traveling in the perrera, but he informed me that the perrera was not going either. What in the world was going on? By 5 a.m., we were told to return to our cellblocks. I called my father and let him know, then got back into my pajamas and read for a little while before falling back to sleep.

When I woke up, my roommates were intensely watching the morning news. Sandra made oatmeal and shared some with me. By 10 a.m. I called my father again and asked him if he had spoken to Miranda and if there was any news. He told me that he had misunderstood. He had thought that I had not been taken to the courthouse but would be taken later on. "No inmates are being transferred today," I explained, to which he quickly replied, "Please call me back in a few minutes," and hung up. When I called him back, he said, "It turns out you do not have to be physically present at your hearing today, so it will be held without you. Call me back at 4 p.m."

In the meantime, I had lunch with Susana, taught Daniela an English lesson, and went outside to write in my diary. I was very nervous knowing that my fate was being decided without me present, but I tried not to think about it behind bars. Finally, I gathered the courage to call my father back, and in the end, the judge had said she wanted me present when she gave her statement, therefore, the hearing had been moved to the following day. Another day, another postponed hearing. My father also said that one of Gaby's friends had walked behind the two Mayora & Mayora attorneys and had overheard one of them say that it was going to be very difficult to keep me in prison. My father then added, "You should pack your belongings because you're coming home tomorrow." I wished I was as sure as he was.

Since I did not speak to my children the previous day, I mustered up the courage to call them that evening; it was great to hear their voices, yet every day that passed it was harder and harder to be away from them.

———

On Thursday, March 10, 2016, my sixty-fifth day in prison, I woke up, jumped out of my top bunk, and got ready for yet another hearing, but when I reached the outdoor holding area, there was a new transportation drama in the air. Two women who had been waiting for four months to be taken to a hospital were returned to their cells. The women traveling to hearings in Mixco, Villanueva, and Escuintla were also sent back to their cellblocks. That left close to twenty women going to the courthouse, with only one available vehicle to transfer all of us, so there would have to be several trips.

The first five inmates to go to the courthouse were called, and they included Carmen and Mari Ro. An hour later, the vehicle returned and was ready to take the second group of nine prisoners, which included me. We were led to a gray, unmarked pickup truck and told to climb aboard. My hands were handcuffed together, as opposed to having one hand handcuffed to another inmate, which made it more difficult to climb into the flatbed, but I managed, as I had managed to adapt to all the new experiences thrown my way during those sixty-five days in jail.

By the time we left Santa Teresa, it was light out. We were traveling with four armed guards in the flatbed with us, while the rest of them squeezed inside the double cab. I climbed into the flatbed first, so I sat with my back leaning against the exterior of the truck's cab. We were packed like sardines, just not as orderly. There was dense traffic on the streets by then, and we had no sirens or police escort to help us navigate, so the trip felt eternally long. Several inmates enjoyed themselves as they yelled out their usual flirty remarks. "The one in the blue shirt, you are gorgeous!" "See you tonight. I'll be in Santa, Cellblock Three!" We went through city Zones 18, 6, and 1.

Many of the inmates recognized acquaintances walking down the street; some inmates hid, while others said hello. Most of us were tired and nervous, going through the fight of our lives, but each one reacted differently to this extremely stressful situation: some were quiet while others resorted to laughter. I was one of the quiet ones, but seeing others laugh in the face of adversity helped lighten the mood, and eventually, even the sourest of guards had to smile because of the things these women said out loud. On the opposite end of the tiny flatbed, was a small, thin, green-eyed woman who smiled at me every time the young women cracked a joke. It was amazing to me how many different ways human bonding can occur under such circumstances.

After what seemed like an eternity, along with all the aches and pains caused by such a journey, we reached the courthouse and were practically pried out of the flatbed, many of our limbs numb from the trip. Even though we were thoroughly searched, one inmate had once again managed to sneak in marijuana and went into the door-less bathroom to smoke it.

She claimed she needed to relax and calm her nerves before her hearing. If there had ever been a time when I could have used those effects myself, it would have been that day, but it has never been my style.

At around 7 a.m., the green-eyed woman eventually grabbed a spot on the cement bench next to me and we started to chat. She had worked for many years for a man I knew of and she could not say enough good things about him, his wife, and their sons. She told me that she had been in Santa Teresa for thirty days now. She had a loving husband, an eight-year-old daughter, and a good job at a pharmacy, but was sent to preventive detention because her former employer had accused her of stealing $820 and a gun from his office. It had all come as a surprise to her. When I asked who could have taken the money and the weapon, she said that her employer had a son who did drugs and a brother whom the employer himself did not trust. They had videos of her opening drawers at the office, but she was the office manager and was expected to handle those drawers. In none of the videos was she handling cash or any sort of weapon, and yet . . . you guessed it: she was in prison. She worried about her current job, about her daughter, about the money her bail and her defense was costing her family . . . the usual nightmares we all faced under these horrible circumstances.

Our conversation was cut short when my name was called. We wished each other good luck, and as I left the holding cell I noticed Miss Congeniality was on duty again. I had my lip balm in my hair bun and my jacket was once again hanging over my handcuffs, so I was expecting trouble, but to my surprise, she searched me lightly and let me through. I climbed the four sets of stairs that led from the basement to the second floor of the courthouse, followed by the two guards assigned to me that morning. My hearing was still twenty-five minutes away, so it looked like I would have some time to spend with my loved ones—that alone was worth the entire morning's hassle. The first one there, as always, was my mother. Slowly but surely, the rest of my team arrived: my father, Rodri, Carlos, Gaby, Pamela, Nathalie, Karla, Annie, Lucía, Karen, Lore, Nena, Chiqui,

Chachi, Claudia, Melly . . . my unconditional liberation army. Meanwhile, Anamaría called me from home and Christie, Kali, and their mother, Lili, called me from New York.

When the time came to go into the courtroom, I did so with my usual "They are not giving me any good news" attitude; however, I was fully aware of the importance of that day's hearing, and my nerves got the best of me. As soon as the judge started talking, my heart began pounding and racing so hard that I felt I needed to hold it inside my chest with my two handcuffed hands. My hands would remain there for the rest of the hearing, trying to keep my heart from popping out or, God forbid, from stopping once and for all. As far as my brain in its current fog could understand, the judge said no to the pretrial motions and no to dismissal or acquittal. Two out of my three opportunities had been denied. The judge kept talking but I could not absorb most of what she said.

Finally, her words caught my attention and my heart skipped a beat. I quickly turned to Miranda, simply gestured thumbs up and thumbs down, to which he answered with a thumbs up! *"You are going home!"* he said to my disbelieving ears. However, the good news was followed by two new dates set by the court: September 12 and September 28, 2016. Yes, the judge had set me free, but she was giving the Attorney General's Office *six more months* to present the specific evidence that Miranda had requested, claiming that the Attorney General's Office had not conducted a thorough and impartial investigation on my case by not presenting these specific documents.

I later understood that the judge had ordered provisional closure of my case, which meant that she had found that the current evidence, or lack thereof, presented by the Attorney General's Office, GFP, and Olyslager was insufficient to merit the opening of a trial against me, and I should therefore be set free immediately. Unfortunately, it also meant that my innocence was not yet proven either, so specific documents were ordered by the judge to be presented to her by the attorney general on September

12, 2016. All the evidence to be presented was specifically requested by Miranda and it all proved my innocence.

Nevertheless, I was finally going to become a free citizen once again. A free citizen who had spent sixty-five days behind bars just to be told that there was no evidence against her, who was needlessly separated from her children, who had to pay for her legal defense, who had lost her employment because of these accusations, and who had her reputation irreversibly tarnished. And all this after my original judge, Jisela Reinoso Trujillo, had sent me home to my children on my own recognizance back in September 2015. Justice is not blind, it is human.

I still did not understand what it was that Olyslager, his attorney Frank Trujillo, GFP, and their legal counsel Mayora & Mayora had gained from throwing me in jail for sixty-five days. Furthermore, even after the judge had announced that I was to be set free because they had not presented enough evidence to warrant a trial against me, this ordeal was not yet over. My emotions were all over the place, but I decided to focus on the positive: God willing, that night, I would smell, feel, hold, kiss, embrace, and love my children in person again—those two precious and innocent children who never deserved any of this.

The judge left the courtroom; before I left, I looked attorney Julio Roberto García-Merlos García straight in the eye and said, "My family and friends are out there just in case you want to apologize for everything you have put them through."

"They should apologize to us for what they have said about us!" he arrogantly replied.

"You know exactly what you have done to me. Scoundrels!" I said, and then turned around and left the room handcuffed, followed by my two armed escorts. As I walked into the short hallway leading to the waiting area, I saw my support team anxiously waiting to hear the news. They had not seen me yet when I screamed, "I am going home!" And they exploded! They cheered, they yelled, they came to me, they hugged me. I tried to break down what had happened in there as best as I could, but it did not matter. We were all elated! Rodri, Gaby, and two of her friends were two floors down at the cafeteria when they heard the commotion, so they dropped everything and ran up to join the celebration. We even managed to take some pictures, handcuffs and all. I was going home . . .

Back down in the basement, I walked into the carceleta, heard the gate lock behind me, took a seat on the bench, and cried. Other inmates usually asked returning inmates how things had gone, but today, maybe because of the tears rolling down my cheeks, nobody said a word. This was perfect because I could not imagine telling other prisoners that I was going home while they had to stay in prison. This was a very personal decision. Most inmates would let us all know joyfully that that day was their freedom day, and we would be happy to hear it. Even when the freed inmate was a stranger, it gave the rest of us hope that one day that could be us. But I just sat there in silence.

Not long after, the green-eyed woman returned from her hearing and sat next to me. "How did it go?" I whispered.

"I will be leaving soon, God willing," she whispered back, explaining that her husband had finally managed to get the $1,370 for her bail, had paid it, and it looked like she would be going home that same day.

"So am I!" I said quietly, as I let it all sink in. Neither one of us wanted to share it publicly yet. Other inmates returned from their hearings sobbing because they'd been convicted, so being openly happy among them about going home was like celebrating at a funeral.

At around noon, the guards informed us that they would be making the first inmate transport back to Santa Teresa, moving the first eight inmates who were finished at the courthouse for the day, which included the woman with the green eyes and me. Once again, and for what I hoped would be the last time, I was handcuffed and I climbed into the back of the pickup truck. When Mari Ro sat next to me and asked how my hearing had gone, I had to share my news. "I'm going home," I said. God willing, she would be going home soon too.

We rode back to Santa Teresa like sardines in the sun for all the world to see one more time, but I did not care. All I could think of was the possibility of seeing my children that night. Other inmates were still in the middle of this heart-wrenching process, and yet others were coming back to Santa Teresa convicted, knowing it may be a very long time before they ever saw these streets again. After what I had experienced, I could only hope that their sentences were fair. I didn't believe in anything anymore. What I do know for sure is that only an innocent person asks God to let the truth come out. Everyone else just wants their story to fit any way possible, as long as it is for their own benefit.

Back in Santa, we jumped off the truck and were uncuffed. As we walked back to our cellblocks, I said to Mari Ro, "I will be waiting for you on the outside. We cannot allow this experience to be in vain. I'm still not sure what I'm going to do with my life now, but I know that all this learning and growing has to serve a better, greater purpose."

"Amen," she said, and we hugged and went our separate ways . . . for the time being.

I stopped by Serigrafía to share my news; the women were all happy for me! Daniela was happy too, but then quickly became sad and frankly, I did too. It's not that I was going to miss that place, the rules, the food, the head counts, but I would miss the people in it. I had been blessed with meeting and sharing my harrowing experience with wonderful women who had my back, and I will never forget that.

After leaving Serigrafía, I walked over to Susana's room and told her the news, then headed to encamamiento and told Sandra and Rina. We all hugged. Lili came in to ask how my hearing had gone and when she heard, she hugged me too, sharing that she hoped to finally be out in a month or so. I was calmer than I would've expected; I suppose I still could not believe it fully. I had spent sixty-five days wondering what that day would be like, and now it had arrived.

Meanwhile, I wanted to let Verónica know, but she was at school until 4:30 p.m. and would then have to go straight back to Cellblock One for lockdown, so I wouldn't have the chance to see her. I asked nurse Lola to let her know that she should come find me quickly, as soon as she was let out of class, but Verónica never made it; however, she did manage to send me a beautiful goodbye letter.

After sharing my news with everyone I cared for, I went back to my room to organize my possessions. I did not have many belongings to begin with, but I could only take home what I could carry out of prison. The tradition was to leave the rest for the inmates of your choosing. So I started going through my things and made separate piles: Daniela would receive my blanket, shampoo, and conditioner; Sandra would get my guacalito, soap, two plastic baskets, my bathroom basket with everything in it, some books, and an unused calling card to call her three-year-old son; Rina would get a Catholic psalms book; Verónica would receive a backpack, food, goodies, a pencil case full of crayons, two plastic storage boxes, a notebook, and my pillow, since Rodri was never authorized to bring one in for her; Pichi at Serigrafía would get the mandala coloring book; and Maritza would get a large pencil case full of stuff. Then I packed two large bags with my clothes, bedsheets, towel, letters, and anything else of importance that I could carry out of there.

Everything that I left behind for my fellow inmates contained a personal letter just for them. I did not have gifts for everyone, but I made sure I said goodbye to each and every woman that I had access to that day. I told Alina that she once scared me because she would not acknowledge my presence, but that all that had changed the moment she and Martina had taken me into their room, when nobody else seemed willing to. I will always be grateful for that. There were so many women with whom I shared a moment of joy or sadness, that I was unable to thank them all. I can only hope they received from me as much as I did from them.

While I concentrated on organizing everything, the women kept asking me why I was not elated. Good question. I concluded that, after all I had been through, I just couldn't allow myself to trust the justice system at all, so I didn't feel I could or should celebrate and let my emotional guard down just yet. It was easy to imagine a guard or some other official arriving at our gate at the last minute to tell me that I could not go home because there was a missing seal of some sort, because the paperwork did not arrive, because there was a missing dot on an "i," or because the person in charge was not available. I would believe it when I stepped out of Santa Teresa a free woman. A big part of my heart had been locked up in safekeeping for sixty-five days in order to survive my time away from my children. I was afraid that if I brought down the walls too soon, my heart would stop and I wouldn't make it out alive.

It would soon be time for lockdown, so Susana came to my gate to chat one last time. Eventually, Carmen came back from her full day of hearings at the courthouse. She had made headlines that day because as an attorney, she was able to question one of her accusers in court. That was important because defendants don't usually do such a thing, but since Carmen had not given up her right to her own defense, she was allowed to do so, on live television, and apparently, she had done a great job. As she walked into Santa Teresa, she felt empowered and at peace. I could only wish her strength and good luck in this process, and prayed that she would go home to her family soon.

Finally, at 9 p.m. my name was called. My heart pounded. I quickly removed the sheets from my bed since I had refused to do so earlier, just in case my freedom did not come as promised, hugged each one of my room-mates, said goodbye, grabbed my bags, and walked out of encamamiento.

As I left the premises, I knocked on Susana's locked door one last time to say goodbye and then exited the hallway into the crisp night. "Freedoms," a nickname given to inmates who were being released, were taken to the warden's office to finalize the exit process. I told the warden that it had been a pleasure meeting her, but that I hoped I never saw her in that place again. She smiled. I did not know that less than a month later, I would be back to visit my friends and to bring the first of several book donations for the library. At the time, all I could think of was finally getting home to my children.

There were three other Freedoms leaving Santa Teresa with me that day: The woman with the green eyes and two other young women. After we all passed through the warden's office, we were escorted by a single guard to the prison's main gate, the one which led to the outside and the public street. It was just past 11 p.m. As we reached the gate, one last set of guards asked us for our names, ID numbers, jurisdictions, and the crimes we were accused of. I suppose this was one more safeguard to verify our identity. When the guard asked me why I had come to Santa Teresa, I couldn't help myself and said, "Because the attorney general and my accusers are a gang of convenient storytellers and I am now leaving because they were unable to prove their lies."

There was an opening in the pedestrian gate and I could see my father and my Rodri waiting for me outside in the dark. I asked the guards if I could go and they said yes. One last guard asked to see a stamp on my forearm before I left, then I took one more step and found myself in my father's arms—my relentless warrior.

The three of us started the long walk past several prisons, including the men's preventive detention prison and a psychiatric ward, toward the car, a walk they had made many times over the past sixty-five days, a walk I was doing for the first time since I'd been thrown in jail. I took my father's hand and, to my surprise, he squeezed back tightly. We walked hand in hand the entire way. I was taking my first steps of freedom between two wonderful men whom God had lent to me so that I could share my life's journey. At forty-seven years of age, I suddenly felt like the safe five-year-old child I had once been.

Throughout this journey, I had confirmed that I was surrounded by an incredible, loving, and unconditionally supportive circle of family and friends. My mother, my children, and my two dogs were safe at home, and God willing, I would soon join them. The truth prevailed and the future was uncertain, but life kept moving and I looked forward to what it might bring next. As I so often remind my children, *God is with you, and within you . . .*

CHAPTER 16

Home Sweet Home

I sat on the back seat of the car, looking out the window, beginning to remember what it was like to be a free citizen, as we began the short drive home. Santa Teresa is a good twenty-five minutes away from my house during the day, but only a six-minute drive at night. However, to get to and from the prison, you are forced to go through areas of Guatemala City that I would normally avoid. Worlds far apart, yet very close.

Although it was the middle of the night, I borrowed my brother's cell phone and spoke to several of my friends who were anxiously waiting to confirm that I had in fact been released. The joy and relief in their voices was as heartwarming as their constant support throughout this entire ordeal.

As we pulled into my driveway, my mother opened the front door, and as soon as I walked inside, I began to cry like a baby. I had spent months erasing this image from my mind in an effort to mitigate the pain, and now it was happening: I was finally home.

After hugging my mother, I ran up the flight of stairs to the second floor, entered Fabi's room, lay down by his side, and sobbed inconsolably.

I smelled him, hugged him, and kissed him everywhere I could, as my mother watched from the bedroom door. He remained sound asleep. I then walked into Nina's room and climbed into her bed, caressing her soft hair and kissing her, while I whispered, "Mommy is home." She slowly turned to me, with barely opened eyes, and gave me a smile I will never forget, before going right back to her dreams.

Not willing to be apart from them for one second longer, I carried each one of them into my room while they slept, and placed them in my bed. We were finally together again. God had heard my prayers.

The following day, at around 6 a.m., my children awoke and found me lying right next to them for the first time in more than two months: The best day of my life! It was also the first time in sixty-five days that I had not had to jump out of a bed at 4 a.m. for a head count, and when I opened my eyes, the first thing I saw, rather than a prison room, was my children and my home. It felt like a dream.

I don't remember what the rest of the day was like. It comes back to me in flashes. Nina and Fabi did not go to school. We took a long hot bath together and spent the day as an inseparable trio. My closest friends called me, and a few came to see me, but, as I later found out, many had decided to stay away for a couple of days in the hope of allowing me precious recovery time with my children.

On Saturday morning, my second full day of freedom, my mother informed me that she was moving back to her home. She was exhausted and needed to rest. Olga was gone for the weekend, so once my mother left, I suddenly found myself home alone with my kids. I had no plans and nothing to do. All I wanted was to be home.

I went about the rest of my morning, trying to reconnect with my old life, when a little before noon, there was a knock at the door. I opened it and found my neighbor Tin on the other side, welcoming me home with a big hug.

"Do you have lunch plans?" he asked.

"No, my calendar is wide open!"

"Great!" he said. "My family and I expect you and the kids for lunch at 1 p.m."

I still had not taken a shower, so I thanked him, but declined.

"Plans or no plans, you still have to eat," he replied, not taking no for an answer. "I'll be back to pick you up at 1 p.m."

I ran upstairs, took a warm shower, got dressed, prepared the children, and at 1 p.m. sharp, Tin was at my door, waiting to walk us over to his house. I am so glad he insisted, as that time with him and his family was precious and I will never forget their grand gesture. It was another life lesson for me; I thought about all the times in my life when I had wanted to approach someone in need, but had shied away because I did not want to intrude, because we were not close enough, or because I did not have the courage, not knowing how big of a difference even the smallest gesture could make in a time of need.

I had no idea how I would feel once I returned home; I hadn't even considered the idea because I didn't want to create false expectations that I would be leaving prison anytime soon. So when the day came, I was ecstatic and also a bit lost. Once again, my life had changed. There seemed to be no old life to jump back into. I had no job, no plans, no schedule. A part of me insisted I had to "throw myself back into life" as soon as possible, while another told me to take my time, to take it easy, to be gentle with myself.

The weekend continued with these conflicting emotions, peaceful, wonderful, because I was home with my children, but also somewhat lonely. When Tuesday came along, I couldn't have been happier; my old classmates had decided they had given me enough time to regroup, and had planned a get-together at one of their homes, inviting only a select group of people because they were worried that I was not ready for too much commotion. That evening, twenty-five of us gathered, hugged, talked, and cheered, with prosecco and wine, the fact that we were together again, celebrating life and freedom, as we have done since many of us were five years old. *I am blessed.*

——

As the days and weeks passed, my safe haven was no longer Serigrafía, it was my home. Family and friends came by on a daily basis, some even bringing groceries and other necessities as they had done the entire time of my incarceration. I was not ready to go out in public much, but I was certainly glad to see my loved ones at my home. I was never alone, ever. And I made sure to express my gratitude to those near and far in my one and only Facebook post on "Justicia para Anaité" on Thursday, March 17, 2016:

Today, thanks to God and to the support of many, it has now been a week since I came back to my house, my children, my family, and my friends. I want to thank you all from the bottom of my heart for your prayers, your messages, your visits, your deliveries, cards, suggestions, support, love, etc. I have been able to thank many of you personally, but I learn on a daily basis about how so many others were vigilant, contributed in some way, prayed, or helped. And to many others whom I have not had the pleasure of meeting but know were by my side through this time, I thank you all.

As many of us have learned throughout this process, this situation does not only happen to an individual; it happens to all her loved ones as well.

Today I am free, but unfortunately, what I have lived has been lived by many before me. We must change our Guatemala; we must thoroughly consider which actions we reward and which ones we punish. Each individual must be responsible for his own actions, not the actions of another.

During this entire process, I have made an effort to keep my eyes, ears, mind, and heart open to discover God's purposes for me in sending this experience my way. I believe I have discovered some, and I remain vigilant to find those I have yet to discover.

I have received and learned so much, that I sometimes feel as if tears run down my cheeks because so much love no longer fits inside my body. There is no better reason to cry.

To all my angels, I am eternally grateful. You know who you are.

And lastly, I want to thank my "colleagues in misfortune" with whom I learned so much and who are still without their freedom courtesy of a pathetic justice system. I have left behind wonderful women in that place, and I pray to God that they go home soon.

Well, I think I exceeded myself.

My children are waiting for me!

Meanwhile, life went on. Being with my children was a true gift from God; however, adjusting to everyday life was an uphill battle. Small tasks like paying the bills or making a supermarket list were difficult at first. Ten weeks away from any routine is tough, especially when one is abruptly taken from everything familiar and dear. And to complicate matters, I found myself in a constant haze, my brain unable to concentrate or even care about simple everyday tasks. I did not know it at the time, but this feeling would last for over a year! Sixty-five days may not seem like much, but they certainly changed my outlook on life, on what is possible, on what certain people are capable of doing for money or to hide their faults, and it showed me how my life could mean nothing to a select few, yet be so valuable to many others. Even for this truth, I am grateful.

I sometimes wonder how I managed to get through it all, and then I remember: *love!*

——

My children and I spent Easter break at the beach with Ed and Vania. We returned to the city on Easter Sunday and enjoyed the traditional family brunch at my mother's best friend's home. Maria Luisa is a second mother to me, and her children are like my siblings. Slowly but surely, my life began taking shape again, but it would never be the same.

Now, as I sit at home writing these pages, and continue to digest everything that has happened to me, and how it has affected my life and my loved ones, I continue to shed tears when I talk about how I felt during that terrifying time when my freedom was taken away from me so suddenly; I continue to wonder when this saga may finally come to an official end, and I worry about the future of my beautiful and beloved Guatemala.

CHAPTER 17

Death of the American Dream

—

E ver since I can remember, being a citizen of the United States of America has been a source of enormous pride for me. As much as I love Guatemala, its natural beauty, its friendly people, and everything I am because of my ties to this wonderful place, nothing compares to my feeling of belonging to the great land of the free, home of the brave, my birthplace, my beloved USA. But this experience has certainly changed my views on that.

The world knows that very little happens in countries like Guatemala without the US Embassy knowing about it, so attaining information regarding a case such as mine should not have been a problem for them; yet they never contacted me while in prison. As a US citizen, I was unfairly incarcerated, and all I heard from the US Embassy was silence. I am hurt, angered, and frustrated beyond words. My father said it best, "*Death of the American Dream*, that should be the title of your book."

A month after my release, while still trying to make sense of it all, I called the US Embassy in Guatemala and requested a meeting. I needed to understand how it was possible that a US citizen had spent sixty-five days in a Guatemalan prison and no one from the embassy had deemed it necessary to enquire about her well-being, or somehow make sure there was no violation of due process in her case. Maybe I have seen too many Hollywood movies, maybe I am expecting too much, maybe I am mistaken, or maybe they truly failed me. What follows is a letter I wrote to the US Embassy, a little over five weeks after my prison release.

April 18, 2016

Ms. Hennessey

Consul General

U.S. Embassy, Guatemala City, Guatemala

Dear Ms. Hennessy,

My name is Anaité Alvarado and I am a US Citizen living in Guatemala. I write to you today, because on April 11th, 2016, I met with Mr. Cano from American Citizen Services at the US Embassy here in Guatemala. After listening to all I had to say, he advised me to write a letter to you regarding my situation.

I was born in the United States of America to Guatemalan parents, which has allowed me dual citizenship. I grew up in Guatemala, left for college at eighteen years of age, returned seventeen years later, and have been living in Guatemala since 2003.

My husband is Jorge Roberto Montano Pellegrini. Back on July 29, 2014, he told me he had gotten himself into financial troubles, something completely unexpected to me because he seemed to be doing very well. Since that moment, my life has changed in ways I could have never imagined. We have been separated for over a year.

His financial troubles seem to be quite massive and as much as I have tried to stay clear of his actions, it became impossible. He still needs to have his day in court, but in the meantime, one of his alleged victims, Mr. Juan Pablo Olyslager Muñoz, gave a statement to the Guatemalan MP [attorney general] claiming that Mr. Roberto Montano, his accountant, and his wife were part of a criminal structure that intended to defraud people of their money. The statement he presented is an almost exact copy of the civil lawsuit he presented against Mr. Montano and his accountant Mr. Cacheo. This statement resulted in a criminal lawsuit and an order to capture the three of us. The order of apprehension took place on Thursday September 17, 2015. Mr. Montano and Mr. Cacheo were conveniently nowhere to be found. The only one still living in the same place, doing the same things, and not hiding from anyone was me. So that is how I was taken by the police to the tribunal tower [courthouse] where I spent the night and learned of Mr. Olyslager's accusations against me.

The next morning, Friday, September 18, 2015, I was brought to Judge Jisela Reinoso's chambers where I was formally informed of my situation. After hearing the accusations of the parties involved (Mr. Olyslager, Juan Ignacio Gómez-Cuevas representing Forestal Chaklum, another attorney representing Forestal Ceibal, and the MP) the judge linked me to due process but let me go home to my children on my own recognizance. She decided I should go to the Attorney General's Office every two weeks to sign that I had not fled the country, and I was not allowed to leave the country without proper authorization. The investigation period was set to three months, ending December 18, 2015.

So this is how I went home to my children (five-year-old twins at the time) in the hope that the truth would set me free.

Monday September 21, 2015, my Judge Jisela Reinoso was taken into custody herself charged with "delitos de lavado de dinero y otros activos, enriquecimiento ilícito e incumplimiento de deberes de declaración patrimonial [*money and asset laundering, unlawful or illicit enrichment, and failure to disclose financial worth].”*

During those 3 months of investigation, my case went through several judges.

January 5, 2016, I had been appointed another new judge, Julia Rivera. The hearing involved a motion from my attorney to take away the requirement to sign the books at MP every two weeks and allow me to leave the country, given that the period for investigation had concluded and I had not failed once to sign the book as the court had ordered. Well, instead of letting me go, she decided I could influence other parties involved and maybe even falsify documents, so she ordered that I should be sent to jail. And that is where I remained until March 10, 2016, at Centro Preventivo para Mujeres Santa Teresa in Zone 18.

During this time, the US Embassy was aware of my situation. I know this because several friends of mine took it upon themselves to inform the Embassy and because Ms. Schofer, ACS Chief, had a meeting she requested with my attorney, Arturo Miranda. Another reason I know the Embassy was aware of my situation is because a US Attorney by the name of James A. Smith representing GFP (Global Forest Partners) came to Guatemala and had a meeting at the Embassy.

Weeks passed and I did not hear from the US Embassy. My friends contacted the Embassy to enquire about my situation and they were told not to call again. And by the time I was finally released, the Embassy was nonexistent.

So I requested a meeting. I wanted the US Embassy to explain what proper procedure is when a US Citizen is imprisoned abroad. Mr. Cano very nicely informed me that yes, the Embassy should have come to see me and make sure I was safe, etc. The reasons given for not doing so were that the Embassy was short on staff during the time of my incarceration, and that since I hold a dual citizenship, it became more difficult for the Embassy to obtain information on my case. He also mentioned that it would have been his responsibility to come see me in prison, but he had arrived to Guatemala not long ago, and his position had been vacant for several months.

I am not sure any of these explanations makes much sense to me, but I am learning as I go through this terrible ordeal.

There are other reasons why I wanted an appointment at the US Embassy.

1. I want to file a formal complaint against Mr. James A. Smith, partner at Foley Hoag LLP. He met with my attorney Arturo Miranda and several lawyers from Mayora & Mayora. During this meeting, my attorney was apparently approached and was asked if I, Anaité Alvarado, was ready to tell them where my husband and the money was so that they would stop charges against me. I consider that extortion and a good indication of exactly what has been done against me.

2. I would like this entire situation investigated because it is my opinion that Mr. Juan Pablo Olyslager got together with the law firm of Mayora & Mayora representing Forestal Chaklum and Forestal Ceibal, to lie about my involvement in this case. Mr. Olyslager's testimony to the MP was part of a strategy against my husband which involved claiming I was part of a criminal conspiracy, in order to have three people involved and making this a criminal case. My process is not yet over, but the truth will remain unchanged.

3. It is my understanding that Mayora & Mayora was hired by GFP to make sure GFP's investments in Guatemala were safe, and to control my husband's management of their assets in Guatemala. It has now become evident by their own accusations that Mayora & Mayora failed at this job and cost GFP millions of dollars. They should not be a law firm the US Embassy recommends to US Citizens or corporations doing business in Guatemala. The US Embassy now knows and should remove them from that list.

In any event, this is a very complicated case and I do realize I have probably left you with more questions than I did answers. I will be happy *to meet with you and answer as best I can any questions you may have regarding my case. I want things right and am hoping you are the person who will help me.*

I look forward to hearing from you,

Anaité Alvarado

The US Embassy contacted me immediately upon receipt of this letter. I met with Rachel Schofer who proceeded to tell me that the US Embassy does not get involved in foreign country's legal proceedings. This surprised me immensely because while I was in prison, US Ambassador to Guatemala Todd Robinson sat in a Guatemalan courtroom, seemingly supporting left-wing judge Yassmin Barrios's foregone conviction of two military men. The case is known as Sepur Zarco.

As I understand it, Judge Barrios rejected official army evidence supporting the fact that the defendant had not been stationed in the place where the crimes allegedly occurred. She admitted illegal evidence for one charge against the defendant, but as soon as that same document contained exculpatory evidence pointing to the guerillas as responsible for the crimes, Judge Barrios refused to admit it, stating that the army was on trial, not the guerilla. In the meantime, Robinson appeared in photographs at the courthouse and at the embassy with Judge Barrios—they were even seen later visiting members of the US Congress. After the trial, Robinson said, "I congratulate Guatemala . . . we hope to see this type of exercise in the future, not only in the courts but in all institutions."

This, and so much other available information, very clearly contradicts the claim that "the US Embassy does not get involved in foreign country legal proceedings." I must have misunderstood her statement; maybe she meant that the embassy does not get involved in proceedings involving insignificant American taxpayers such as myself.

Ms. Schofer also said that the law firm of Mayora & Mayora was no longer a firm recommended by the US Embassy, and that the reason my friends had been asked to not contact the Embassy again was that the Embassy did not share such information over the telephone.

Ms. Schofer then explained that due to my dual citizenship, it had been difficult (if not impossible) for the US Embassy to obtain any information regarding my case. The US Ambassador to Guatemala spent three years blatantly interfering in Guatemala's internal affairs, yet the Embassy claimed it had a difficult time getting information on my case. Therefore, it came as no surprise when this ambassador, who has publicly strengthened US ties with the same ex-guerillas whom my beloved United States helped defeat decades ago—known guerillas and their sympathizers whom he has helped into positions of power within the Guatemalan government—publicly declared on behalf of the American people he represents that, "The issue of sovereignty is the last on the list of my concerns . . ."

Needless to say, I will never feel the same way about my embassy again.

Epilogue

—

I do not know what the future holds. One never does. What I do know is that there is unimaginable beauty and promise within imperfection. Only with imperfection do treasures such as wisdom, unconditional love, loyalty, personal growth, self-awareness, and clarity flourish and become evident.

These last chapters of my life have been among the toughest so far, and yet they have been among the most enriching. I may never come to understand why my husband made the choices he made, what fear, anger, or hate drove Juan Pablo Olyslager Muñoz to lie about me, what Mayora & Mayora is hiding or protecting by insisting on my guilt, or what GFP knew or did not know about their company's involvement in this entire case. Yet, I no longer need to know. I free myself of all the unwelcome and unsolicited drama they all willingly and knowingly brought into my life. Their actions will always say more about them than they ever will about me. And as I have also learned, the truth stubbornly refuses to remain concealed forever. So, I shall continue my journey and let it all naturally come to light.

The darkness may seem vast and overwhelming sometimes, but it is easily destroyed by any speck of light. Today, with a legal process still in place against me, my life irrevocably changed, and this experience under my belt, I find myself thinking . . .

And just as she thought her life was over, she discovered she had wings to fly!

UPDATES AS OF MAY 2018

From Prisoner to Visitor

Since my release, I have visited my dear friends in Santa Teresa several times, and I will continue to do so as long as they are locked in that place. I now know what a show of affection can do for a person locked behind bars.

Santa Teresa

I have recently been told that as of August 2017, Santa Teresa has been housing 1,300 inmates. It was originally built to house 236.

The Library

My permit to bring book donations (which keep pouring in) into Santa Teresa never arrived. On July 18, 2016, Captain Byron Lima, accused and convicted of the 1998 murder of Bishop Juan Gerardi, was violently murdered at the prison where he was serving time, and many changes came about within the penitentiary system. According to Marta, these changes are the reason why my permit was never approved. This meant that I had to stop receiving donations for the library because my home had become a book warehouse. Eventually, I did manage to bring most of the books into the prison on encomienda day and I fully trust that Marta did a wonderful job with the prison library. As of today, both the Education Department and the Social

Services Department at El Centro de Detención Preventiva para Mujeres Santa Teresa in Guatemala City each have a complete set of encyclopedias for the women to use. Marta has since been transferred to another prison. Today, I continue to receive book donations and manage to send them to Santa Teresa thanks to Ashley Williams's help.

Ashley Williams

Ashley has since moved on from the foundation she cofounded in Guatemala and continues to focus on her passion for justice work. Serigrafía is now called Serigrafía de la Gringa and continues to provide a source of work and dignity to a select few in Santa Teresa. Ashley has since completed her first year of law school at URL, with the second highest scores in her class. In January 2017, she began her second year of law school and is on the school's Honor Roll. Besides school and work, she dedicates much of her time to speaking at different venues. She is frequently invited to speak on radio and TV shows, and is featured in print media. Her commitment to her cause and her resolve to change the system in order to prevent the incarceration of innocent people, continue to grow. She recently turned thirty years old and has already accomplished so much in the service of others.

Carmen

Carmen has since been transferred to another prison and is still going through her legal process. She has now spent three years in preventive custody, a total violation of her human rights.

Lili

Lili has been released and is back home with her family.

Daniela

Has since been released and is currently employed and a productive member of society. She is an example of a life transformed and a testament to Ashley Williams's work in rehabilitating women. She is expecting a baby girl.

Mari Ro

After her second trial, Mari Ro was set free once again. One of the three judges who deliberated during her second trial stated that accusing her of such a crime when she herself had been in harm's way was senseless. In October 2016, she attended a court hearing to find out if the Attorney General's Office was finally desisting from its accusations against her, or if they would appeal. They appealed and a three-judge panel denied their request for a third trial. The Attorney General's Office appealed to a higher court and won. Mari Ro will most likely be subjected to a third trial. We continue to be in touch.

Verónica

During one of my visits back to Santa Teresa in August 2016, Verónica told me that her sentence had been reduced and had been affirmed. When I visited the prison in September 2016, I was told that Verónica and Jenny had been transferred to another prison for the remainder of their sentences. I like to think that by now she has been released. I can only hope she is well and will contact me one day soon.

Susana

My dear Susana is still behind bars, waiting to hear about an appeal filed by all the accused in her case. Susana was sentenced to eighteen years and eight months. As of September 2017, she had served five years and eight months in preventive custody in Santa Teresa.

On March 8, 2017, forty-one girls died during a fire at a government-run safe house (Hogar Seguro Virgen de la Asunción) for girls who were declared by the court to be victims of violence. Since that incident, much has been said about child adoption, the adoption laws passed by the Guatemalan Congress that prevent international adoptions, and the absurdity of allowing an irresponsible government to be in charge of the nation's most precious beings, our children. I hope that one day soon, unwanted children in Guatemala will once again be given the oportunity to become members of loving families, and that the atrocities commited under those adoption processes will be reconsidered. It is my opinion that incarcerating people like Susana has not benefited Guatemala's unwanted children.

Meanwhile, Susana calls me every week and we talk about anything and everything and laugh a lot. She is one of the most amazing people I know and I will always be a friend of hers. I hope that she and her three cats go home soon.

Martina, La Patrona

On May 20, 2016, Martina escaped from prison only to be found later in the wooded area adjacent to Santa Teresa. She apparently fled through the barred windows of the room we once shared. Alina was transferred to solitary confinement and Martina was transferred to another prison. On May 11, 2017, the day of my last hearing, she escaped once again. She was later aprehended in El Salvador and from what I heard, is now in solitary confinement in Santa Teresa.

Abuela

On my visit to the prison in September 2016, Abuela came over to me. She looked better than ever and we had our first sensible conversation. After greeting me and telling me I looked well, she asked me if I was going to visit the neighboring male prison that day. She said she had no way of contacting her daughter, no means of sending anything to her, and no family to help them. I was glad to finally have a connection with this woman whom I had thought was unwell in the head, but my heart shrank a little when she confirmed her predicament. All I could do was give her the goodies that I had brought for Verónica, who had already been transferred elsewhere.

Mimi

Mimi has since been transferred to serve out her prison sentence at C.O.F.

Mariana

I never saw Mariana again.

Arturo Miranda

Apparently, in another display of unprofessional behavior, one of the partners at Mayora & Mayora made it clear at a third-party meeting that he would not attend a client meeting if Arturo Miranda, who was also invited, was present. Miranda also claims that he has been blocked from several legal consulting jobs as a direct result of having been the attorney on my case. I can only say that although client-attorney relations tend to get tense during cases such as mine, Arturo Miranda did everything in his power to defend me in a professional and appropriate manner. The justice system is plagued with evil, greed, and corruption, and sometimes the road becomes dark and difficult to travel. So today, I want to publicly thank Arturo Miranda and his team for everything they have done for my family and me during one of the worst episodes of our lives.

My Husband

As of May 2018, my husband's location is still unknown to me.

Juan Pablo Olyslager Muñoz—My Accuser

Olyslager was vice president of BMI Insurance Company in Guatemala, is still a member of EO (Entrepreneurs Organization), has since become a father, and now claims to be an actor.

Mayora & Mayora—Global Forest Partner's (GFP) Law Firm

Many people have mentioned to me that it is their belief that if this law firm's founder were alive today, their actions in my case would most likely have never taken place. During one of my meetings at the US Embassy in April 2016, Rachel Schofer from the Embassy's Citizen Services Department provided me with paperwork that showed that this law firm and the son of the law firm's founder were no longer on the Embassy's suggested list of local attorneys.

Julio Roberto García-Merlos García

According to one of his own tweets, this trial attorney hired by Mayora & Mayora to prosecute me has since had another child. I hope every time he sees that baby in her mother's arms he remembers that in this country, anyone can accuse his wife for her husband's actions. May he never forget what he was a part of.

Jisela Reinoso Trujillo

The judge who presided over my hearing in September 2015 and decided to send me home has since been convicted of money laundering and illicit enrichment, and sentenced to thirteen years in prison.

Frank Trujillo—Juan Pablo Olyslager's Attorney

As far as I know, he is still awaiting trial in prison. He turned himself in to the authorities due to the warrant for his arrest regarding the SAT case.

CICIG

CICIG is still active in Guatemala, continuing to imprison citizens who have been accused but not convicted by a court of law. The prisons are full, especially the ones housing citizens held in preventive custody, while they await their day in court. Legal proceedings are slow, untrustworthy, and CICIG has yet to have a solid conviction under its belt. In the meantime, CICIG's credibility among Guatemalan citizens and the world continues to diminish in spite of the full ideological and financial support of the UN and countries such as Sweden.

People are beginning to question CICIG's use of protected witnesses in lieu of hard evidence, many of whom have eventually recanted or had their testimony declared inadmissible in court. Two of the most famous cases are: former Guatemalan Chief of Police Erwin Sperisen's case, whose life conviction was recently reversed in a Geneva, Switzerland, court; and the Rodrigo Rosenberg case in Guatemala, in which witnesses have since declared that CICIG coerced them into giving false testimonies.

On August 27, 2017, Guatemalan President Jimmy Morales declared CICIG's Commissioner Iván Velásquez persona non grata for, among other things, interfering in Guatemala's internal affairs, and ordered his immediate expulsion from Guatemala. This decision caused much turmoil and division among Guatemalan citizens who either supported President Morales or supported the CICIG commissioner. Many forgot that the battle was about neither one, but rather against corruption and about protecting Guatemala, its constitution, and its laws.

A few days later, a judge closed an eight-year-old case against the Valdés Paiz brothers, accused of having been involved in Rodrigo Rosenberg's murder/suicide case. The judge declared that it had been demonstrated that the Attorney General's Office and CICIG's accusations against them were false, based on witnesses who had been forced to lie; one more blatant example of the way CICIG has been persecuting citizens in Guatemala. The brothers had spent three years in prison.

Medical Care for Inmates

On August 16, 2017, a well-known gang leader was taken from prison to one of Guatemala's public hospitals. While there, gunmen stormed in and opened fire, in an assault staged to free the imprisoned gang member. At least seven people were killed and many were injured. Among the dead: two prison guards, a doctor, two patients, and a five-month-old baby boy.

As I witnessed, regular inmates are rarely taken out of prison to a hospital. Why then was this known gang leader taken to a state hospital without the proper escort, without proper security, endangering innocent lives?

Once again, Guatemala's citizens became enraged, claiming all inmates should die in prison, and that the death penalty should be brought back. I agree that some members of society deserve the death penalty, but I have been an inmate, I have experienced our justice system, and

I cringe at the thought of these judges, attorneys, prosecutors, and international organizations having the power to take my life.

Guatemala

Guatemala continues its battle to survive in freedom and under the rule of law. Every day presents new challenges, new situations, and new uncertainties. While a select few fight to gain power or remain in power, with all the personal benefits it brings, most citizens struggle to survive. CICIG has been "fighting corruption and strengthening Guatemala's institutions" for ten years now, but as far as I can see, and after millions of US dollars spent, the country is in worse shape than ever.

———

This experience has definitely changed me, not into a different person, but into a person who is more committed than ever to fight for what is right. May this book be the beginning of many good changes to come. Thank you for reading my story.

TIMELINE

—

Date	Event
2014 JULY 29	My husband informs me that he is having financial trouble.
2015 SEPTEMBER 17	The public prosecutor arrives at my home with a warrant to search my house, a warrant to arrest my husband, and a warrant to arrest me, and I am taken to the courthouse. I am later informed that my employment contract at the foundation where I was raising funds to benefit children with cancer in Guatemala was not to be renewed.
2015 SEPTEMBER 18	After spending the night in the carceleta, I have a hearing with Judge Jisela Reinoso Trujillo, who declares that there is no evidence of money laundering and no report from IVE. She decides to give the Attorney General's Office three months to investigate the other charges against me and releases me on my own recognizance, ordering that I not leave the country without the court's authorization and that I sign the book at the Attorney General's Office every two weeks to certify that I have not left the country.
2015 SEPTEMBER 21	Judge Jisela Reinoso Trujillo is taken into custody. My long list of temporary judges begins.
2015 DECEMBER 18	The court-ordered investigation is finished. No more evidence may be presented past this date (or so I was told).

2016 **JANUARY 5**	I attend my hearing at the courthouse. My new judge, Julia Rivera, decides that I might tamper with evidence and communicate with the other people involved in the case if I remain at home, so she orders that I be taken into custody at El Centro de Detención Preventiva para Mujeres Santa Teresa.
2016 **JANUARY 12**	The public prosecutor is a no-show; the hearing is postponed.
2016 **JANUARY 18**	The judge is a no-show; the hearing is postponed.
2016 **JANUARY 27**	Court hearing: My attorney presents strong arguments showing my innocence and pushing for my release from prison, yet the judge decides that nothing has changed and I am to remain behind bars.
2016 **FEBRUARY 18**	The judge is a no-show; the hearing is postponed.
2016 **FEBRUARY 23**	The justice system fails to present sixteen of the forty reports requested by the judge, so my attorney and I decide to postpone the hearing.
2016 **MARCH 3**	The public prosecutor is a no-show; the hearing is postponed.
2016 **MARCH 8**	After a very long court hearing, the judge decides to reconvene the next day.
2016 **MARCH 9**	There is no police support available for the penitentiary system to transfer inmates to the courthouse and the judge does not want to proceed without me present; the hearing is postponed.

2016
MARCH 10

Court hearing: The judge decides that there is not enough evidence to merit a trial against me. My attorney claims that the Attorney General's Office has failed to present specific crucial evidence regarding my involvement. The judge decides to send me home—*I'm free!*—however, she gives the Attorney General's Office six more months to present the requested evidence.

2016
MARCH 11

After sixty-five days in prison, I wake up at home with my children.

2016
APRIL 18

I write a letter to the US Embassy in Guatemala explaining my experience and requesting information on the Embassy's policies regarding US citizens imprisoned abroad.

2016
SEPTEMBER 12

Date established by Judge Julia Rivera for the Attorney General's Office to present the evidence requested, but none is presented by the 3 p.m. deadline.

2016
SEPTEMBER 16

I learn that the Attorney General's Office has requested that the judge grant them another six months to continue their investigation. My attorney requests that my case be dismissed once and for all.

2016
SEPTEMBER 28

The scheduled court hearing is canceled because the Attorney General's Office did not present the evidence they were ordered to obtain. We await decision on a new hearing date.

2016
SEPTEMBER 29

My father turns seventy-five years old!

My attorney calls to let me know that the new judge declined the Attorney General's Office request to investigate my case for six more months.

2016 OCTOBER 4	My original judge, Jisela Reinoso Trujillo, is sentenced to thirteen years in prison.
2016 OCTOBER	The Attorney General's Office appeals the judge's decision and refuses to request an acquittal. The public prosecutor tells my attorney that the State would insist on a minor accusation against me so that my defense could easily fight it. The question remains, why not let it be?
2016 OCTOBER 31	My attorney informs me that the next hearing regarding my case has been set for February 2017. I decide to publish my story.
2017 FEBRUARY 2	The public prosecutor is a no-show at the scheduled hearing; the hearing is postponed.
2017 APRIL 25	The public prosecutor is a no-show; the hearing is postponed and I find out I have a new judge on the case: Carlos Guerra. My attorney and I make a formal complaint against the attorney general's public prosecutor Jeowan Stuardo Vasquez. He failed to appear in court January 12, February 1, March 3, and April 25, 2017.
2017 MAY 11	Another hearing. The public prosecutor forgets his files. Miranda lets him borrow his copy of their accusations against me. The public prosecutor presents only one of sixteen forms of evidence requested by a judge a year earlier: my marriage certificate. The judge reprimands the public prosecutor but grants the Attorney General's Office ten more months to present requested evidence. A new hearing is set for March 11, 2018.

2017
June 10

My attorney presents an *amparo*, a legal complaint asking an appellate court to review and dismiss the judge's new ruling, which gave the Attorney General's Office ten more months to investigate.

2017
October

Hearing with the appellate court magistrates regarding our complaint against the judge.

2017
November

The magistrates rule that my rights were violated by the judge's decision to award the Attorney General's Office more time to present evidence against me. The Attorney General's Office appeals to a higher court.

Hearing with the appellate court magistrates regarding our complaint against the judge.

2018
February

Hearing at the Court of Constitutionality. My attorney and Mayora & Mayora present their cases before the five magistrates. We await their decision.

2018
May

As of May 2018

I am still waiting to hear the following: Acquittal

When the judge formally certifies that the accused, Anaité Alvarado Sánchez, is free from all charges against her, as far as the criminal law is concerned.

ACKNOWLEDGMENTS

—

I once thought this story had been written while I was in prison, but little did I know how much work and effort is required for a book to be born.

I want to thank Denise Leal for being the first person to take this journey with me by working on the first transcription of my original handwritten notebook. I want to thank Karla Pemüeller, who in this time of trouble has been a constant source of love and encouragement. She visited me on a weekly basis while I was in prison, made sure I had a notebook to write in, pens to write with, and kept my writings safe until I was released. Her help was indispensable in the process to self-publish my original book, *Back Where I Belong*. For her existence and our friendship, I am eternally grateful.

My thanks also go to Cristina Apóstolo, who sent my original story to Alex Merrill and Julia Abramoff at Apollo Publishers in New York. Thank you, Alex and Julia, for reading my writings, for taking a risk on me, for believing that my story had value and should be known.

My gratitude also goes to a Cecilia Molinari, who accepted the challenge and agreed to be my editor. It has been an unending journey of learning and growth for me, a journey that would not have been the same without so many angels by my side.

And to all who have accompanied me throughout this difficult, yet enriching, chapter of my life, I thank you. No words could ever express the gratitude I hold in my heart.

"Never be afraid to raise your voice for honesty and truth and compassion, against injustice and lying and greed. If people all over the world . . . would do this, it would change the earth."

—WILLIAM FAULKNER